PLATE I: WOMAN WITH NECKLACE, *by* HENRY TONKS

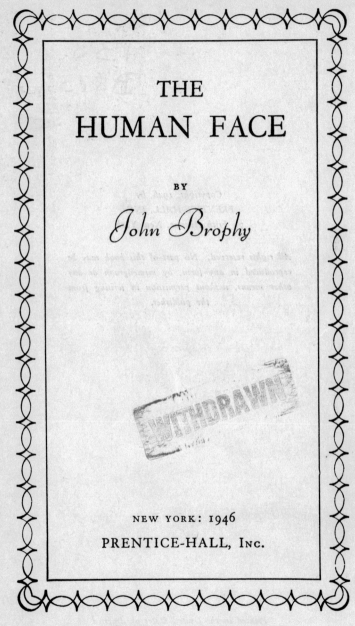

THE
HUMAN FACE

BY

John Brophy

NEW YORK: 1946

PRENTICE-HALL, INC.

ACKNOWLEDGMENTS

My best thanks are due to Captain B. H. Liddell Hart for reading my text in the typescript stage, and for allowing me to draw on his exceptional knowledge of the history of fashion, and in particular on certain lectures and as yet unpublished essays. I have also to make grateful acknowledgments for advice in selecting and arranging the illustrations to Mr John Rothenstein, Director of the Tate Gallery; Sir Owen Morshead, the Royal Librarian at Windsor Castle; and Mr Cecil Phillips, Mr Oliver Brown and Mr W. Donlevy of the Leicester Galleries.

For permission to reproduce pictures and drawings I express my thanks to: M. Jean Vallery-Radot, Conservateur of the Bibliothèque Nationale, Paris (Plate II); Mr Eric Kennington (Plates IV and X); Mr Mervyn Peake (Plates V and XXI); Mr Alexander Akerbladh (Plate VII); Dr A. M. Hind, Keeper of Print Room, British Museum (Plates VIII, IX, and XII); Mr John Wheatley (Plate XIII); Mr Robert Greenham (Plate XV); Mr Augustus John, O.M., and Mr Michael Redgrave (Plate XVI); Mr K. T. Parker, Keeper of Prints, the Ashmolean Museum, Oxford (Plate XXIII). I am grateful to Mr H. L. Holman, the owner of the portrait of Miss Vivien Leigh, for allowing me to have part of it photographed for reproduction, and to Miss Leigh for assenting: as I pass these proofs for press I hear that the painter, Mr Dietz Edzard, has emerged safely from a Nazi prison camp, and I hope he will confirm the arrangement made with his agents, the Leicester Galleries. I have been unable to trace the present owners of the two Tiepolo drawings (Plates III and XX), which were formerly in the Wendland Collection in Switzerland; nor has it been possible to trace the ownership of any copyright which may exist in the E. R. Hughes pastel (Plate VI) and the Tonks drawing (Plate I).

J. B.

iii

CONTENTS

ILLUSTRATIONS

CHAPTER ONE

THE STRUCTURE OF THE FACE

So MUCH has been written and said and thought about the human face, in rapture, in disillusionment, or in spite, that one might imagine a whole library exists on the subject. Far from it. There are books about portraiture, books about facial diseases and injuries and remedial surgery, and books which profess to give instruction in the art or science of reading character in other people's faces—or even, should the reader be temerarious enough, in his own face. And there is Johann Kaspar Lavater, the mystical eighteenth-century Swiss who published a tome called *Essays on Physiognomy*, embellished with hundreds of indifferent drawings of real or imaginary faces. A study of these essays, with the accompanying illustrations, and perhaps the "Hundred Physiognomical Rules," ought to make every human face an open book which none could misread or mispronounce. The sad fact is, however, that Lavater is of little help nowadays: his treatise is an oddity, full of out-of-the-way information, little chunks of it embedded in long and dull disquisitions, but the precise science he sought to establish now seems inexact, rickety and—to be blunt—unscientific. And that's about all. It has been a source of considerable toil and lamentation to me that in preparing this book of my own over a period of nearly fifteen years, I have not been able to find even one established authority to use as a springboard for my own inquiries and speculations.

At first sight it may seem inexplicable that a subject of such universal interest as the human face should have escaped thorough and concentrated scrutiny by all those authors, professional or amateur, profound or superficial, conscientious or merely on the look-out for popular success, who among them have wrapped up almost every aspect of life in endless lengths of woven words. But the subject is not so obvious after all. It does not stare us in the face. Rather it lurks behind the face from which we stare. Most of us, I fancy, if we undertake a little introspection, soon discover that there is a psychological barrier between our thoughts and our faces considered objectively. That, indeed, is what we find it remarkably difficult to do: to consider the face objectively. For it is the face which, even more than the voice, the words we speak, the emotions we express or suppress, and even the mannerisms we produce unconsciously, presents our ego to the outward world, to the rest of humanity. "If we really had modesty," says Raymond Mortimer in his *Essay on Clothes,* "it is our faces that we should conceal. By comparison our legs are anonymous, our bellies uneventful." Think of anyone you know, and you are almost forced to think of his face. Old Duncan, in *Macbeth,* complains that "There's no art to find the mind's construction in the face," and it cannot be denied that faces may be enigmatic, bewildering, or even downright deceitful. And yet in everyday experience the face is the index by which we all read other people's behavior, and by which our own is read, with or without sympathy. But this is comparatively a simple process. Not one of us can look at his own face in a mirror and see it dispassionately, as an object, an assembly of flesh, blood, skin, and hair. Our own face is too much part of our self, our ego, too much identified with our thoughts and emotions, for the mind, unless compelled and directed, to achieve the act of detachment from which exact observation proceeds. We think a good deal about faces: about our own with vanity and anxiety, about others with love or envy, dislike, repulsion, amusement, or hatred. But almost invariably we feel as well as think, at one and the same time. For images and associations of faces are mixed deep and confusedly in our most private and precious existence, as well as in our lifelong everyday intercourse with others. The plain fact is that though that unseen blood-pump, the heart, forms the most popular symbol for all human emotions and aspirations, it is the face, visible to every passer-by, which identifies each one of us and sets us apart as an individual, a little or a lot different from the rest of our kind. Without our characterized faces we should hardly be human.

For all these reasons we find it difficult to realize the face as what, considered objectively, it is: a specialized part of the body, the frontal aspect of the head; and the head is an upward prolongation of the spine in which are gathered together, for convenience, a remarkably large number of the most important instruments needed for the business of living. These instruments include the brain (which is the consummation of the spinal cord and is protected by the hard bone of the skull, and in wartime by a steel helmet); the principal organs of the senses, sight, hearing, smell, and taste, the sense of touch alone being distributed over the whole surface of the body in varying degrees of sensitivity; and the lips, teeth, and tongue, which serve, by one of those admirable or embarrassing economies that Nature delights in, the dual purpose of stoking the body with food and drink and enabling us to communicate with our own kind through speech and even song. The body is a unity, as St Paul in one of his acute analogies pointed out, and its parts are interdependent. Yet there is a scale of relative importance even where the most intimate relationships bind all the members together: and among the parts of the human body primacy must go to the head.

This primacy of the head has long been implicitly recognized in the customs and even the languages of mankind. The very name for this topmost portion of the body is everywhere employed, by a metaphor so ancient that it passes for literal statement, to mean principal or predominant. We speak of the head of a school or a college, the head of the river in rowing races, the head of a family, the head of a state, and no one has any doubt that we mean the chief, the foremost, the best, the leader, the ruler. Even the word we use for the most important city, the seat of government in any country, 'capital,' is derived from the Latin for the bodily head. It is true that the head cannot live without the rest of the body, but whereas a good head can get along pretty well with an inadequate, a maimed or a sickly torso and limbs, the most splendid physique becomes only

3

an object for pity if it is surmounted by an inferior kind of head. Our forebears were brutally direct, for their public executions disdained the thrust to the heart. Life was removed from the condemned by a stroke of the ax or sword, the severing of the head visibly symbolizing the abrogation of the deposed statesman's or general's power and authority. With an equally brutal logic, execution at the block was, right into modern times, considered a privilege of the notable and the well-born, a final mark of honor; for heretics the bonfire, and for base malefactors and nonentities the hangman's rope.

If the head is, both traditionally and scientifically, the most important part of the human body, and the part most intimately associated with the impalpable mind, its expressive qualities are concentrated into its frontal aspect, the face. All faces have much in common, and it is not hard to assort them into categories—long, broad, flat, beaky, swarthy or pallid or rosy, plain, ugly, or beautiful. Yet each face is peculiar to its possessor. No human face is wholly true to type, and none is completely identical with another, except occasionally with unicellular twins, where we may have something like a duplicate personality. To the Western eye one Chinese may look much like another, and so with Arabs, Negroes, Japanese, and other non-European races. But this is due to lack of practice in discrimination. Those who live among Asiatic and African peoples soon learn to tell one person from another by a glance at the face. The rule is universal to humanity: the face is the readiest identification of the individual.

The physical function of the face is to present the chief organs of the senses to the world and to operate them with the utmost advantage. This arrangement is common to all animate creatures, for animals, birds, fishes, reptiles, even insects, all have heads placed in a lofty and forward position, with more often than not the sense organs compactly organized to form a rudimentary or, in the higher vertebrates, a well-developed and recognizable face. The nearer animals approach to the status of man, the more likely they are to exhibit something akin to individuality in their faces—although there is a notable exception in the elephant, which is said to be highly intelligent and yet (no doubt because of its thick skin) carries a face of primeval and clumsy massiveness. In the great apes the approximation to human complexity and subtlety of expression is most marked, and in their mobile brows and introspective eyes it is perfectly possible to trace not only basic emotions akin to ours but the progressive urgency of thoughts striven for, achieved, understood. To draw a line of demarcation between the highest animal and the lowest human is no easy task, but once we pass on to civilized man the human face is clearly identifiable by its extreme range of individuality and by its ability to communicate subtle varieties of expression, with or without conscious intention.

We will consider the face, then, as an object, as an assembly of bone, gristle, muscle, skin, hair, blood, blood vessels, and other organic matter. It is surmounted invariably (unless baldness intervenes or depilation is undergone for the sake of high principles or fashion) with a crown of hair which can only artificially be kept short. It seems that, among peoples of European heredity at least, the head hair of women grows longer than in men. Nevertheless, we know from pictorial records of the past, as well as from Indian and other contemporaries, that the hair of a man, if allowed, will grow to a length sufficient to fall below his shoulders, and of a thickness to cover the face like a curtain let down from above. At the present day—and, indeed, it was so in most of the civilized ages of the past—the custom is for the man's hair to be cut short at frequent intervals, thus providing a cropped carpet over the top and back of the skull; incidentally, haircutting adds another trade or profession to the many which, in a fine confusion, serve to keep those inadequately explained activities, economics and finance, going. Men's hair is cut short for convenience, to leave the vision unobscured and perhaps to preserve the weaker sex from the steamy and oily tortures of permanent waving. Women take another way out of the dilemma, and, whether they let their hair attain its full natural length or trim it, as at the present day, till it is rarely more than a foot long, they dress and bind and pin it in various arrangements at the top, the side and the back of the head, thus leaving the eyes uncovered and at the same time adding a border decoration to the face itself. The head hair, by one means or another, has to be kept out of the way.

Whether at any time in the past women (except by some cruel freak of misbehaving glands) ever grew beards, and why the lower part of their faces should apparently be ordained to be hairless, are questions to which I have not been able to discover satisfactory answers. Some Chinese men never need to shave, and are said to attribute the hairlessness of their faces to the effect of long centuries of highly refined civilization. Assuming this theory to be justified, it may be that if, as we are frequently told nowadays, the Stone Age or the Bronze Age or both of them were eras of lasting peace, golden with a primal innocence, women were glad to be kept in caves while their menfolk went hunting or tended their domesticated herds. It is therefore possible that women in the distant past were thus able to evade the worst inclemencies of the weather, and, sheltered against rain, toasted by the family bonfire, taken outdoors only when the sun was shining or during a mild shower of summer rain, beneficial to the complexion, their facial skin lost the power of putting forth protective hair, and so, as generation succeeded generation, and century century, women became (facially, at least) creatures of a softer sort. At any rate, I find it pleasant to think that humanity may, by chance or design, have had some such peaceful millennium in its past history—the rest of the record is bloodthirsty enough—and thus, out of creature comforts and soft living, evolved woman as we know her: that fine flower of æsthetic fancy, that criterion of desirable beauty without which the pictorial and poetic arts would hardly be conceivable.

Just the same, it is odd and inexplicable that the hair should continue to sprout from the top of a woman's head and not from her chin. But I am very glad that is the way of it. In this preference

I am at one with the poets and historians, who when they speak of a woman's hair mean the hair which grows from the crown of the head. And in most ages men have believed that the more hair a woman carries the better. "If a woman have long hair, it is a glory to her," said St Paul. In view of this opinion, which he recorded in his First Epistle to the Corinthians, it is ironic that he should usually be evoked as the scriptual authority behind the insistence of vergers that women should wear hats whenever they enter a church. Puritans, more often than not, are people in whom the senses are very easily stimulated, and Milton, notoriously Pauline in his attitude to women, may have had in mind some unrecorded personal experience, or merely the wistful dreams of longing, when he inlaid magic into his scholarly phrases:

> To sport with Amaryllis in the shade
> Or with the tangles of Neæra's hair.

Browning was obsessed by women's hair, gold and very long:

> Dear dead women, with such hair, too—what's become of all the gold
> Used to hang and brush their bosoms?

In *Porphyria's Lover* and *Evelyn Hope,* and, of course, in *Gold Hair,* the woman's hair is rhapsodically described as golden or yellow, and it must have been disconcerting at times for Browning to remember that Elizabeth Barrett's was brown.

Poets delight in women's hair, and will seek far and wide for appropriate adjectives. Milton, always suspect as an ascetic, gave Sabrina a "loose train of thy amber-dropping hair," braided with lilies, presumably water-lilies. The Elizabethan Chapman (another enthusiast for gold) wrote of Berenice's "ever-burning hair," but Swinburne was, for once, less definite with "subtle-colored hair," which might be unkindly interpreted as mousy. Tennyson, in *A Dream of Fair Women,* put red hair on his swarthy queen with the "bold black eyes": playing a sequence of clever modulations on the

7

difficult *b* sound, he describes her as "brow-bound with burning gold." In the sixteenth century black hair was unfashionable, perhaps because Queen Elizabeth (who disliked competitors) was sandy, and Shakespeare in several sonnets lamented his misfortune in falling in love with a "black woman." Red or reddish-gold hair perhaps reached the height of its popularity in late Victorian times, Browning leading the way and Rossetti following hard, with paintings as well as poems. His Blessed Damozel has hair "yellow like ripe corn," and for some may achieve an unfortunate resemblance to a barmaid when she leans out "from the gold bar of Heaven." And William Morris's Rapunzel (whose name seems to have become in the United States a generic term for Miss Veronica Lake) had "golden" and "glorious" hair which she let down and wept through. Red-gold hair became almost a Pre-Raphaelite monopoly, and its persistence can be seen in the pastel *Woman's Head,* by E. R. Hughes (Plate VI, page 42): in the original the hair lifts like tangled flames out of the dark background. Poe, however, gave Helen of Troy black hair, though he disguised the attribute, for the reader without a dictionary at hand, by using the adjective "hyacinth." On the whole the poets have been wisest who held to color images for women's hair. Solomon, for example, drew a strange comparison when he rhapsodized over his beloved: "Thy hair is as a flock of goats, that appear from Mount Gilead."

Below the roots of the hair the face proper begins, with the forehead or brow flanked on either side, above the ears, by the temples, traditionally vulnerable—it was through the temples that Jael drove the nail or tent-peg, pinning Sisera to the ground. There the Old Testament is easily understood, but Solomon again produces another incongruous image when he compares his beloved's temples not to a pomegranate, but to a piece of a pomegranate: which surely implies a section cut open. It seems a fair assumption that in the long, slow course of evolution the human forehead has become upright or almost upright, instead of sloping sharply back, and has also increased its height. As human experience extended itself over a wider range of external and mental activities, and was at the same time intensified and subtilized, the physical apparatus necessary to accompany so much thinking—the brain—would be enlarged and so, slowly, imperceptibly from generation to generation, the skull would be forced to augment its accommodation. Part of this annex would be created by extending the front of the head forward and upward. At any rate, a high forehead is commonly regarded as a sign of intellectual capacity, and even of noble character: low foreheads to Shakespeare (himself handsomely furnished) were "villainous," while the prestige of the high forehead has been a great consolation to many men who in middle age find their appearance transformed by the encroachments of baldness. It is perhaps a wanton or unconscious insult which has made taste at certain periods—the dictum is explicit in certain nineteenth-century books—hold that a low forehead in a woman should be a positive sign of beauty. But at other times the 'lofty brow' has been admired equally in both sexes, notably during the Renaissance in Italy. In surviving paintings some prodigiously high foreheads are to be seen. Erasmus reported that many aristocrats in Venice (a city where haircutting was proverbially drastic) shaved their heads all over. A century earlier Florentine ladies are known to have shaved, or plucked with tweezers, the hair clean away from the front of their heads, in order to give the illusion of a steepling brow. This may be part of the secret of the attraction of Filippo Lippi's Madonnas.

The eyebrows beneath the forehead follow the ridge-lines of the upper part of the eye-sockets, and one of their physiological functions is still performed: they serve as a barrier-trap against sweat or rain which otherwise might flow down to the eyelids and obscure vision. The capacity of eyebrows for retaining excessive moisture is, however, limited; sweat hard enough, and some of the salt liquid will seep through. Those who believe that nature's moderations should be taken as danger signals will see in this a warning against excessive physical labor, at any rate in hot weather. The other primary function of the eyebrows is no longer universal, and not every one has controllable and flexible muscles in this part of the face, or eyes pitted sufficiently deeply to be able to lower and contract the brows as a screen against the glare of the sun.

Beautiful eyebrows have long been admired, though the selection of particular characteristics making for beauty has varied from time to time. In men shaggy or tufted eyebrows—as, indeed, hairiness in general—are looked on as a sign of virility in the young, and of authority and venerableness in the aged. In women a more moderate growth is generally considered desirable, and brows and lashes darker than the hair of the head are always admired—partly because they serve to emphasize the brilliance of the eyes. Poets and lovers (in Elizabethan times the words were almost synonymous) tend to concentrate their attention on the shape of their beloved's eyebrows. This shape is subject to fashion and can, within certain limits, be altered artificially. In the early Middle Ages women counted themselves fortunate, or clever, who could exhibit dark eyebrows, heavily arched, and tapering sharply at the outer ends: rather like crescents drawn in charcoal. This fashion probably came from Byzantine icons and mural paintings in Greece and Turkish Europe. A little later, taste demanded that a beautiful woman's eyebrows should be wide, and hardly arched at all; sometimes they were run together over the bridge of the nose, making a continuous and almost straight line. Later the eyebrows were widely separated, and thinned above and below, by shaving or by the use of the tweezers. This Renaissance fashion was widely revived in the nineteen-thirties, and fantastically developed until smart young women would have their eyebrows entirely shaved off, so that they could mark on artificial substitutes with black or blue cosmetic pencils, sometimes varying color and shape according to the time of day. Eyebrows which are exceptionally wide and rise at a steep angle from the center help to produce the conventional aspect of the Devil or Mephistopheles. This association, I believe, arose from Goethe's *Faust,* and still survives in productions of Gounod's opera. It is reinforced with a scarlet silk costume, hollow, clean-shaven cheeks, a swarthy complexion, and flashing eyes.

PLATE II: LOUIS DE BÉRANGER, *by* FRANÇOIS CLOUET

PLATE III: YOUTHFUL HEAD, *by* G. B. TIEPOLO

And one of Shakespeare's most extravagant, and successful, images calls bright eyes "lights that do mislead the morn." Browning's Lost Leader had a "mild and magnificent eye," and the eyes of Milton's Adam were somewhat unspecifically "sublime."

Spectacles are a modern and complicating addition to the appearance of the eye, which they may hide by reflecting too direct a light. They are not so modern as all that, however. The monocle and the lorgnette belong to the late eighteenth century, and there are portraits by Velasquez and Murillo, nearly a hundred years earlier, showing gentlemen with rimmed spectacles. In *Lear* we find the old King sardonically advising Edgar:

> Get thee glass eyes;
> And, like a scurvy politician, seem
> To see the things thou dost not.

In color, blue wins hands down and all the time; green eyes, unjustly, are often held to betoken a jealous or a sinister disposition, except when they are purloinable emeralds inset in a "little yellow god"; brown eyes cloy when they are called "liquid" or "melting," the metaphor apparently having strayed from a cookery book; or else they may be likened, after Homer's example, to cows' eyes. And black eyes—if any eyes can fairly be called black—are almost put out of the poetic count by the ill-luck of the idiom (and Charles Coborn's popular song) which uses the phrase for the flesh over the eye-socket, bruised and discolored by a blow. Solomon makes an estate-agent's comparison—"Thine eyes like the fish-pools in Heshbon"—but the color he thus praised must remain uncertain. Robert Louis Stevenson did his best by yellow or tawny eyes when he described his wife as possessing "eyes of gold and bramble-dew." But blue is the universal favorite.

The primary function of the eyes is obvious enough: it is to transmit images of the external world, reflections of light falling upon objects. That is why the eyes are set high in the face, itself poised at the summit of the body. This process of vision is not, however,

The eyebrows surmount and screen the eyes, the most brilliant and expressive feature of the face. Without the eyes, or even when they are hidden by the lids, a great part of the face's vitality is lost. So powerful is the effect of what we perceive with our senses, as contrasted with what we know by study, that it is difficult to realize or remember that the eyes are globular in shape: "vile jelly," Cornwall in *Lear* calls them. What is revealed is the pupil and iris, and part of the white, framed in the irregular ellipse formed by the eyelids; and when we speak of small or large eyes, or of their shape, it is to this frame of thin flesh that we refer. It is truly a frame, for the creasing of the lids both above and below the visible eye produces the effect of a double line. Æsthetic requirements are fairly stable: beautiful eyes are those which are not noticeably small or deep sunk, not set closely together, not dull or out of focus, and not abnormally protuberant. Within these limits the eyes may be blue, brown, gray, or that dark gray known as hazel, tinged greenish or tawny or reddish, or speckled like a trout, and still be sure of finding admirers. And this comprehensiveness applies to both sexes. Blind eyes have pathos; eyelids reddened or swollen by weeping may be regarded as either pathetic or displeasing, although Shakespeare, in *Antony and Cleopatra,* invests Bacchus, quite unreproachfully, with "pink eyne." The color and brilliance of pupil and iris are enhanced by contrast with the white of the eyeball, which should not be discolored except, perhaps, with a faint tinge of blue.

Dull eyes—'lack-luster' was the word Shakespeare invented for them—deny themselves the potentiality of beauty: a torpid mind can make them almost as blank as the eyes of the dead. Brilliance is the essential quality. Tom Moore, who elsewhere celebrated his Lesbia's "beaming eye," and some other girl's of "most unholy blue," chirpily proclaimed that

> The light, that lies
> In woman's eyes,
> Has been my heart's undoing.

simple either in operation or in its scope. By means of the eyes we are informed instantaneously not only of the color and shape of things, but of their distance from us, their movements, and their speed of movement. It is because of the faculty of vision that we are able to carry on a freely mobile physical existence among our fellow creatures. This primary function of the eyes is one in which human beings are superior to animals only in so far as they can use the visions recorded in their brains as a basis for mathematical and scientific calculations—all science depends ultimately on the evidence of the senses—or make them yield æsthetic and emotional pleasures which, so far as we know, are peculiar to man.

But the eyes perform a further function. They not only transmit reports on external objects: they emit reports of the state of mind of the person who, insubstantial, intangible, a mystery even to himself, may be described as living behind the eyes. The eyes indicate— more vividly, if not so precisely, than words or even the intonations of the voice—our moods and emotions. Sometimes the information is given with the free will of the mind; sometimes in spite of it. If we wish to know what someone is really thinking (although by 'thinking' we usually mean 'feeling') we try to scrutinize his face, and especially his eyes. It is the eyes which reveal instant and secret reactions, often very different from what is ostensibly professed. The eyes can indicate affection, desire, defiance, contempt, hatred, indignation, melancholy, or joy—all the emotions. They can be used to intimidate and to seduce. They have a lover's language all their own—and a rebel's. Not for nothing does the British Army enumerate, among the military crimes of subordinates towards those in authority, "dumb insolence," which may be defined as looking what one dare not speak.

But it should be emphasized that, although the eyes can thus make vivid communications, their power of expression is confined to indications: they can plead but not argue; they can state but not analyze; they can declare effects, but are helpless to explain causes. The glance of the eye can be an act of intimacy, sanctioned or not, a penetration into others' lives, a disclosure of one's own. It may be casual, light-hearted, or flirtatious. But if the glance is made seriously, and interlocks with the glance of another person, each pair of eyes staring into the other, the meeting cannot be sustained for long without an intense relationship being set up. Normally, one or the other of two persons who thus confront one another quickly looks away; for while glances are held together there is a spiritual nakedness—privacy is surrendered and with it a certain amount of free will. Gladly or uneasily we are aware that we are no longer alone. Come close enough to another person, and you will see in each of the dark eye-pupils opposite yours a tiny image of your own face. And you may be sure that in your eyes similar miniatures are showing. This was what the Elizabethans, expertizing on lovers' habits, called "seeing babies." It is an exercise in sustained intimacy proper only to lovers, for behind the lustrous eyeballs lies the brain; and the brain, though it is not the mind and soul, is the most delicate instrument they use. The brain remains invisible, at least while we are alive; and it is through the eyes therefore that we come nearest to communion with each other, and step closest to the ultimate mystery which locks us, each separately, for as long as life endures, inside the prison-house of one body, whence we may shout and listen to other prisoners, and out of which the only peephole is the eyes.

In the face considered structurally the eyes surmount the cheeks—tracts of plastic flesh which may be concave or convex, creased or smooth, and are to a certain extent mobile where they adjoin the mouth. The cheeks change their appearance, at different periods from infancy to old age, as much as any of the features. They may be sucked in or distended; they may be so broad as to present most of their extent to the frontal view, or they may recede at a sharp angle. In a baby they may be almost globular, and in the fat or unhealthy they may become pendulous, sagging below the line of the jaw. From them the upper portion of the beard is grown, and across them, a decorative diversion, the mustaches may spread,

twisted and pointed perhaps with wax. They are sometimes diversi-
fied with one or, more rarely, two dimples; and it is perhaps worth
noting, whatever the explanation may be, that women with dimples
are to be seen much less frequently than even twenty years ago.
Pallor in the cheeks denotes sickness; an exceptional rosiness health
or a resolute use of rouge. Youth shows in the complexion of the
cheeks as vividly as in the eyes, and upon the form and plasticity
of this middle tract of the face depends to a large extent the first
general impression it makes on the observer: it is the field or background against which the more often noticed features are drawn.

Between the cheeks descends and projects the nose, of all the parts
of the face the one which most often provokes ridicule from unkind observers and humiliation in those who consider themselves
unfortunately dealt with by nature. Scientists tell us that the sense
of smell is almost atrophied in civilized man: because we no longer
need to sniff the wind to scent approaching danger we are no longer
alert or discriminating in smell. And what faculty we have left, as
with the taste in the palate, we overwhelm with tobacco smoke.
Yet man has lived an urban life for several thousand years, and if
he has lost the full use of the sense of smell I would rather ascribe
it to a merciful dispensation, making him oblivious to the open
sewers and undrained privies which, until quite recently, were
universal in cities, towns, and villages, and in more modern times to
the odors of gasoline and factory smoke. The theory of an atrophy-
ing sense of smell does not, to my mind, account for the facts any
more satisfactorily than Coleridge's suggestion that the basic reason
for the existence of the nose was to take snuff. For the more primitive races of mankind, who might be supposed to depend on an
acute sense of smell for food and self-preservation, almost all have
flattened noses nearly level with the cheeks; whereas the nose of
civilized man is a jetty: it thrusts forward well ahead of the rest
of the face.

However, it may be accounted for scientifically (and the theory
in favor at the moment will, almost certainly, be reckoned out of

date in a few years' time), the prominence of the adult civilized nose is a fact which must, like the rest of the universe, be accepted. Even small noses, admired in pretty women and men of conventional good looks, reach at least an inch farther forward than the brows and mouth, and many which are rightly considered no disfigurement jut far more decisively than that. A woman, to pass as beautiful, is required to have a smaller nose than a man. But smallness is not enough: her nose must be elegantly shaped. This is to conform to the more delicate structure of the feminine face, as well as to the softer and clearer texture of the skin. A handsome woman can successfully 'carry' a high-bridged nose, but it will look incongruous in an otherwise pretty face. Indeed, no feature of the face can be considered by absolute æsthetic standards: the effect, pleasurable or repellent, interesting or dull, depends on the relationship to other parts and to the face as a whole. So a pretty woman must have a pretty nose—which is to say one that does not attract attention to itself by undue size or odd shape or coloring. A moderate snubness —Tennyson's "tip-tilted," frenchified by the genteel as retroussé—is pleasing: it lends an air of mischief and impertinence. But it will not do for a tragedienne: Marie Tempest could never play Lady Macbeth or Mrs Alving, and, contrariwise, Mrs Siddons, we are told, was unwittingly tragic in comedy.

For men who desire to be attractive and impressive much more scope in the size and prominence of the nose is allowed. It is commonly held, indeed, that a large nose lends character to the face. The Roman or aquiline nose—not that many Romans appear to have possessed it, and not that it really resembles an eagle's beak—is regarded as a sign of a determined and martial character. The first Duke of Wellington (who in coloring and facial shape was characteristically Irish) possibly owed some of his promotion and a good deal of his early popularity to the high arch of his nose, making an angle in front of his blue eyes like a bend in a plumber's pipe. On the other hand, the saintly and erudite and argumentative Cardinal Newman had a face in which all was subordinate to the nose, a prodigious beak; and Erasmus, all his adult life, seems to have carried before him a nose exceptionally thin and forward-reaching. Viewed from the front, even the biggest nose loses some of its effect as it merges into the general perspective of the face. From this aspect, the width of the nose is more important. Too thin or too broad will not do; and again shapeliness is necessary if criticism is to be avoided. Some noses descend from bridge to tip in a ridge which has the aspect of painful bony upthrust against the skin; in others the ridge makes a flat surface, as if between two parallel lines. Other noses spread abruptly and excessively to splay the nostrils wide, and others again enlarge at the base into bulbousness. The nostrils, both on the lower and upper curve, may be high or low in arch, and either pinched or distended. It is perhaps a fine point to enthuse over the precise formation of the nostril vent, which is but a subordinate part of the whole end of the nose.

Viewed in profile, the nose takes on a new and more important aspect, for this way it is released from the obscuring background of the face. It sketches itself vividly on the air. It charms or it impresses, or else it disappoints by its failure to achieve any decisive effect. The upturned nose, if it tilts too far, passes beyond mischief into clownishness, and the impending arch of the Roman nose loses majesty if the tip descends too low towards the mouth and chin. Yet there are infinite variations on the theme of profile beauty to be drawn by noses. "Cleopatra's nose, had it been shorter," said Pascal, "the whole history of the world would have been different." Presumably he meant that with a different face Cleopatra might have failed to capture and hold the successive loves of Julius Cæsar and Mark Antony, rulers of the world. But, so far as surviving medallions show, Cleopatra (who was a Ptolemy, and therefore Greek) had a heavy-featured face, and notably lacked that single sweeping profile line from the top of the forehead to the tip of the nose which the classic Greeks, if their sculptors are convincing evidence, held so precious.

The praise of other features may give us more pleasure, but there is none concerning which we respond so sensitively to criticism. The red nose, of drunkenness or indigestion, the long nose, the hook nose, the bulbous nose, are all part of the stock-in-trade of stage comedians, and the snub nose painted white belongs to the clown's insignia. Cyrano de Bergerac gave Rostand and a succession of nineteenth-century actors the chance to make a romantic gesture of defiance against the fore-ordained comicality of the egregious nose. There is one parallel to Rostand in the history of art: the portrait of an old man with a small boy by Domenico Ghirlandhaio, in the Louvre. The old man has a nose enormously swollen by some disease and covered with crimson pimplings: just such a disability as the millionaire, J. Pierpont Morgan, suffered from. Yet the effect of the picture is in no way ridiculous; it is moving because of the simple and direct sincerity of the affection evident between the child and the old man. In general, however, a nose that is ill-shaped or vividly colored is considered a legitimate and inevitable subject for laughter, and the possessor of such a nose who aspires to be taken seriously is in a pitiful position. Falstaff, by tradition, is played not only with a paunch but with a drunkard's big red nose—though he must not outshine Bardolph with his face "all bubukles, and whelks, and knobs, and flames of fire"; and perhaps the opulent rosiness prepares for the final pathos of Falstaff's reported end: "his nose was as sharp as a pen, and a' babbled of green fields."

The nose is unique in one way: it is the only part of our face we can, if it is overlong, see directly without the aid of a mirror. Here I need not depend on the testimony of others, for I am bound to admit that, by focusing my eyes downward and inward, and with a little strain, I can see the end of my own nose, which must be classified therefore as unduly prominent. It is also, at the end, too broad in proportion to the upper part, and for my own taste (which I would like to hope is not universal) it is clumsily and displeasingly shaped. It was not always so with me: as a boy I had a nose of modest proportions and some symmetry, but then heredity took me literally by the nose. The power of heredity over the face is a subject which must be discussed later on. Here I will say no more than this: though I have a grudge against this humiliating determinism, this biological bullying, I recognize that I might have fared worse at the distorting hands of heredity, for on the other side of my family there is a long, narrow, inquisitive nose (said to derive from a remote Spanish ancestor in the West of Ireland) which it is true might have some aristocratic elegance but for the fact that it invariably slants across the face in a disconcerting diagonal. And before I forget, for those who have never made the experiment there is a variation on the trick of looking down at the end of one's nose: this is to look down, but to close first one eye and then the other, when the ridge line of the nose may be seen in profile, from just below the bridge to the tip. It is an ingenious game, but rather harmful to the vanity. After the experience life is never quite the same again.

The nose occupies a place between and in front of the cheeks; the ears lie behind and beside them, almost always visible from a front view. Like the nose, the ears depend for beauty on size and shape, but the shape is more varied, complex, and often more delicate. It is evident that the sense of hearing in man has not been diminished by civilization to the same extent as the sense of smell; indeed, it is often exquisitely refined by the appreciation of music and spoken language. But until recently, at least, we have not needed our ears to preserve our lives from danger, and doubtless it is for this reason that they have in the course of time, except for a few unfortunates, become folded back to lie almost flat against the side of the head. Most people have also lost the animal faculty of being able to flap the ears outward the better to listen to distant sounds. It remains to be seen whether the further experiments of civilization with the gasoline engine and high-explosive missiles will induce humanity to re-equip itself with outstanding and adjustable ears.

The ear varies in shape most noticeably at the top and the bottom. At the top it may describe a shallow or a high arch, and the turn-over of the rim may be narrow or coarsely broad: or again the top of the ear may describe a curve so sharp that it is almost angular, thus imparting a touch of the faun to the face—a touch alleged by Mr Aldous Huxley and other satiric novelists of the nineteen-twenties to be erotically stimulating to female observers of manly beauty. The bottom of the ear may droop into a lobe, full or restrained, or it may join the neck without any pendant at all. White or faintly pink ears are most admired, but only a small minority of women apply cosmetics to this part of the face. This is odd in view of the fact that widespread ears are notoriously apt to glow scarlet in cold weather, and face powder at least, so freely applied to the nose, might surely be ventured here. Earrings and eardrops are worn sometimes to draw attention to the ears, sometimes to distract attention away from them; and women who have no lobes, or insignificant lobes, to their ears are said to wear pendant eardrops to create an illusion of length. The custom of piercing the ears is or was widely believed to have a beneficial effect on eyesight, and many sailors and fishermen still wear earrings.

The whorls, or convolutions, of the ear (properly, the outer ear, for the process of transmitting sound is done inside the head) are often compared to those of sea-shells, and their reproduction on canvas or paper has long been troublesome to portrait-painters. Many artists, despairing of catching a faithful likeness, have, in the past at least, evolved each his own formula of brush- or pencil-strokes, so that when you sat for your portrait what you got at the side of the head on the canvas or panel was not so much an image of your own ears as ears of a kind that particular painter found it easiest and most effective to paint. Now the attribution of unsigned (and sometimes of signed) pictures done in the past is a matter for learned argument and dispute, and can be as fascinating as a detective story. It was first put on a scientific basis towards the end of the nineteenth century by a Swiss connoisseur who specialized in Italian pictures of the Primitive and Renaissance periods. His name was Giovanni Morelli, but for some reason he chose to write as a Russian, as one Ivan Lermolieff. Perhaps this was because he set himself to overthrow and expose certain attributions made by a German scholar of ponderous mind, Dr Wilhelm von Bode. One of the principles on which Morelli worked was to study the details of authenticated paintings and drawings by certain masters, notably Filippo Lippi, Titian, Raphael, Botticelli, and Giovanni Bellini, thus establishing the formulas or conventions they used for certain recurrent subjects. Dr Bode called him a "surgeon" because he compared so minutely the hands and, most often of all, the ears in different pictures. Morelli won his case, and on the basis of his work the catalogues of most public art galleries were thoroughly revised. He was never forgiven by Bode, who once was rash enough to commit himself to the dogmatic opinion that a certain bust was indisputably the work of Leonardo da Vinci. On his advice the bust was bought for a Berlin museum, and a little later, broken by accident, it was found to contain, embedded in the wax, fragments of a nineteenth-century newspaper!

The ears, boneless and the only part of the head not integral in its structure, are apt to be regarded, by brutish people in authority, as easily removed appendages. Defoe, it will be remembered, had his cropped for pamphleteering, and Fouché, one of the vilest sadists let off the leash by the French Revolution and later Napoleon's Chief of Secret Police, used at one time to ride about with ears cut from his victims' heads fastened to his cap. And then there was that perverse ingenuity of madness which prompted Van Gogh to slice off one of his own ears, parcel it up and dispatch it through the post, and afterwards paint a portrait of himself with his head bandaged. In *Hamlet* the whole action of the play springs from the murder of the old king by poison administered through "the porches of the ear." And in *A Midsummer Night's Dream* the metamorphosis of Bottom is made most vivid by Titania's infatuated willingness to kiss "the fair large ears" of the ass's head clapped upon him. In general, however, writers incline to the ear in the abstract, as a symbol for sounds which delight them, rather than to the ears as material objects of flesh and blood. If we add to Nick

Bottom the fable of Midas, and the apotheosis of Chesterton's donkey, with "ears like errant wings," it will be seen that in the treatment of this part of the face literature has done better by the ass than by normal humanity.

The mouth, the most flexible and, next to the eyes, the most expressive of all the facial features, is a composite. It consists of two lips, but this word is used sometimes of the red surfaces continuous with the inner mouth, and sometimes of the adjoining planes of the face which link the red to the nose and the chin; the teeth and the tongue also have their place, intermittently, in the visible mouth. It is easiest to consider the mouth—as, indeed, the whole face—in repose, when its stable shape can be studied and what it seems to signify is more likely to be a lasting, recurring, ingrained complex of traits than an evanescent reaction to outward events. The mobility of the lips in speech varies not only between persons but between nationalities: it has a constructive and amending influence on language. There are also many ways, some of them unlovely, of putting food into the mouth and masticating it, and of swallowing drink. And the adjustable shape of the mouth may betoken many emotions: the phrase 'down in the mouth' explains itself, while lips upturned at the ends, halfway to a smile, indicate good humor. The mouth is also, with the chin, a traditional symbol of will power, as with the 'stiff upper lip.' Lord Chesterfield, a preceptor whom few admire nowadays, held that a gentleman ought never to laugh: sufficient if he unfurled his lips gracefully and moderately in a smile.

Then there is the most emotional of all the uses to which the mouth is put, for the giving and receiving of kisses. Kissing is by no means a universal custom, and we have all heard of South Sea Islanders who prefer to rub noses. Erasmus was astounded, and pleased, in the course of his first visit to England, to find that casual visitors were kissed by the womenfolk of the house (the custom is long out of fashion), but there is no record whether these conventional kisses were of the full or deflected kind. For there is a world of difference between the kiss performed mouth to mouth and the kiss which falls on cheek or forehead. To judge from Shakespeare's account of Henry V's wooing of Princess Katharine, it would have been considered shocking for a girl in France to kiss or be kissed by her fiancé before marriage; but not so in England. On the other hand, to this day in France and some other Continental countries men may still be seen on festive and ceremonial occasions embracing one another and dabbing their mouths at or alongside each other's cheeks; but again the custom has fallen out of favor in British countries and in the United States. Women, however, are still expected to exchange kisses, with or without enthusiasm, at appropriate times. But by and large, the full kiss, mouth to mouth, is reserved for lovers. The reason for this limitation of privilege is crude but sound. The full kiss brings together delicate and sensitive skin surfaces, where the stimulation of contact from another person is direct and dynamic to the whole nervous system, and so to the emotions. Self-denial, by reserving the full kiss for comparatively rare occasions, thus preserves and refines the voluptuous effect, and those who are chary of their kisses thereby set a higher value on them.

The beauty of the mouth lies partly in its color. A mouth too pale will not do; nor will a surface over-wet and glistening, or one broken into flat facets by dryness or chapping. Any dark shade of red short of purplish may be admired. Once the expression is mobile, with the mouth open, provided too much gum or discolored, broken, missing, or protruding teeth are not revealed, the mouth loses some of its importance in the face as a whole. The beauty of the mouth is best seen in repose, when the lips lie together and a shape is established athwart the lower part of the face: "the dear red curve of her lips," in Masefield's phrase. In recent times most women have taken to concealing and altering the shape of their mouths with lipstick, and considering all the adverse criticisms passed by men it must be difficult now to maintain the argument that women adapt their appearance to please masculine taste. Lipstick may have been originally designed to repair inadequate coloration, but in practice what it does is to paint another and false mouth on the face: a mouth, moreover, unduly prominent yet makeshift, obtaining a startling effect at twenty yards' distance and a repulsive one at close quarters, and on top of that establishing a false standard of color by which the natural hue of the lips is apt to be judged paler than it really is.

Apart from this intemperate folly, which may prove not to be lasting, the shape of the mouth offers an interesting series of variations. Breadth is traditionally regarded as an indication of generosity and good humor; narrowness passes as a sign of either demure femininity or pettiness of nature. Whether these are justified assumptions or not, both narrow and broad mouths may be beautiful: everything depends on proportion to the rest of the face and on shape. Some tastes prefer lips which are roughly of even depth; others are better pleased if the nether lip is the fuller. Some like a pronounced double curve, the 'cupid's bow' shape; some like to see the ends of the mouth curve upward; some prefer an approximation to the straight line. The lower lip which droops slightly and the upper lip which pouts a little, revealing part of the front teeth, can both be charming. In some mouths both lips protrude slightly outward, curling back from each other; in moderation, this also can be attractive. But the pursed or the bitten-in mouth can hardly be deemed beautiful, because it destroys and conceals shape. Moreover, in mature faces the mouth gains or loses by the natural frame provided by the cleft or double line, from the nose to the middle of the upper lip, and the facial creases sketched or channeled from the nostrils downward and outward along the cheeks. The mouth can hardly be isolated: consider the trite similarity of those lipstick impressions left by film actresses as mural decorations in an American restaurant. Its expressive power is best seen in immobility, but this depends on its conformity or its contrast with other parts of the face, and in particular with the mobile and expressive eyes.

The most marked characteristic of the chin is its position relative to the mouth. If it recedes it detracts from the dignity and the effect of strength of the whole face; if it juts forward too far it is apt to convey an impression of aggressiveness rather than determination. In women a rounded chin is considered desirable, particularly to complete the oval shape of the classic face, but angled and dimpled chins are judged attractive in both sexes. A deep recess under the lower lip may emphasize the chin into a boss. For beauty, one chin is sufficient, although—to judge from portraits of Nell Gwynn and the Duchess of Portsmouth—Charles II did not think so. The chin merges upward and outward into the face, and the jawbone may or may not be visible under the flesh. Generally, an emphasized line of the jaw is more admired in men than in women, though not more common. Plumpness of flesh under the jaw, which in later years tends to sag and crinkle into folds and bags, is a product of over-eating and insufficient exercise. In all countries a pouched under-jaw is a mark of the urban well-to-do class, and is perhaps particularly noticeable in the United States of America, where it is by far the most common characteristic in portraits of 'big business-men.'

Finally, the head is set on a flexible pillar, the neck, which enables it to turn from side to side. Here again, to please the eye there is a scale of proportion which must be maintained. Too long, too short, too thick, or too thin, and the effect of the most beautiful face may be ruined, although taste varies from place to place and time to time; some Burmese tribes encourage their women to elongate their necks with brass rings; but in 'white' countries the swan-like throat and the bottle-neck shoulders which so often accompanied it are no longer admired as they were in the middle of the nineteenth century. The endurance of the fashion of collars and ties for men is partly due to the fact that by this means the natural misfortunes of neck and throat may be partly concealed and amended.

The face is the only part of the body—for the hands are often gloved—which is always on view to the public gaze, and, as a later discussion will show, a vast amount of thought, time, and ingenuity have been expended on techniques of presenting the face to the world so as to emphasize its advantages and minimize defects and deficiencies. Good, bad, or indifferent, the face inescapably remains that part of ourselves by which we are most really identified and, as often as not, brought up for instant judgment.

PLATE IV: HEAD OF A GIRL, *by* ERIC KENNINGTON

Author's Collection

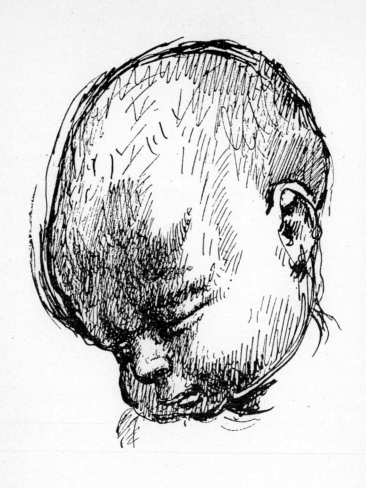

PLATE V: STUDY OF A BABY, *by* MERVYN PEAKE

Author's Collection

CHAPTER TWO

ADORNMENTS

MAN turns his face towards wherever his attention is drawn, and out of certain instinctive movements of his head he makes symbols, nodding it up and down to signify assent, shaking it from side to side to indicate refusal or denial, although in Arab countries these meanings are reversed. In moments of exaltation he tilts his face upward: "I will lift up mine eyes to the hills, from whence cometh my help." To express devotion he bows his head, sometimes abasing the whole body with it, and often prays with his face covered by his hands. The assumption that what is high is morally superior to what is low seems to be inherent in human thought, like the preference for right hand over left hand which gives the word 'sinister' its secondary but now principal meaning. Paradise, as the abode of God and the reward of the good human life, is universally conceived as in the skies, and hell as subterranean. Linked with this is the association of good with light, and evil with darkness. It is doubtless because of these assumptions that the face tilted slightly up, as if to the sky, normally indicates aspiration and solemnity. Leonardo discovered, or at any rate explicitly stated, the chief variation: the face bent slightly aside and downward. This posture was used most frequently for pictures of the Virgin, and it is natural to a mother with her child at the breast or cradled in her arms. But Leonardo used it also for men, making it symbolize meditation.

Apart from these classic positions, the face is normally seen and thought of as looking forward, at eye level, for here the face is viewed in either a full or a three-quarter aspect. Profile is rather different, for then the face is observed but is observing elsewhere. We think of our own faces almost always as if seen from the front, in a mirror: few of us (except actors and actresses, who have to

27

study the use of their appearance as part of their stock-in-trade) maintain a clear conception of our own profiles. The profile is indeed but half a face, and one-eyed at that, yet it may achieve graces not promised in the full view; or again, it may disappoint expectation. The profile is often so different that it may be regarded as an additional and independent face. It is easier to study other people with detachment if they are seen in profile, for there is no meeting of the eyes, no disconcerting clash or communion of self-consciousnesses. The profile has more draftsmanship and less perspective than the full face: it is sketched, momentarily perhaps but sharply and decisively, against a background, and, because the whole head is seen poised on the column of the throat, the profile may well be a more lucid exposition of personality than the full face. But an intimacy is lost when the direct glance of both eyes is avoided.

Since civilization began men and women have striven, with considerable ingenuity and pains, though not always intelligently, to present their faces to others at the best advantage. While women tend their complexions and experiment with cosmetics, men have usually confined themselves to variations on themes executed by the razor and the scissors. For without barbering the mature male face would be visible only in part. In many places and at many times the beard has been revered as pertaining to the personal dignity, and often as a sacred emblem of virility—a quality which few of our forefathers (and foremothers) learned to take for granted. In the old story the Roman senator suffered in statuesque silence the close inspection of the invading Goth, but struck a blow, which he knew must bring about his own death, as soon as his beard was touched; he was prompted by an instinct powerful in the ancient world far beyond the limits of the Roman Empire. In the Middle Ages, also, to pluck a man by the beard was a gross insult, and one which King John can hardly have committed unintentionally when he visited the Irish chieftains. Even later, Sir Francis Drake, himself bearded, vividly summarized his piratical impudence at Cadiz as "singeing the King of Spain's beard." It is because of the long tradition associating the beard with personal dignity that it easily becomes a matter for mockery: where there is no tradition of reverence there can be no sacrilege. The youths who in the nineteen-twenties played the game of counting beards among passers-by were, as youths so often do, embroidering an old tradition rather than establishing a novelty. This game of Beaver (the title has hardly been accounted for) survives only as a freak of the period, commemorated by passing references in fiction. It is said to have originated, like excessively wide flannel trousers and other foolish extravagances, in the University of Oxford, but with what justification I do not know. Until a few centuries ago men swore, without facetiousness, by their beards, and even today in Moslem countries influenced by Western customs, although the beard is as out of fashion as the face-veil for women in sophisticated circles, it is still conventional to take a sacred oath by the Prophet's beard.

The razor may have come into use with the Bronze Age, or, even earlier, men may have shaved themselves, roughly and painfully, with knives chipped out of flint or some other hard stone like obsidian. In the earliest civilizations shaving of a sort, without a hollow-ground or wafer blade, and without lathering soap, seems to have been practiced off and on. The later Romans are said to have eked out the razor's crop with pumice-stone. Thus there have always been the still prevailing variations in the appearance of the masculine face. It may be full-bearded, with mustaches; bearded with the beard trimmed to different shapes by clipping; mustached; whiskered (that is, with the chin shaved but not the cheeks and jaws); or clean-shaven. Fashion, vanity, and sometimes religious or secular custom dictated the choice. There is a tradition that Adam was created with a ready-made beard. In old Nineveh beards were curled and oiled, and in Persia they were plaited with golden threads; but in ancient Egypt men were nearly always clean-shaven, although on solemn ceremonial occasions they wore artificial beards, these denoting by size and shape the social rank of the wearer. In Greece Zeus was conceived as bearded, and so were many of the legendary heroes, but, to judge from statues, by classic times shaving was well established. In Republican Rome a beardless face was apt to be regarded as effeminate, but not so under the Empire. Augustus was clean-shaven, but most kaisers, emperors, and despotic kings—and some quite undespotic—have been bearded. This is probably a prudent arrangement, for the majesty of monarchy, until recent times at least, forbade that a king should shave himself, while to risk his throat under a hireling's open razor must have seemed an encouragement to a *coup d'état*.

At the time of the Norman Conquest beards were out of favor not only among the Normans but among that already hybrid nation known as the Anglo-Saxons or English. Long mustaches and bare chins were worn by both sides at Hastings. A little later Crusaders brought back from the Near East a temporary fashion for beards, and at all times foreign travel and wars have, as by-products, effected remarkable changes in the appearance of the home population. During the Middle Ages beards—particularly forked beards—mustaches, and clean-shaven faces contrived to exist side by side without causing any undue resentment: as we know, people had then plenty of other things to quarrel about. It was perhaps the classical influence of the early Renaissance which brought about the bare-face fashions of the fifteenth century in England, but later on Henry VIII grew his own distinctive kind of beard: broad, brown, and not too thick over the front of the chin. By the time Elizabeth came to the throne every adult man seems to have worn a beard: Cecil, Raleigh, Bacon, Drake, Spencer, Shakespeare, all the great Elizabethans were bearded. But monotony was avoided by trimming the beard to various shapes, many of them fantastic. Philip Stubbes in 1583 lists the French, Spanish, Dutch, and Italian cuts, the new, the old, the bravado, the mean, the gentleman's, the common, the court, and the country cut. And he tells us that barbers could 'lay out' the moustacios "almost from one ear to the other," and turn up the ends. Elizabethan beards were often drenched in perfume, or dusted with powdered orris root, or starched. They could be spun into ringlets with curling irons. And many were dyed. Bottom was not thinking only of false hair from the theater wardrobe when he offered to play the part of Pyramus in "either your straw-color beard, your orange-tawny beard, your purple in-grain beard, or your French-crown color beard, your perfect yellow."

Charles I introduced a new mode when he shaved most of his face and wore a tapering chin-beard with mustaches. This style, widely copied by gentlemen of the time, and the single small tuft below the nether lip, are both perpetuated in innumerable Van Dyck and Lely portraits, although they are best known from their nineteenth-century revival in France by Louis Napoleon. Charles II elected to be restored to the throne with a shaven chin and thin, elegant, dark mustaches, but by the time of Queen Anne neither beards nor mustaches were often seen, and both stayed out of fashion for more than a century. This was because it became customary for every adult male who could afford it to wear a wig, and beards and mustaches do not consort easily with detachable falls of gray or white artificial hair. Wigs have been in use, it is estimated, for 100,000 years, mostly by women to supplement or cover their own hair, considered insufficiently thick or long. They were also used by bald men, by actors, and as a disguise: Messalina wore a yellow wig when she visited the stews of Rome. The periwig or peruke began in the seventeenth century, in France, as a simulation of natural hair, but was soon stylized in silver, gray, or white, and developed, for evening and court wear at least, to a full-bottomed wig drooping over the shoulders, a wig such as is still worn by judges, who are thereby pretty well condemned to shave all the shavable parts of their faces. To accommodate the heavy wig of the late seventeenth and early eighteenth centuries men began to crop their hair short, and even to have the skull razored over. This probably accounts for the oddity of certain informal portraits of the period in which the sitter is portrayed without a wig, but with his head swathed, turban-like, in a white cloth. This, by the way, is an effective headdress, and it was used by Orpen in one of his best self-portraits, perhaps in imitation of the portrait of William Cowper by Romney.

Under George III wigs ceased to be universally worn, the natural hair, at first, being arranged to resemble a pigtailed peruke. Sailors dressed this pigtail with tar, and wore the thin collar, square at the back, which still survives in the Royal Navy, to protect their uniforms from tar stains. The black cloth 'flash,' depending from the back of the tunic collar, worn by the Regiment of Royal Welsh Fusiliers, has a similar origin. The Church, the learned professions, and the fighting services, conservative by instinct, held on longest to their wigs. But by the early nineteenth century soldiers had brought back from the Netherlands and Spain not only mustaches but short side whiskers descending in front of the ears; the side-whisker fashion was revived for a few years in the nineteen-twenties, perhaps under the influence of the film actor, Rudolph Valentino, and worn by some men of taste and serious outlook; but the mode passed soon after it was taken up and vulgarized by young men frequenting the cheaper dance halls and a few who wished to pass for artists of bohemian temperament.

At the period of Waterloo side whiskers were worn by officers and men of line regiments, but the mustache was regarded as the perquisite of the cavalry and the horse-gunners. The early Victorians were mostly beardless, but in the eighteen-fifties veterans of the frosty Crimean winter campaign brought back to London not only woolen or fur Balaclava helmets (which presumably they displayed rather than wore) but long beards. From that time onward the Victorians, soldiers, sailors, and civilians, were predominantly bearded men. The beards were of many shapes but rarely fanciful, the most extravagant being the Dundreary (forked and straggling); the weeper (long and sparse); mutton-chop whiskers (worn by Mr Gladstone); and the Imperial, named after Louis Napoleon when he moved up from President to Emperor. It was a variant of the Imperial which Disraeli and Abraham Lincoln wore, and from the

United States, or at least from New England, came the abrupt tuft below the chin known as the goatee.

By the eighteen-nineties many of the younger Victorians were noticeably tiring of Victorianism, and one of their rebellious ventures was an effort to restore the clean-shaven face to favor. It was a young man's and to some extent a dandy's mode: Oscar Wilde, Aubrey Beardsley, Max Beerbohm, all burst bare-faced upon the shockable bourgeoisie. Bernard Shaw, as so often, was an exception, and Kipling no doubt grew a mustache because of its military associations. The clean-shaven fashion took on, and between the death of the Queen and the outbreak of war in 1914 there was a visible cleavage line between the generations, for while some of the older men might be beardless, practically all the young men went clean-shaven. The mustache had never gone utterly out of favor; special cups, with perforated shelves fixed at one side below the inner lip, were provided to keep drooping hairs from absorbing too much tea, and every barber sold tubes of French pomade for the mustaches of such as preferred to twist the ends into solid cylinders. But those who in the eagerness of their youthful patriotism rushed to volunteer themselves into the Army were, in the last months of 1914, peremptorily ordered to grow mustaches—or rather, in military fashion, the order was framed: "The upper lip will NOT be shaved." Mere abstention from the razor could not, of course, inevitably produce a visible mustache, and before long the order was rescinded. Still, many soldiers did grow mustaches, and a new model came into being: the toothbrush. This did not mean that the hairs were necessarily grown to the length of the bristles on a new toothbrush: they were usually cut much shorter. The similarity lay in the general narrow oblong shape across the upper lip, and in the stiffness. I do not know if anyone has ever stated the reason for the popularity of this form of mustache; it was due to the unhygienic conditions of trench life. The 1914–18 was an excessively dirty as well as blood-thirsty war: soldiers consequently kept the hair of the head cropped short in order to reduce the nesting area for egg-laying lice, and the same precaution was applied to the mustache in conditions where water for washing was often unobtainable for weeks on end. The toothbrush style survives chiefly as the mark of a generation now middle-aged.

A variant of the toothbrush style popular with some subalterns during the period 1914–18 was the Charlie Chaplin mustache, small, grown clear of the upper lip, and necessarily dark if it was to be visible at all. Mr Chaplin had established himself as the leading film comedian, with a series of short silent films, just before 1914; but to the best of my knowledge the mustache he wore in front of the camera was always gummed on. Ridicule killed the Charlie Chaplin as a potential fashion, and it was rarely seen, except as part of the stage properties of comedians, until Hitler's photographs began to appear in the world's newspapers. From the late nineteen-twenties, however, a further apparently new model appeared: this was the mustache thinned to a very narrow streak across the full width of the upper lip, with shaven skin clearly visible above and below. Sometimes it tapered towards the ends. It was popularized, if not introduced, by the late Douglas Fairbanks in his costume films. It still has a Hollywood look about it, although it is actually a revival of a mode established by Charles II—who, by the way, would surely have enjoyed himself immensely in Hollywood. This narrow-streak mustache is capable of both handsome and effeminate effects. The full-grown mustache, occupying the whole of the upper lip, and brushed away to either side, is generally known as the Guardee. Its recent popularity dates from about 1935.

Up to 1939 the beard had almost disappeared, except among old men. It was seen for a time in Dublin and other Irish cities during the 'troubles' of 1920–22, when many conceived it their patriotic duty to let all the hair on their faces grow, whether they were or were not active members of the Irish Republican Army, so that the police, in or out of uniform, might be confused by the sight of hundreds of beards and baffled in their attempts to trace suspects. In

34

the 'thirties the beard was worn by a few painters and literary men in London and Paris. In America it had been reduced almost to the sign of a hillbilly or a hobo. But when the Hitler war began British sailors serving in submarines found it impossible to shave every day, and, rather than start to hack at weeks-old stubble, they took to growing full and handsome beards, brown, black, yellow, or red. The British Army has long had a rule: no beard or whiskers; either a mustache or a clean-shaven face. In the Navy the rule has been: clean shave or beard *and* mustache; but until the exigencies of wartime submarine service violently changed the custom the great majority of naval men elected for the razor. In Burma, soldiers fighting in the jungle grew beards, but shaved them when they returned to the amenities of camp. It remains to be seen whether the Australians after serving in the Pacific will carry their beards home with them. If they do they will no doubt be remembering the fine figures cut by Ned Kelly and other bushrangers.

In these ways men have played about with the appearance of their faces, adapting their tastes as capriciously, if not quite so frequently, as women. Sooner or later, and probably in his youth, almost every man goes into a brief secular retreat in order to prove to himself that he can grow a beard: which may indicate that the old idea of the beard as an emblem of virility still persists. It would be rash to argue that the beard will never return to general favor, but on the whole there are few signs of that happening just now. Bearded young men have a habit of suddenly reappearing transformed. Doubtless, if properly and frequently washed, a beard is quite as cleanly as a shaven chin, but, if my own experience is general, it does not feel so. Bothersome and painful as the daily shave may be, it is a habit one misses, and the automatic clippers known as an 'electric razor' do not at all, in my opinion, produce the sensation of a close shave, which, indeed, bears some resemblance to the dual nature of the sex-relation in its subtle exploitation of the pleasure-pain principle. I see from advertisements in American magazines that only one man in five in the United States is estimated to shave every day. In Great Britain there can be very few who do not shave before they set out for their day's work or, if that hour is too early, in the evening. The discrepancy is difficult to account for, especially as in America so much emphasis is laid on plumbing, deodorants and other hygienic devices, and 'electric razors' are more popular than wafer or hollow-ground blades. When American forces came to Britain voltages had to be altered in many camps and billets to accommodate the shaving requirements of the troops. And possibly this urban habit accounts for the stubbled faces shown in so many photographs of Americans on active service.

Many factors work in favor of the shaving habit, and in particular two professions or vocations. These are the church and the stage. Since the eighteenth century the Popes have been clean-shaven, and most of their clergy have followed their example; the most notable exceptions are the Franciscan monks and missionaries, who have, I believe, a tradition of wearing a beard as a sign that they have returned from sojourning among barbarians: the origin of this word is obvious. Similarly, at one time at least, Roman Catholic priests in Dalmatia were permitted to grow mustaches in deference to local prejudices. Church of England priests, except for some Victorian side-whiskers, have been clean-shaven since the bewigged eighteenth century. So are most Nonconformist clergymen, though some grow mustaches. The reason is probably a feeling, conscious or not, that a beard, covering so much of the face, may be used to conceal expression, and the clergy must be open in every aspect of their lives. As for actors, they have to be clean-shaven because their faces are raw material for their profession. Easier to add false hair than to grow it exactly as the part requires. The actor's consistent face, by which he wishes to be known, is necessarily clean-shaven. It is this face which is most often photographed, most often reproduced in the press, most often admired by women and envied by men. Thus the stage always exercises a strong influence towards a fashion for the shaven face.

The whole face of an adult man could not be revealed without the razor or some other instrument of depilation, and in civilized history man has vacillated between concealment, clean-shaving, and partial disclosure of what lies between the upper cheeks and the throat. There can be little doubt, I think, that in these decisions men are prompted chiefly by the desire to make their appearance attractive or impressive. Masculine vanity is no less powerful than feminine, although it may reveal itself less obviously and courageously. But the promptings of vanity, not simple in themselves, are further complicated by auxiliary motives. The conceit of the individual may be overruled by the conventions of his time and environment, for few men care to defy fashion, and masculine unconventionalities are apt to flow along conventional channels of rebellion. And besides vanity there is comfort and convenience, which most men will take a good deal of trouble to achieve.

Here, perhaps, I may pause to explain that I myself have grown a mustache, of the toothbrush model, and maintained it, with one brief interval, for a quarter of a century. I started the growth in 1914, under military orders, and very immature and unconvincing it then was. As soon as the order was withdrawn I began to shave my upper lip, and continued to shave it, whenever conditions permitted, till 1919, when I left the Army. This was largely due to cussedness, for, although no compulsion was exerted after 1914, there was a strong and continuous moral suasion exercised on soldiers to let their mustaches grow. The shaven upper lip became for me— and, I feel sure, for others—a small but precious symbol of unconquered individuality. On that upper lip I have a birthmark, not large enough to be a disfigurement, but very easily cut by a razor. From those cuts blood invariably flowed profusely and persistently, an irritation and a waste of time. In the Army I had to carry with me, wherever I went, a styptic pencil to stanch the blood. Demobilized, morally and physically a free man, I saw no reason to suffer this daily botheration; so I let my mustache grow. I cite this as an example of the complicated motives which may go to make up the decisions every man has to take about his own face. Lest I be thought to claim exemption from vanity, however, I must confess that, after ten years or so of carrying a mustache, I wondered one morning if the birthmark on my upper lip had lost any of its vulnerability, and further, what I would look like, a decade older, without what had come to be an integral part of my appearance. With scissors and razor I removed the mustache, and was careful not to shed any blood. But the new revelation did not please me at all, nor my wife, nor my friends. It seems that I have the long Irish upper lip, somewhat prominent and clearly marked out by the facial creases from the nostrils to the edges of the mouth, the same upper lip which caricaturists easily exaggerate into a monkey-like mask. After a few days, to make sure of the worst, the mustache was allowed to grow again and has never since been removed. Here, beyond a doubt, is vanity in a defensive mood. But if anyone should wish to know why I keep my mustache clipped short the answer is: partly old habit, and partly convenience, for whenever I let the hairs grow more than half an inch long they begin to curl and intertwine untidily, and moreover to twitch and fidget on my face, as if each had a separate life of its own, setting up an intolerable irritation.

Part of the reverence paid to the full beard is probably due to its concealing effect, for what is hidden, though known to exist, is apt to be mysterious. It is for this reason that God the Father, in almost all the great religious paintings of the Renaissance, is depicted as an old man with a long beard. And so with patriarchs, prophets, and Fathers of the Church. The beard is an indispensable adjunct for the fullness of venerable majesty. The face must never be wholly revealed: its expression must be concentrated in the eyes and the brow, features which fulfill no purposes of carnal appetites, like the mouth and the jaws. No beard, however, has succeeded in hiding the nose from view, and that brings us to the scientific problem of why, out of all the skin surface of the face proper (for the ears are appendages), only the forehead, the nose, and the area round the eyes do not produce a natural growth of hair. And the only answer

I can offer is that hair would impede the exercise of sight and smell
—but then long hair growing on the crown of the head, unless it is
artificially cut short or bound up, easily falls over the eyes and the
nose. So as an auxiliary answer I suggest that evolution may not
after all be the logically perfect and explicable process many assume
it to be. But if there is no satisfactory reason for the hairlessness of
the forehead, the upper cheeks, and the nose, at least the exemption
is something all men (except perhaps manufacturers of razors and
soap) ought to be thankful for.

Women, spared the ordeal of the daily shave as some compensation for their monthly periods and the pangs of childbirth, are able
to transform their faces at will or whim much more comprehensively
than men. Climate to a large extent determines their natural complexions, but that is only the beginning. Here again nature offers
compensations, for the changeable and much abused weather in
Great Britain does provide most of the women who live there, and
who care to expose their faces to fresh air untainted by factory
smoke, with a facial coloring exquisitely blended of red or pink with
white or various shades of brown. To the traveler's eye, when he
returns from Central or Western Europe, English women are apt
to seem not only divinely tall but divinely complexioned—unless the
traveler moves farther west, to Ireland, when he will decide that the
English are, after all, only halfway to godlike perfection. Sunnier
climates produce a durable, even tan, light or dark brown, and this,
though it has its attractions, may seem monotonous in comparison
with the subtle English variations on roseleaf coloring. A fresh
complexion is an advantage which most Englishmen share with
their women, as may be seen by comparing a body of English soldiers, sailors, or airmen with a similar body of Americans: the absence of red tinting in the American face can hardly be overlooked,
and æsthetically it is a loss.

But women have never been content to accept nature's handouts.
Powder, rouge, lipstick, and endless creams are put to work to
amend the unsatisfactory complexion. Sometimes little attempt is

39

made to imitate any effect observable in nature, but in general what is aimed at is a similitude of a clear complexion in which the blood mantles through the translucent skin. That is to say, the model is the natural English (or better still, Irish) complexion. The women of Crete, Greece, Egypt, China, and other ancient civilizations are known to have used cosmetics, but details are hard to come by. Oily and scented unguents, replaced in modern times by skin creams, were applied to soften the texture of the skin and to keep the surfaces of the lips supple. Apple juice (the original 'pomade'), lemon juice, and other acid tinctures were used for whitening the skin, and wealthy beauties have not merely washed but bathed hopefully in milk. Paint was often put on in coats. Many of the Roman satirists direct their criticisms as fiercely against women's toilets as against their morals. The ladies of the Middle Ages rouged drastically, and by the sixteenth century painting the face had become extremely fashionable: Queen Elizabeth in her later years laid it on, it is said, half an inch thick, and not only on her face but on her throat and breast. The fact that Shakespeare dared to make Hamlet say to Ophelia: "God hath given you one face, and you make yourself another," may be taken as contributory evidence that the play was not produced till after the Queen's death in 1603. Face-painting of this extravagant sort continued among great ladies and courtesans into the Victorian era. Then for some time it was looked on as a foreign and immoral habit even by the London aristocracy. It revived in the 'nineties, when Mr Max Beerbohm, a *mondain* youth, was able to publish his *Defence of Cosmetics*. A decade later the popularity of Queen Alexandra was in no way diminished by her reputed habit of enameling her face a bright pink, her choice of color being commemorated by the artificial wild roses still sold every June on a day named after her.

Since the First World War the use of cosmetics has become much wider spread and at the same time much more moderate. It is rare, except on theater and cinema stages, to find nowadays a face which is painted, apart from the application of lipstick to make an artificial mouth, and, more rarely, a blue or black tinting of eyelids and some darkening of the eyelashes. The intention seems to be to treat the skin with creams and then to cover it lightly with powder of what is held to be an appropriate shade. The effect is to allow the texture of the skin to show clearly under a light dusting of powder, sometimes reinforced with rouge over the cheekbones. The eyebrows may be shaped in various ways, but few women now darken them with pencil, or clog the eyelashes with mascara. Mascara is an Oriental cosmetic, like kohl. Kohl, which may be powdered antimony or burnt almond-shells or frankincense, darkens the eyelids and so makes the eyes appear more lustrous.

Cosmetics modify the coloring and skin texture of the face, but only by suggesting the presence or absence of shadows can they affect its modeling—unless depilation by chemicals or tweezers or electrolysis be reckoned a cosmetic process. In the twentieth century, however, women have been enabled to do something toward altering the shape of their faces. Massage and the wearing of chin-straps during sleep are both said to diminish unwanted plumpness and the sagging of muscles and tissues due to age or unwise eating. The attempt to restore the illusion of youth is more drastic when it is undertaken by a surgeon, who will 'lift' a face by cutting the skin, removing certain tissues, and sewing the face up again more tightly. The surgical scar is usually tucked away under the chin and the turn of the jaw. Actual amendment, as distinct from restoration, of the facial appearance is normally confined to the ears and the nose. Outstanding ears are sometimes readjusted closer to the head, and the shape of the nose can be altered quite unrecognizably. This facial surgery in aid of vanity, which flourished among the fashionable women of Europe and America during the nineteen-thirties, was extended first to Chicago and New York gangsters who needed to change their appearance in order to defeat police investigations, and more recently (picking up the British pioneer work of 1914–18) it has been used, by the grafting of skin from other parts of the body, to restore the shattered or burnt faces of wounded sailors, soldiers, and airmen. And I dare say that there are some poor women, suffering from facial injuries in air raids, who may feel remotely and ironically glad that their wealthier sisters in prewar days went, with check-books in their handbags, in and out of the consulting-rooms of enterprising surgeons in search of their outworn or dissipated youthfulness.

PLATE VI: WOMAN'S HEAD, *by* E. R. HUGHES

PLATE VII: STUDY OF A HEAD, *by* ALEXANDER AKERBLADH

Author's Collection

CHAPTER THREE

∿

FRAMING THE FACE

So FAR I have considered the face very strictly, never roving beyond its narrow boundaries. But, as every hairdresser and milliner knows, the face is only on rare occasions presented to the world in such isolation. It is surmounted and sometimes partly enclosed by the head hair, and poised upon the throat. The hair must be kempt to one degree or another, and may be surmounted with a hat, while the throat gets a collar or other adornment most of the waking day. Again, the whole, or some part, of the face may be concealed behind a veil or mask. These accessories or some combination from among them provide a kind of frame for the face, emphasizing it by enclosing it wholly or partly, and—if they are skillfully chosen and arranged—considerably modifying its æsthetic effect.

First, the hair. Except at certain periods and in certain places, there has generally been a marked distinction between the sexes in the length of the head hair, and only in the Napoleonic period and again recently have any considerable number of women cut their hair drastically short of its full natural length. In the decade before the First World War young girls wore their hair plaited into one or two ropes or pigtails, hanging down the back, the ends finished off with bows of black, white or colored ribbon. (These pigtails have been seen more often in the past few years, though they are not almost universal as they once were.) Before that, girls of school age let their hair flow loose over their shoulders (much as many grownup women do nowadays), or else they bound it with a ribbon at the back of the neck. The Germans called such pigtailed adolescent girls *backfischen*. The British and the Americans called them 'flappers,' the name no doubt deriving from the girls' habit of swinging the pigtail as they skipped or ran about, and sometimes flipping it, with a jerk of the head, from the back to the front of the shoulder. Between 1910 and 1918 the flapper became a symbol of precocious and rather shocking youth, because the young girls of the period were held to become forwardly interested in boys and men at an age when their mothers, under the spell of Victorian decorum, had been supervised and closely chaperoned. The flapper possessed many of the noisy and unruly characteristics of the 'tomboy,' but in addition she represented an active emancipation of her sex from the over-ripe Victorian ideal of submissive and characterless modesty. The moral relaxations of the 1914–18 war lent a strong impetus to this movement of defiance, although it was not often carried to the extreme lack of self-respect observable occasionally in London during the Hitler war. On the subject of other people's sexual behavior it is always rash to make generalizations, and probably only a minority of flappers conducted themselves as shamelessly as the majority were by some alleged to do. And at all times it has to be noted that, so far as such wide generalizations can be made, there has never been in Britain any license of behavior comparable to that reported in America by Americans. The balance between puritanism and profligacy is more stably maintained.

Within these roughly marked limits the flappers of 1914–18, with their beribboned pigtails and scarlet tam-o'-shanter hats (forerunners of the beret), are to be seen as instituting a novel and precocious competition for the attentions of young men. And partly in response to this stimulus young women of eighteen or more years of age, instead of rejoicing in the once-coveted privilege of putting their hair up, began to cut it short. The process was known as bobbing. It consisted of combing and brushing the hair away from the top of the head and shearing it off level at the nape of the neck and round to the ears or a little below. Sometimes the front hair was pulled forward over the forehead and cut to a horizontal fringe parallel to the eyebrows and only a little above them. The fringe and the bob can both be seen in the Tonks drawing (Plate I, frontispiece). The usual excuse was convenience, especially for war work; the likeliest motive was vanity mixed with a desire to try out a novel effect.

Many young women, however, held out against the bob, either from conservatism, fear of criticism, regard for the beauty of their full-grown hair, or doubts about the shape of the backs of their heads. It was some time before women over thirty had their hair cut short. The fashion for bobbed hair held precariously into the nineteen-twenties, when it was succeeded by the shingle, which had many variations, and the short-lived Eton crop, which approximated to a man's haircut and was sometimes made more noticeable by plastering the hair close to the head with gums or unguents. In both the shingle and the Eton crop the nape of the neck was un- covered by the use of clippers, supplemented by a razor.

Today most women keep their hair a good deal shorter than its natural length, but the shaven nape is rarely seen. Instead, the back hair is curled up into a tight roll, or curled loosely up, or left to bunch or to flow, sometimes netted or sacked in a snood. There is some survival, too, of the Victorian (originally Greek) chignon, or loosely gathered and curled bunch of hair poised on the nape of the neck. The variant of this, however, in which the hair was piled on top of the head, at the back of the crown, is rarely if ever seen. More popular still is the Edwardian coiffure (associated in my boy- hood memories—how I cannot explain—with barmaids) which erects the front hair high above the forehead almost vertically, like a cliff or a sea wave. But because no special value is now set on the length or quantity of the hair, these adapted revivals of old fash- ions have not brought with them the very old custom of inserting concealed pads of wool, horsehair, or other soft material to fake an abundance. Nor are lengths of false hair, carefully matched, any longer woven and pinned into the natural hair.

From the earliest times women have dressed their hair around and above their heads, holding it in place with ribbons or fillets, cords, strung beads, as well as combs and hairpins of bone, ivory, metal, or wood. For many centuries hairdressing was comparatively simple, playing variations on one or other of two models: the Græco-Roman, or classic, which swept the hair aside over the ears, usually from a center parting, and piled it, high or low, tight or loose, at the back of the head; and the Teutonic, which braided it into long plaits, sometimes binding those round the brows. Before the later part of the Middle Ages the Church kept women under severe restraints, which included prohibitions against showing their hair in public. Women, indeed, had a somewhat servile status until the romantic technicalities of chivalry set a new value, at least on ladies of high birth. The Renaissance brought in some remarkable elaborations, when the hair of both men and women was sometimes twisted into spirals, like elongated corkscrews, and fixed in shape with gum or starch. By the late sixteenth century someone had conceived the idea of building up the hair into a superstructure, brushing it up straight from the forehead and the ears till it had the appearance of a solid cap, as high again as the whole face, as in Clouet's Versailles portrait of Diane, Comtesse de Gramont.

Not very long afterwards (the impetus came from the Court of Louis XIV) fashion decreed that as men wore powdered gray or grayish-white wigs, women should dust their heads thickly with rice-powder or flour. In the seventeen-seventies the faces of fashionable women, thickly overlaid with paint, were dominated by vast and extravagant hairdressings, often twice as high as the face itself. It was said that a lady's face at this period often appeared where one would expect her navel to be. To achieve this top-heavy elegance grease was rubbed into the hair to clog it, and the whole mass was then built round a frame of linen and wire, and stiffened and whitened with powder or flour; the sticky hair was then drawn up over big pads of wool on top of the head, worked into fantastic shapes, and powdered again. For ceremonial occasions these hairdressings might be decorated not only with ribbons, jewels, and feathers, but with ornaments representing butterflies, birds, even coaches-and-horses and ships in full sail. The outer dressing of powder could be renewed once or twice a day, by the lady's maid, though this was a messy operation, and had to be done inside one of the narrow cupboards known as powder-closets which can still be seen in many Georgian houses. A lady so got up sometimes went to the ball kneeling on the floor of her coach, with her head out of the window; and when she began to dance she had to take care that her hair did not collide with the chandeliers. The actual structural erection of the hair was a long job, with a technique of its own. It could be performed only by a highly paid barber, who was called in every few weeks. Meanwhile the lady's hair and scalp, unwashed and clogged with edible matter, provided an excellent breeding-ground, and the barber's first job, when he took down the hair, was to kill off thousands of lice and their eggs. Those elegant antiques, consisting of a slender ivory or gold stick with a forked end, known as back-scratchers, were more often used for relieving the irritations of the scalp. Pitt perhaps struck no more valiant blow for England's good than when in 1795 he imposed a tax on hair powder.

Before the end of the century Englishwomen, led by the Duchess of Grafton, began to wear their hair in a more cleanly fashion, binding it close over the head, unless it was frizzed with hot irons, and hanging it in thick corkscrew curls at the back and beside the ears. Meanwhile the women of Paris, under the Directoire, and afterwards under Napoleon as Consul and Emperor, sometimes wore their hair cut fairly short, but more often in Grecian styles, to match the classically cut and sometimes transparent gowns then in fashion. These Greek styles also influenced fashions in England and America, and, with variations of Teutonic hair-plaiting, survived through the puritanism of the middle century. In the 'nineties and the Edwardian era the hair was piled on top of the head again, with smaller pads to plump it out, but without powder. And so to the age of world wars, the brief reign of the 'bob' and the 'shingle,' and the general fashion for cutting the hair to less than its full length.

Each period likes to evolve its own prevailing style or styles of hairdressing, but there are always obstinate conservatives holding on to outmoded fashions, as well as individualists who devise, or have devised for them, styles to please their own taste and flatter their own appearance, so that it is not always so easy to ascribe a painting or even a photograph to a particular year as cursory students of fashion-plates may like to believe. In recent times fashions change more rapidly than ever before, and in any one season at least half a dozen hairdressing styles may be simultaneously considered fashionable. Moreover, modistes and coiffeurs have become highly conscious of history, and are continually reviving, with or without minor modifications, the half-forgotten ventures of the past. In general, however, it may be said that most of the methods of dressing women's hair fall into three classifications. First, there are styles which keep the hair flat and smooth over the crown of the head, thus revealing and emphasizing its shape; both the Græco-Roman and the Teutonic plaited techniques belong to this subdivision, as well as the simple contemporary style which brushes the hair down to shoulder length and dispenses with pins and ribbons. Second, there are styles which dress the hair over the crown in curls or waves so that the surface is undulating or embossed and the shape of the head is half concealed by ornamental bands, bunches, ringlets, or curls; the Edwardian hairdressings, and their recent revivals, belong to this classification. Third, the hair may be piled up into a complicated superstructure which by its height and apparent solidity attracts the attention away from the face itself; such styles are at present completely out of favor, and there is no reason as yet to suppose they will be revived. The modification of women's haircutting to approximately shoulder length is a compromise of some practical value: it reduces the weight borne by the head and yet enables the hair to be arranged in ways which are not likely to be confused by those adopted by men. Elderly gentlemen, however, are apt to lament the change, and to pity the younger generation of their own sex because they are robbed of the nightly transformation in the appearance of wives and mistresses taking down their hair and brushing it to flow luxuriously down their backs, and, a little later, over the pillows and sheets.

The current shortness of men's hair restricts the number of ways in which it can be dressed. At certain times in the past it was not so. The hair was grown thick and long round the head, and cropped hair was the mark of the slave. In the fifteenth century there was a fashion for growing the hair fairly long except over the ears and the nape of the neck, where it was shaved; the hairdressing style worn by Laurence Olivier in the *Henry V* film was authentic to the period. During the Renaissance men's hair often fell in curled or ribboned locks below the shoulders. Cromwell's Roundheads are said to have had their hair cut by the barber clapping a pudding-basin over the head and snipping away whatever had remained visible below the rim. The Victorians on the whole, while they kept their hair clear of their shoulders, grew it thick. The Prussian military habit of having the hair clipped short all over the skull was a revival from the eighteenth century (no doubt they gave the credit to Frederick the Great), with the iron-spiked helmet replacing the periwig.

At the present day practically all European and American men have their hair trimmed short by a barber every week, fortnight, or three weeks. Variations are found only in the parting over the crown, the angle at which the hair is brushed, and the shortness at the nape and above the ears. Generally, the hair is parted at the left of the head, high or low, and brushed into an asymmetrically divided carpet, which becomes progressively shorter towards the ears and the nape of the neck. The center parting, often seen in the early years of the century, has almost disappeared. A few men dispense altogether with a parting, either because they are bald or because their hair grows very stiff and upright, either straight or curly, so that it can be combed and brushed *en brosse*. This is by no means a new fashion, as can be seen in Clouet's drawing, done in 1570, of Louis de Béranger (Plate II, page 10). Sometimes the hair, comparatively short, is brushed across the crown, parallel to the line of the eyebrows; sometimes it is grown long over the crown and swept back to the nape; if it is straight and impregnated with oil or brilliantine and a fixative cream it forms a kind of smooth, solid, glossy skull-cap. When I was a boy I formed the opinion that long hair greased and swept back in this way was a mark of vulgarity, and I still find it surprising that men of education and otherwise of good taste should so present themselves to their fellows. Yet I remember also that in my boyhood very short hair was a standard joke, and taken as the sign of a recently released convict. The two great wars in which the majority of young Englishmen have served no doubt helped to kill this prejudice. Only at the Universities and in self-consciously artistic communities do the majority of men still grow their front hair six or more inches long; and it is quite easy at a football match between a University and a Services team to distinguish one side from the other, even if the significance of the colored shirts is not known: the University men (mostly, in wartime, medical students) will soon have their hair flapping about their ears and in front of their eyes, like the witches in *Macbeth*.

Baldness, complete or partial, is likely to give a man the appearance of exceptional wisdom, by adding the illusion of a high forehead. The recession of hair, to right and left at the front of the crown, above the temples, is generally regarded as advantageous to the looks of the not-so-young. The effect can be studied in the Clouet drawing, which also shows the sixteenth-century ruff in comparatively simple form as it first evolved from a lace collar. Gray or white hairs over the ears are by many believed to improve the looks of the middle-aged. If the front hair is not swept back it may be left moderately short and brushed across, but nowadays it is rarely erected into a comb or coif, in the Edwardian manner, or brushed down flat over the forehead in the bear's-lick lock cultivated by some of the soldiers of Queen Victoria to set off their pill-box caps. Often, however, a man may be seen whose hair, whether it is fine or coarse, straight or wavy, grows naturally thick and resilient immediately above the forehead. This is a characteristic of Irish ancestry (I possess it myself), and is said to be a survival of the 'glibbe': in the Middle Ages the Irish were forbidden by English law to wear

any form of armored headdress, and so in self-defense they grew
their hair thick and long in front, plastering it with fat or resin till it
coagulated into a mass sufficiently solid to blunt or divert a sword-
stroke.

All forms of hairdressing, both for men and for women, have to
take account of the natural state of the hair. Their starting point is
its color, its texture, its tendency or inability to ripple and curl, and
its oiliness or dryness. In the past men have been as ready as wom-
en to dye their hair for the sake of vanity or fashion—but not today.
And for some odd reason women are more prone to bleach than to
darken their hair. In countries where black hair is common an
especial value is set on fair and red hair. Gregory the Great, mar-
veling at the blondness of captured Saxon slaves, made his notorious
pun: "Non Angli, sed angeli"; and where the red hair of the
women that Titian painted came from cannot be known, unless
they had Jewish blood. But dyes were often used, and Italian wom-
en liked to sit about in the sun, hoping in this way to become
blondes more naturally and lastingly. Really red hair, however, is
rarely seen except in Ireland, Wales, and the Highlands of Scotland.
Today the dyeing of hair is undertaken usually to restore or fake
the original color lost by age, or to achieve the obviously artificial
pallors of ash and platinum blond. Some women go to the hairdressing salons to have their hair permanently whitened: another
reversion to the standards of the eighteenth century. And there are
occasionally to be seen in the West End heads tinted to chemical
blues, greens, and oranges. Dark hair bleached or reddened is
easily detectable, even if the roots cannot be inspected. A more
pleasing variation is the custom of bleaching a single strand or
streak of gold or light brown into dark hair over the forehead.

Shampooing and artificial waving, not so noticeable in their effects as henna or peroxide, are now part of almost every woman's
routine. The shampooings are administered either domestically
(one manufacturer created a catch-phrase by associating his brand
of shampoos with Friday night) or in the hairdresser's cubicle. The

permanent wave, which is certainly not permanent but relaxes as the hair grows, is produced by more or less trained operators. The process is reported to be a lengthy one, in which the hair is baked into patterned ripples and curls, and the undulatory effect has to be restored at intervals of a few weeks by the briefer and less expensive operation of 'setting.' Immediately after these treatments the hair manifests considerable gloss, but the waves or ripples have a rigid, starchy look, and are harsh and brittle to the touch. This also disappears comparatively quickly, but on the whole the artificial waving of women's hair seems to be the sort of investment which brings in profits only after a lapse of time. Like lipstick, it is designed to impress the casual observer rather than those on sufficiently intimate terms to come to close quarters; which may, or may not, be an indication that modern women, in making themselves decorative, seek to please the community at large rather than their husbands and lovers.

The throat, the flexible pillar on which the head is poised, is left bare on some occasions and on others covered and perhaps adorned. One of the most striking changes effected by the twentieth century in the dress of men has been the lowering and softening of the collar, and for sports and informal summer occasions its virtual supersession by opening one or more buttons at the neck of a shirt of which the collar is an integral part. There were few or no high collars in the Ancient World, and men in the Middle Ages, when armor was not worn, made do with collars cut low in a circular or square shape, like present-day undervests. In Tudor and Stuart times, however, the top of the shirt was heightened into a collar, which folded down, sometimes ornamented with lace, over the neck of the doublet or jerkin. An elaboration of this was the ruff or ornamental and detachable collar of lace or fine starched linen, matched with ruffled cuffs at the wrist. Under Elizabeth the ruff grew in size and complexity, often being widened into a great spread of fine starched lace which stood up behind the head and expanded over the front of the shoulders. In this form it was stiffened with wires. Legal penalties, and the denunciations of Puritans, failed to put a stop to the fashion for extravagant and expensive lace. Women often managed to combine vast and imposing ruffs with low-cut bodices which displayed the greater part of their bosoms. Another form of sixteenth- and early-seventeenth-century ruff, popular all over Western Europe, was shaped like a disk, the neck being in the middle; this was built on a concealed frame, and layer after layer of almost transparent starched cambric was added, sometimes with vertical intersections, till the ruff looked like a wheel with a multiplicity of spokes. Specially long spoons had to be provided at banquets to enable ruff-wearers to feed themselves. These goffered cartwheel ruffs needed very delicate ironing, and the starch had either a blue or a yellow tinge. Rembrandt, Rubens, Hals, Van Dyck, and other Dutch and Flemish painters excelled in the fine brushwork needed to depict such disk-like ruffs, on which the face was deposited as if it were John the Baptist's on Salome's charger.

With wigs, lace ruffles and, later, cravats came into fashion. The stiff linen collar belongs to the nineteenth century. Single or double, with or without a winged front (folded back to form two triangles), the starched linen collar persisted well into the twentieth century. Gladstone gave his name, perhaps unwillingly, not only to a small handbag but to a high single stiff collar sufficiently loose and wide in front to give free play to the Adam's apple. Collars of paper, thrown away when soiled, and others of celluloid, shining and apt to grow gray but alleged to be washable, provided cheap substitutes for laundered linen. Like the made-up tie, and the dickey or false shirt front, they were regarded as signs of poverty and vulgarity—two qualities which in the late Victorian and Edwardian periods many people considered almost synonymous. Schoolboys were incommoded by the spreading Eton collar, which often made the back of the neck red and sore.

In the 'nineties and early nineteen-hundreds linen collars were usually very tall, the top rim touching the chin and often the lobes of the ears. Aubrey Beardsley, a rebel against most aspects of Victorianism, nevertheless wore these 'chokers,' as several photographs and Sickert's portrait reveal. And they were just as tall and stiff in America. Yet, grotesque as they may look, tall collars have a kind of harmony with the silk hats and bowler hats of the time. Certain conventions are not to be defied piecemeal, as was made evident by the spectacle of Mr Benjamin Britten in 1945 conducting an orchestra at the Albert Hall with a soft collar creasing and flapping over the lapels of a tail-coat. The soft collar, later in certain versions slightly stiffened with starch, began to appear about the time George V came to the throne—1911. It had still to be affixed to the shirt with a front and back stud. It was a double or folded collar, and was fastened in front with a clip pin slid under the knot of the tie. Since then the soft collar in various forms has passed into universal use, as the cut of men's clothing has relaxed into greater comfort. Up to 1939 stiff collars were worn only by a few professional and business men at their work, by undertakers, by men attending the more formal sort of weddings, and with evening dress. In wartime, with laundries collecting and delivering only once a fortnight, no domestic help procurable, and clothing severely rationed, the soft collar had it all its own way.

During the nineteenth century the collar and tie together became a mark of class distinction. Manual laborers wore mufflers or, in the summer, open shirt-necks without collars. Forty years ago the distinction began to vanish, and nowadays, except when the kind of work undertaken forbids, all men wear the collar and tie. This may be taken as an example of Tennyson's "Freedom slowly broadening down from precedent to precedent." The movement has at last reached the British Army, for late in 1944 the noncommissioned ranks were permitted to wear khaki collars and ties when out of camp or barracks. This was a belated concession, for the Royal Air Force uniform, since long before the outbreak of war, had incorporated collar and tie for all ranks. And the private soldiers in the British Army, intensely respectable in all their instincts, especially resented the fact that Service women, in the A.T.S., the

W.A.A.F., and the W.R.N.S., all wore the collars and ties which in civilian life are the mark of the male sex. Whether the Navy will ever decide to let its seamen cover up their fully exposed necks I dare not guess.

By comparison with men, women—except in the period of elaborate ruffs—have usually adorned their necks quite simply. More often than not they leave them bare of clothing. One exception was the high-necked blouse fashionable from the 'nineties to the Edwardian era, when collars of transparent lace or net were worn which fitted close all round the neck and stood as high as the linen collars worn by men at that time. These transparent collars were usually held in place by vertical insertions of thin white whalebone. A little later blouses still buttoned at the neck and had collars, but these stood only an inch or two high, or else were folded down in the Peter Pan or Puritan style. Sometimes a masculine effect was imitated with a knotted or a bow tie; sometimes the collar was decorated with a brooch. And at most periods women have for certain occasions worn scarves of heavy or thin material, wound tight or loose round the throat; the scarf affords possibilities of almost infinite variations of drapery, besides throwing a splash of color into the general appearance.

Long strings of beads, chains with jeweled or metalwork or enamel pendant brooches, and looped ropes of pearls hardly modify the appearance of the throat, as they carry the eye lower, to the breast; and pearls or other jewels worn in circlets round the throat form in effect a collar. But the single line of jewels or beads worn fairly tight round the throat is another matter. By brilliance and color it may draw attention to the complexion and texture of the skin, and by its position it may help to make a long neck seem shorter or a thin neck broader or fuller. In the chalk drawing by Tonks (Plate I, frontispiece) a further studied or unconscious effect of the circlet of beads can be observed: it emphasizes, by duplicating on an almost parallel line, part of the soft curve of the chin, and, a little lower down, the fold or crease to be found in many feminine throats. An old tradition maintains that this crease—it is often named after Venus—in the flesh of the throat is an indication of latent or cultivated sexual proficiency. There is a similar popular belief about fine but profuse hair on a woman's upper lip. The circlet of beads, by paralleling the Venus crease, has certainly been used by some women to emphasize an attraction they were proud of. A variation is a band of narrow black ribbon or velvet worn tight round the throat, usually fastened at the back with a clasp or tied in a bow. This was seen as recently as 1920, and toward the end of 1944 American fashion designers were making an effort to revive it. In the *Olympia* picture, with which Manet scandalized Paris in the 'sixties, the model has this narrow band of black ribbon round her throat; it is knotted into a bow under the chin. Otherwise she wears nothing at all. In an earlier picture, *Le déjeuner sur l'herbe,* which also caused a rumpus, Manet depicted himself and a man friend picnicking alfresco with a young woman, who wears not even a piece of black ribbon. Both pictures have long since attained the respectable status of classics, and those who are curious enough may, on their visits to Paris, spend a few minutes examining these famous nudes and tracing the skill with which the painter has indicated on the necks of his models the line of alleged erotic significance. Possibly this minor detail was not overlooked when the pictures were first exhibited to the public, and the outraged French bourgeoisie may have had a better idea of what it was protesting against than some critics imagine.

The most powerful modification of the appearance of the face, however, short of concealing it completely, is obtained through the hat. Here is a subject so vast that even histories of costume lavishly produced in a number of volumes can treat it only in outline, and illustrate no more than a fraction of a percentage of the kinds of hats known to have been worn in the past. Originally, no doubt, the hat developed from a loose mantle worn over the whole body, including the head. Its function was to afford protection against rain, wind, and sunshine, but it must very quickly have evolved into a form of ornament, for one of the ways in which man distinguishes himself from the animals is by his decorative faculty. Add a brim to a close-fitting cap, and the first step has been taken toward creating a hat with a design pleasing in itself.

In ancient Greece, as in Rome, the mantle was often used to cover the head, yet there were localized fashions in hats, and one—the sock-like Phrygian cap—was later adopted as a symbol by the early enthusiasts of the French Revolution; it can still be seen in costume dramas of the stage (*The Pirates of Penzance,* for example) and the cinema, made of knitted scarlet wool, and worn by buccaneers and smugglers. The Middle Ages evolved some highly complicated hats, mostly for men, and the warrior went out to battle in an elaborate and expensively wrought helmet. There was a fourteenth-century fashion for hoods with attached collars spreading over the shoulder and a stuffed tippet, which could be wound round the head like a turban, or round the throat like a muffler. The traditional jester's cap, parti-colored, is one form of these hoods. Women, outdoors and in fine weather, swathed the whole head in a wimple of white linen or fine colored silk, arranged so as to leave only the oval of the face exposed. This was to conform to the strict edicts of the Church. The headdresses worn by some orders of nuns today are an austere survival of this medieval fashion; yet the wimple sometimes became extremely ornate, with a high conical underframe, and gold, silver, or jeweled embroideries.

With the Renaissance came some extravagances, at first worked out within a small range of shapes. Both men and women wore chaplets, or wreaths, of flowers, either real or imitated in metalwork. The Duke of Urbino, in Piero della Francesca's portrait in the Uffizi Gallery in Florence, exhibits his imposing profile under a hat shaped like an inverted cylindrical plinth. And the Doge Loredano, in both of Giovanni Bellini's famous portraits, wears an exquisitely embroidered hat (over a kind of skull bandage) which rises into a kind of horn from the back of the crown. But it is probable that these are only variations of the plain scarlet or crimson cylindrical hat, worn high or low, to be seen in so many paintings of Renaissance gentlemen, and this was very likely imported from Moslem countries into Venice when she held "the gorgeous East in fee."

In the early sixteenth century, as armor was going out of use, all costume, for those who could afford it, became fanciful in color and shape; although—to judge from portraits by Holbein, Dürer, and Bronzino—the floppy cap of black velvet, fuller cut than the beret and worn, unlike the tam-o'-shanter, straight on the head, was popular in most parts of Europe. A little later conical hats, large or small, with or without a brim, and decorated with feathers or jewels, were all the rage. These were usually put on at an angle. And at last women began to take courage: it is only from the end of the sixteenth century that it became common for middle-class women to match their men in peacock extravagances out-of-doors. In Rubens' National Gallery portrait of Susanne Fourment (known as *Le chapeau de paille,* although the hat does not appear to be made of straw at all) we see a young woman wearing a hat with an exceptionally wide brim, turned up on the left side, and decorated with a fine confusion of feathers. On the other hand, there is another Rubens portrait, in the Louvre, of Susanne's sister Helen (Rubens' second wife), which shows her wearing, perched high and askew on her head, a tiny, grotesque-shaped felt hat, which might easily be worn today at a cocktail party. But big crowns and broad brims were more in favor.

It was the wig, however, rather than the hat, which dominated the seventeenth and most of the eighteenth century. Englishwomen of the nineteenth century, following a little after the women of Paris, began to go in for millinery, with 'trimmings' as we know it today, and in the eighteen-twenties big hats, broad-brimmed and extravagantly decorated, were all the rage. With their wigs, eighteenth-century men had first cavalier or wide-brimmed, high-crowned hats, and then hard black three-corner hats with or without cockades and lace; if the wig was a full-bottomed one the hat was usually carried everywhere under the arm. At the end of the eighteenth century cocked hats came into fashion, with the wide brim fastened up to the crown on the sides, eventually transforming its appearance. Napoleon and Wellington unintentionally signified their antagonism on their heads, one by wearing his cocked hat crosswise, the other perching it edgeways over his hook-nose.

But already, before the Napoleonic era, something like a top hat, a hard cylinder with a curly stiff brim, had come into use; it was associated with democratic and republican sentiments, and a convincing version of it was worn not so long ago by Sir John Martin-Harvey in *The Only Way*. At first fawn-colored and made of beaver fur, in the middle of the nineteenth century and almost to the end the topper was standard formal wear, in glossy black, for all respectable men, and compulsory, with starched linen and tailcoats, even for clerks who could ill afford the initial price and the cost of having the nap ironed from time to time. The topper survives at funerals, on the heads of Bank messengers, and at that hardly less modernized institution, Eton College. The bowler hat (known to Americans, ever ready to love and commemorate a lord, as the Derby) was held at first to be a less formal alternative to the topper. It can be regarded now as the compromise of a transition period, and a man who wears it in these days, except for horse-riding, goes in danger of looking a little too well dressed. The name of the bowler is enshrined in slang, as a verb in the passive voice: a professional soldier who is put on half-pay and so relegated to civilian life is said to have been 'bowler-hatted.' With the bowler has departed the stiff straw, the 'boater,' at least in Britain; the United States still holds to the custom of making hot weather still more uncomfortable by clapping on the head a hard, tight-fitting construction of plaited straw and ribbon, which leaves a sore red crease on the forehead and encourages sweat to evaporate under the crown.

The so-called soft hat for men began with the curly brimmed Homburg, popularized by Edward VII and revived in the nineteen-thirties, with minor modifications and solely in black, under the patronage of Mr Anthony Eden and officials of the Foreign Office. But this is the most formal version of the soft hat. Others have 'snap' or flexible brims, and crowns which can be punched or fingered into various shapes, including the 'pork-pie.' The soft hat, or Trilby, is, perhaps, a felt descendant of the fine straw Panama hat, now rarely seen; it is worn in black, blue, green, brown, gray— the sober hues allowed to modern men. Anglers and a few others sometimes put on soft hats of tweed cloth; but the deer-stalker, with side-flaps buttoned on top of the crown, survives only in illustrations to the Sherlock Holmes stories, although a khaki version of it flourished about 1915 as a trench cap. The more ordinary cloth cap is little worn nowadays, and then mostly in the country: from the late nineteenth century to the nineteen-twenties it was a social uniform, worn on all outdoor occasions by 'working-class' men, and often, with a long hat-pin pushed through the crown, by their women. Since its early days the cloth cap has widened its side-pouches and developed a stiffer and bigger peak or visor.

It was the nineteenth century which made men's clothing drab-colored, the only notable exception being full-dress military uniform and sports costumes. The Guardsman's bearskin, the Hussar's busby, the flat-topped Lancer cap (copied from the Poles), may be seen again after the war, but khaki is more probable. Now that the ugly forage cap, the fore-and-aft, is being replaced by the beret, the change may be an æsthetic advantage, for the handsome shako (originally Hungarian) disappeared in the nineteenth century, and was replaced at different periods by the spiked helmet (copied from a Prussian model), the absurd pill-box, worn on the side of the head, the fore-and-aft forage cap, and the Brodrick, a peaked cap, not unlike that in which the British Army went uncomfortably to war in 1914. The beret has every advantage over them all. Many men now go hatless, for choice, even in the hard winter months; this may be for reasons of hygiene or comfort, but there is at least a suspicion that it is due to resentment against the convention which forbids individuality in the shape of hats, and any bright colors except on the cricket field.

Until the seventeenth century men do not appear to have thought it necessary to doff their hats on paying a visit, except in the presence of a monarch. And the usual greeting when meeting friends out of doors was to push the hat back a few inches off the forehead and let it fall again. This survived into the nineteenth century in the farm laborer's symbolic 'tipping his hat to the squire.' The military hand salute, like military uniform, is also modern. It was instituted in England in 1745, in place of hat-raising, but at that period had to be accompanied by a bow.

Victorian sobriety, which tamed the masculine fancy so effectively that it has never been ebullient since, let women off the leash. The craft of millinery flourished in thousands of shapes, small and large, millions of 'trimmings,' and now that fashions change every few months there are always large numbers of basic types to be seen about the streets. Hardly a woman so poor in purse or spirit that she has not half a dozen hats to choose from every time she goes out. Even in the depths of the wartime austerity movement which followed Dunkirk the British Government, rationing clothes as strictly as food, dared not ration hats. The couponless hat was the outstanding, and highly successful, bribe or stimulus to maintain feminine morale: and it is worth noting that it is the hat, far more than frock or gown or coat and skirt, which permits excesses and adventures of fancy.

Yet the Victorian age began timidly with the poke-bonnet, reacting, no doubt, from the vast circular-brimmed hats which Gainsborough made famous. The poke-bonnet, usually of straw, projected far forward not only over the head but on either side; later on it was seen in a less rigid and more attractive form, made of linen, as the sun-bonnet. Even when they became tiny and narrow, and were perched high on the head, Victorian hats were often known as bonnets, a name now reserved almost exclusively for hats worn by old ladies. But whether they called them hats or bonnets Victorian women wore dainty and complicated and infinitely varied constructions of straw, felt, velvet, and silk adorned with ribbons, artificial flowers and fruits, feathers and lace. Millinery became an industry. At the beginning of the twentieth century hats grew bigger, as hairdressing styles piled higher and broader. The Edwardian age was a time of 'picture' hats, wide, insecurely fixed, often tilted forward, and laden with a profusion of ornament which often included whole dead birds. By 1916 hats, though hardly more beautiful, had become smaller and simpler. The cloche hat, close-fitting and covering the ears, was fashionable in the 'twenties, and hideous. From the nineteen-thirties onward many women have elected to go hatless outdoors. Others wear a bandeau or narrow scarf round the head—a custom taken from the Wimbledon tennis courts and in essence a broader revival of the Greek fillet. Others again wear a scarf to cover all the hair, letting it hang behind, triangular, between the shoulder-blades; this is derived, like so many fashions, from the peasant costumes of Central and Eastern Europe. Today there is no one prevailing style in women's hats, though they are generally small; but taste has improved enormously in the past fifteen years, and the fanciful hats, or 'bits of nonsense,' which can be seen in immense variety everywhere have most of them the courage and skill of somebody's ingenious imagination.

Even such a rapid and selective survey as I have made of hairdressing, beard-dressing, shaving, the use of cosmetics, collaring the throat, and behatting the head, must indicate that men and women habitually spend a lot of time and energy in preparing their faces for others to look at. If this is merely vanity, and vanity a sin, we are all sinners, and not likely to reform our ways. What we seek to do every day is, as we say, to make the best of our faces, to induce them to conform as nearly as possible to our own particular conception of what is pleasing and proper. In this endeavor none of us has a free hand: we must work with the raw material of the face bestowed on us by circumstance, dearly though we could wish for even a temporary change. And, consciously or not, we are likely to modify our own conception of facial beauty or impressiveness to meet the taste of the time and place we live in.

The toilet, then, is a continually renewed attempt to improve the appearance of the face, and the indirect approach is just as important as the direct. For few are so handsome that their looks cannot be either enhanced by skillful framing—the frame being the hair, the hat, if it is worn, the throat and whatever is used to adorn it. Every woman knows, or quickly learns, the elementary principles of this craft: how soft, waving, and broken lines in the hair and the hat can offset the severity of a long or lean face; how hair draped over the ears, a tall-crowned hat, or pendant earrings, can make a plump face look longer; how to distract attention from ill-favored features by throwing shadows across them or placing some bright or unusual ornament close by, to which the observer's eye is attracted; how to produce the illusion of a longer neck by means of a skillfully arranged corsage, and how to emphasize the color of the eyes by matching them in ribbons and jewelry. And most men, after a time, learn the same basic principles, but within a smaller, less adventurous compass of effects.

Human beings, it seems, are vain of anything in their personal appearance which pleases them or arouses the admiration of others. Yet their vanity springs from a subconscious modesty. Few of us are more than momentarily satisfied with our faces, and in this activity, as in so many others, humanity can be seen as conducting an eternal pilgrimage. The quest is for perfection, for an ideal which continually changes and is never realized. Anything and everything which promises improvement is tried, adopted for a time, and then replaced by a fresh experiment. In another aspect the quest takes on the nature of insoluble internal conflict. In modifying the appearance of the face, as in all political and economic organizations of the community, human nature seeks two irreconcilable ends. It seeks submergence in the crowd, the security of being unnoticeable, by following the conventions of the fashion of the moment. And at the same time it hopes, if only by the disposition of a detail here and there, to achieve the status of individuality, to be separated at a glance from the rest of the crowd. These two divergent motives are recurring elements in all human behavior, and neither appetite is ever fully placated without the other reviving its urgency. The fluctuations of fashion in the toilet, with each one of us striving at the same time to conform and to rebel, form a minor but illuminating sub-clause of the most difficult of all modern problems: the mutual adjustment of the State and the individual.

The presentation of the face, however, is only superficially a minor subject for serious thought, for the State is something even less tangible than the sum of the individuals who compose it: it is an abstract idea, powerful though that may be, and it has no way of manifesting itself in concrete form except through individual human beings. A great deal of the trouble is due to the fact that individual human beings, when they function as representatives of the State—as civil servants, diplomats, statesmen, police, armed warriors—are apt to appear to themselves, as well as to others, symbolic figures. And so they lose many of the attributes of humanity. Their faces, when they are visible on official occasions, become like coins of the realm, hard-graven, immutable, almost identical one with another. Against this trend towards dehumanized uniformity, fashion, despite its commercial exploitation and its occasional absurdities, launches an incessant counter-attack. Fashion decorates the whole body, but in particular it draws attention to the face, the expressive aspect of the sovereign head, the supreme sign of individuality, one version for each person. Fashion imposes its own conventions, but they offer a wide variety of choice; and within every convention each of us is free to assert himself as different from others. The assumption on which we work is that the human face is a picture, a portrait, a minor work of art capable of yielding pleasure or at least interest to others. We frame the face with some care, dressing our hair this way or that, taking trouble over collars, ties, beads, brooches, choos-

ing and adjusting our hats with forethought, and all in order to say
to the crowd: "Look at me, I am myself, I am unique, and in my
face may be read secrets not to be found anywhere else." Each
face may make many concessions to good taste, the current expectation of the community, but in the last resort it is always slightly different from other faces, a defiant assertion of the individual against
the uniformities required by the State.

CHAPTER FOUR

～✲～

FORMS OF BEAUTY

ACCORDING to the old adage beauty is no more than skin-deep. If facial beauty is meant the statement is a half-truth, for artists do not study anatomy out of whimsy or a love of unapplied science. The physical beauty of the face lies only partly in complexion; shape and structure, the plastic surface-molding of the flesh, are largely dependent on the bone formation of the skull. Another deposit of traditional, and doubtful, wisdom tells us that beauty lies in the eye of the beholder: or, in more modern terms, that when we judge a face to be beautiful we are registering a merely subjective reaction. Here again one element is unwarrantably expanded to account for a highly complicated process, and the explanation is unsatisfactory. It is true that toward what one person admires lavishly others will remain indifferent, and that the irrelevant intrusions of desire and affection make it exceptionally difficult for us to achieve a balanced and impartial judgment of facial loveliness. Yet there are faces which everyone concedes to be beautiful, and this presumes an absolute criterion or criterions somewhere.

To define beauty, either as an abstract principle or in its particular manifestation in the human face, would be a dangerous and, I fancy, an unrewarding task. A few specific examples (and they will be given in due course) may forward the discussion better than protracted metaphysical or scientific analysis. Wiser to go side-stepping, and on tiptoe, past this bottomless gulf, and obtain a little preliminary clarity by roughing out some fairly obvious but useful subdivisions of the subject. The beauty of the face may be either physical or spiritual: that is to say, it may gratify the visual and tactual senses (for touch can be exercised imaginatively through the eyes and even felt, without contact, in the finger tips), or it may evoke responses from the unsensuous and unintellectual departments of the mind, those faculties which we sum up conveniently as perceptions of the spirit and the emotions. Some faces satisfy on both counts, and they are very lovely indeed; but for the present it will suffice if we note the distinction between physical and spiritual beauty. Second, in both kinds there is a difference between what is commonly and traditionally considered proper to men and to women. Similarly there is an appropriateness of beauty to the different stages of growth. Elements that contribute to the beauty of a woman would be marks of effeminacy in a man, and the soft, unformed mouth which charms us in a child's face, if retained when the child grows up, becomes a blemish. Consider in Mervyn Peake's tender, precise, unsentimentalized drawing (Plate V, page 27) how inappropriate, how utterly transformed in effect the baby mouth would be if it were found in the face of a man or a woman. And, third, every face has two distinctive aspects: when it is in repose and when its features are mutable from moment to moment, animated by the energy of speech or laughter or, more subtly, by the play of attentive expression.

The physical beauty of the human face is a delicately balanced composition of many elements, chiefly the configuration of the whole face, the complexion of the skin, the coloring of hair, eyes, and lips, and the shaping and relative sizes of the features. But first, for æsthetic satisfaction, the face must be pleasingly proportioned to the head, and the size of the head to the height and breadth of the body. An unduly small head, whatever its graces, is apt to look insignificant, and even to put the observer in mind of an insect, whereas an uncommonly large head may be impressive, even majestic—at least on a man. In the nineteenth century, when men wore their hair longer and often wilder, popular writers were fond of using the adjective 'leonine'—the hair having something of the effect of a mane—for large and handsome heads. Beethoven had such a head, and so had T. E. Shaw (Lawrence of Arabia), although as I remember him he kept it more trimly barbered. Alan

Dent, the dramatic critic, also has an impressive head, broad-browed and of three-dimensional bigness. For women who are to be judged beautiful there is less latitude in the relative proportion of head to body, and for them it is necessary that the head should be clearly upborne, not sunk into the shoulders. Yet a thin neck, in both men and women, is likely to resemble the stalk of a flower, and to look pitiful and overbalanced. In men of mature age a short neck, or at least a thick one, does not detract from the imposing effect of the face, as may be seen by studying portraits of Mr Churchill, President Roosevelt, and Generalissimo Stalin.

Variations from the normal in the size of the face relative to the size of the head are less frequent. Baldness alters the proportion notably, and may transform a round or square face into a long one. Some faces are foreclosed by a low or sloping forehead, with the hair seemingly marching down to join the eyebrows; it is amusing to compare photographs with painted or drawn portraits of Henry Irving, and see how the artists have tried to mitigate or even to idealize away the great actor's shallow and sloping brow. Other faces are apparently mutilated by a receding or inadequate chin. Others again reveal, as the head is turned into profile, that the ears and the angled line of the jaw-bone are set exceptionally far forward. As a general rule it can be said that the face, viewed from the side, should occupy about two-thirds of the width of the whole head; otherwise it becomes a mere façade. Round or nut-shaped heads are commonly smaller than those which are long, whether the length is measured vertically or horizontally, and they require smaller areas for the face, and smaller features. Napoleon's outstanding physical characteristic was a large face set on a small round head: whereas Leslie Banks, who played the Emperor some years back in Conal O'Riordan's play, *Napoleon's Josephine* (and played the part admirably and with skillful make-up), presented to the audience a normally proportioned face and head. Here was a very minor discrepancy, not likely to trouble any but a minutely attentive spectator; yet it illustrates the difficulties of simulating historical characters on the stage and the fundamental importance of relative sizes in the characterization of the human face.

An harmonious proportion is essential also in the features. Sometimes all are too small for the space occupied by the face as a whole, and although each feature may be exquisite in itself the general impression conveyed is of over-refinement, and—rather unfairly—of a niggling and petty nature, inadequate to tackle the problems of life. Sometimes only one feature is unduly small. A narrow mouth set in a broad or even an average-sized face is a not uncommon defect; so is a small or a very thin nose, and small eyes (the smallness is only relative) are often compared, with an unjust implication, to pig's eyes. In the nature of things it is hardly possible for all the features to be over-sized, but perhaps the majority of faces are spoiled for beauty by the largeness of one or more features. Big eyes, protuberant and with the whites visible all round the pupils, are said to be the product of disease; they lend an air of over-intensity to the face, although this may be turned to advantage by players of the stage and notably the cinema—witness Bette Davis. Large and wide-set ears are another defect, for everyone is agreed that ears should not draw attention to themselves. A big nose, by reason of its central position and prominence, is a fell destroyer of beauty, especially if it be misshapen. Here, however, there is a compensation, for the common opinion is that a large nose, provided it is not downright ugly, will pass as an indication of strong character. Height and breadth of forehead rarely offend, and the mouth may be very wide—short of a clown's grin—without departing from beauty. A perpetually damp surface to the lips, however, or excessive thickness or protrusion, are not regarded as attractive, except perhaps by sensualists. Relativity is the master rule, and what is a pleasing feature in one face would be a defect if transferred to another.

In shape and measurements faces vary only slightly, but within this limited scope a remarkable number of distinctive appearances are possible. In women the standard of beauty, by which all are

subconsciously judged, as conforming or achieving a pleasing variation, is undoubtedly the classic oval, a traditional idealization which
dominates Greek and Roman sculpture and much of the painting of
the Italian Renaissance. It is not a precise, geometrical oval, being
broader at the brows than at the line from the jaw to the chin,
but its characteristic is a symmetry of continuously blended and un-
accentuated curves. The classic oval can be seen in the Roman
copies, in the Vatican and at Munich, of the Aphrodite of Cnidus
by Praxiteles—and even better, perhaps, in the portrait head in the
Leconfield Collection at the British Museum, which may be an
original by Praxiteles. Raphael's, Leonardo's, and Luini's Madonnas
conform to this model, with very minor modifications, such as the
elimination of the long, bridgeless Greek nose, and so does Michelangelo's in the unfinished *Madonna and Child, St John and the
Angels,* in the National Gallery. In the classic face there is little or
no indentation of the outline at the side of the eyes, and the features
maintain a mathematical proportion, each being subordinated to the
oval shape of the whole. The eyebrows and the lips curve regu-
larly. The structure of the face is built up almost entirely of convex planes, so that there are practically no flat surfaces and the general effect is full-fleshed, of a moderate plumpness.

The classic oval is a face designed for repose: it is almost invariably depicted with a contemplative if not a dreamy expression.
In pictures the tinting of the complexion (although this is generally
of an even golden hue) and the coloring of hair and eyes and lips
may add to its complexity, but they are hardly essential to its beauty.
The extraordinary quality of the classic face is that, dependent on
symmetry as it is, and with its main proportions strictly limited, it
can be made by skillful artists to yield so many variations of charm.
Subjected to very minor modifications, it has persisted in art almost
to the present day. It is the basic model, smoothed out, of the
odalisques and fashionable women portrayed by Ingres, and reappears, with the curves more accentuated, a thinned and tilted nose,
and a hint of dimpling, in the foremost circus girl in Tissot's *Chariot*

Ladies (Plate XIV, page 122), painted towards the close of the nineteenth century. Real life is another question altogether, and it may be doubted whether even the Greek Phryne (said to have been Praxiteles' model), were she living today, would be regarded as outstandingly beautiful. Conceivably, she would to modern eyes seem no more than a pleasant-faced woman, for the inherent strength of the Græco-Roman ideal—its symmetry—has proved also to be its limitation. The classic face is just too perfect: the balance is too minutely adjusted, no one part of the face attracts more attention than another, and the result, when observation has become familiar, is apt to be a dilution in the intensity of interest. Bluntly, the classic face in real life can be a bore.

Two reasons suggest themselves to account for this. One is that the complexity of modern life, the immense confusion of knowledge and experience which now beats on and in the mind (for example, psychological novels and drama, journalism, radio, the cinema, millions of scientific inventions), have left a record, however imperfect, in the modern face. Consequently, when we are confronted with the Græco-Roman ideal we look in vain for countless subtle indications of common and individual modern experience of which it is completely void; for when the classic face becomes conscious of these things it ceases to be classic, just as Leonardo's *Gioconda,* with its notoriously enigmatic smile, has already begun to say farewell to the ancient world and so is classic only in a decadent sense. The second reason may be that our instincts, necessarily sophisticated in no trivial or vicious sense, cannot any longer be satisfied by physical perfection of this simple, symmetrical order. Once we have discovered the exquisite pleasures to be got out of skillfully regulated departures from the obvious or the familiar, what is faultless, even in the grand style, may strike us as inadequate. "There is no excellent beauty," said Francis Bacon, an early exemplar of the modern spirit, "that hath not some strangeness in the proportion."

Yet the classic oval, although when carried unaltered into modern art it may seem a disappointing anachronism, nevertheless remains the true norm, the point of reference from which we take our bearings whenever we develop and modify new contemporary conceptions of the facial beauty of women. One variation is a lengthening of the oval, usually by increasing the height of the forehead and the depth of the cheeks. Almost inevitably this produces, together with a new delineation of full face and profile, flatter planes to the whole face, especially over the cheeks, which may be slightly hollowed. These changes often add to the graciousness of the face, producing an air of natural aristocracy, and in the expression a hint of pensive self-withdrawal. This longer oval in the delineatory outline of the face can be seen in the Botticelli *Venus* (Plate XVIII, page 154); and in the superbly modeled head by Eric Kennington (Plate IV, page 26) the oval is slightly and subtly modified from the Græco-Roman standard.

Instead of being lengthened, the classic face may be apparently squared off; the squaring is an illusion, for, apart from a leveling of the planes, all that happens is that the delineatory curves, without ceasing to be curves, approximate a little nearer to straight lines and so—especially where they meet, and when seen in profile—they convey a suggestion of angularity. At one extreme the flesh of the face, pallid in color, may cling so close to the bones that it suggests emaciation. It is an effect not necessarily so repulsive as in Lautrec's studies of hard-living women. El Greco used it to depict saintly ecstasies, and it becomes highly romantic in some of Picasso's canvases of the Blue and Harlequin periods. Again, if the oval is blocked out till it seems to resemble an oblong a woman's face may acquire a masculine, even a martial, aspect. Otherwise the illusory oblong shape is likely to produce an extremely handsome, dignified, and imposing appearance, which is traceable in such oddly assorted manifestations as the Du Maurier and Dana Gibson 'girls,' in the lady who plays the foil to the Marx Brothers in most of their films, in the elderly Society women of Peter Arno's cartoons, and, of course, in the models from which they all derive: English and American hostesses at the end of the last and the beginning of this century. But the deviation of curves into some approximation to the straight line is not necessarily a loss of feminine grace and delicacy, as can be verified by a glance at the profile portrait in pastel (Plate VI, page 42), by E. R. Hughes, which reveals the influence of Burne-Jones, and the water-color study, full-face (Plate VII, page 43), by Alexander Akerbladh.

Instead of being squared off, the basic oval may be further rounded and foreshortened, till the full-face outline is almost circular. At worst this results in a cat-like face, but it is a variation full of potentialities for charm and intimacy. The *Woman with Necklace*, by Tonks (Plate I, frontispiece), has been studied to evoke the subtleties inherent in the circular outline, and Renoir, when he was not painting portraits on commission, almost invariably chose models with round heads and faces. A bolder and more majestic version of the round face is to be found in the Tiepolo drawing (Plate III, page 11). Concerning beauty, it is futile not only to dispute but to try to set up any single standard. Besides the long oval, there is the short one—the heart-shaped face, in which the classic outline is slightly reduced in length, although the indentation at the side of the eyes is usually accentuated and the planes of the cheeks may be flattened, or even hollowed. Some of the most beautiful actresses of our time, including Vivien Leigh, Claudette Colbert, Greer Garson, and Myrna Loy, have heart-shaped faces, and the same shape can be seen in the justly admired Victorian portrait of Mrs Collman, by Alfred Stevens, in the National Gallery. Finally, there is what is best described, from the overriding impression it conveys, as the 'piquant' face. In outline this may follow any of the normal variations from the classic oval, but it obtains notice chiefly by some sharpening or delicacy of the features, particularly the nose and the mouth. Watteau excelled in depicting piquancy of this kind, at least in the drawings (see Plate IX, page 75) which he made for his own enlightenment and satisfaction, as distinct from the artificial mythologies he painted to please the Court of Versailles. And there is piquancy, too, in Rubens' drawing (Plate VIII, opposite) of his first wife, Isabella (or Elizabeth) Brandt.

Every human face approximates more or less to a type, the individual characteristics being worked out within definite limits set by heredity and environment; and men's faces, long or classic ovals, squared or rounded or sharp-featured, may easily enough be classified into a small or a large number of typical forms. It is not so easy, however, to analyze masculine beauty systematically, for two faces different in shape may nevertheless convey a similar impression of physical beauty. Beards, whiskers, and mustaches obtrude new considerations; maturity and experience write their records more forcefully, if not more lucidly, than on women's faces; and the possession of physical beauty is not, in common opinion, so important an advantage to men as it is to women. The kind of face, however, which most often marks a man as handsome is also derived from Græco-Roman models or idealizations: that is to say, it gives pleasure to the eye by the symmetry of its outline and the balance of proportion between the parts. In its purest and almost abstract form, this masculine symmetrical face can best be seen in the head of the major figure (Hermes) of the statue of *Hermes with Dionysus* in the museum at Olympia. This marble has survived (with the loss of an arm and the legs below the knees) from the fourth century B.C., and is the only fully authenticated example of the work of Praxiteles. The crown of the head is covered with short, close-growing curls, the forehead is broad and impends in a boss over the eyes, merging into a straight and tapering Greek nose, and so, diminuendo, to a curly mouth and a narrow, round chin. To a modern eye, the features of this anthropomorphic god look rather small for the area occupied by the face, and, as so often with nude statuary, the face lacks significance and intensity of expression, and demands no more than the precise fraction of the observer's attention warranted by its size in relation to the rest of the body. Nevertheless, here is a masculine version of the classic oval, and were the

PLATE VIII: ELIZABETH BRANDT, *by* PETER PAUL RUBENS

British Museum

74

PLATE IX: HEAD STUDIES, *by* ANTOINE WATTEAU

hair longer and dressed differently, the head would not seem out of place on a female body. This is the prototype from which many later models of good-looking young men have sprung, including most of the romantic 'juvenile leads' of the theater and cinema. The curves will usually be straightened, the planes of the cheeks sometimes flattened, the nose given a bridge, and the chin enlarged and squared; but the indestructible symmetry of the face will remain, the features, shapely in themselves, subordinated by precise proportions to the whole. It is the schoolgirl's dream, from realizing which most men, as they grow adult, are thankful to be delivered.

The man of today who is considered handsome, rather than a lovely boy, usually has his face constructed to a different order. He is not so much beautiful as commanding, and the aloofness and peremptoriness of his expression springs in part from a comparative largeness and a severe shaping of the features. The nose, for example, may be high-bridged, like the first Duke of Wellington's; it will certainly not be small. The mouth will have no pronounced curve, and the jaw will be broad and prominent. There will be symmetry in the face, but not the softly blended symmetry of the Greek ideal. And even so, poor man, he is more likely to please women than critics of his own sex.

Boldness or bluntness of feature is, in the general view, no detraction from the beauty of a man's face. The jut of the nose and the jaw, and a fairly coarse modeling of brow and cheek, are regarded as signs of virility, for there persists, among all the scarcely noticed assumptions in which human instincts are rooted, an almost universal belief that the nature of man is more active, originating, and adventurous than the nature of woman. This belief is perhaps stronger in women than in men, and stronger in young than in older women. One of its most notable confirmations is to be found in the popularity of those male film stars who, short of personality and talent, attain an hysterical fame for a year or two, and then are hustled off into obscurity by newcomers no better and not remarkably different. The most important function of this kind of photographer's idol is to embody the desirous aspirations of romantic women: to be, vicariously, anybody's and everybody's sweetheart, forestalling the arrival of a lover in real life or compensating for his defects if he has already arrived. Beautiful faces should not be looked for among the sort of men women choose as their husbands, for in the setting up of intimate personal relationships many other factors are influential as well as the æsthetics of the face; besides, for most women the range of choice is limited, and the man who eventually goes to the altar or the registry office and the double bed may owe his fortune, good or bad, to lack of urgent competition. The physical facial beauty which attracts young women is, on the whole, more symmetrical and in the boldness of the features more apparently virile than any of the types of beauty which most men possess or would wish to possess: for there is buried in the mind of the average man a fearfully confused psychological complex about masculine beauty, a complex made up of irreconcilable elements of envy and aversion.

In shape and structure, indeed, men's faces differ less from women's than is commonly supposed, except that they more rarely come within reach of attaining any definite standard of beauty, as can be demonstrated by observing how many plain or downright ugly men are able to conduct successful love affairs. A woman, seeking a mate for a permanent or temporary alliance, more often than not has to resign herself to a low standard of looks among the whole assortment of men available to her. The excessively virile face passes as more handsome than it actually is because it stands out as an exception, a primitive survival, in the civilized world. The head of Praxiteles' Hermes, as has already been noted, would not look discordant on a female body. And the youthful face drawn by Tiepolo (Plate III, page 11), which a little earlier was cited to illustrate the round formation of a woman's face, is, in fact, catalogued as *Head of a Youth;* while if the beard and mustaches were removed from the portrait of Louis de Béranger by François Clouet (Plate II, page 10) the face might be that of a young woman. These parallels, however, arise from similarities of structure and plastic surface. In real life, men's faces are easily distinguished from women's not only by their capacity for growing hair, whether it is shaven or not, but by the tinting of the complexion and, even more important, the rougher texture of the skin. Apart from this practical differentiation, it seems that in modern times, so far as the face is concerned, facial dissimilarities between the sexes have been considerably narrowed. A woman with an over-feminine face, one which draws attention to her function as a female animal, is apt to seem voluptuous, if not sensual; while a man whose face is formed on a harsh, aggressive pattern is in danger of being looked on as a kind of savage. The greater part of humanity lives happily between these two extremes, and complexion and skin texture, together with the accidentals of dress and toilet, are sufficient to distinguish the sexes to the eye: which is more or less what we are entitled to expect in a civilized society.

There are, however, some minor problems lying unsolved just beyond the margins of this exposition. How is one to account for the admiration fairly and honestly won by many women whose faces are not beautiful, not even comely, but who succeed, in a world where lovely women are neither rare nor undervalued, in attracting men of discriminating taste? To answer this would take the discussion outside the range of its present subject—physical beauty—for clearly both character and temperament are involved; so the anomaly should be noted, though its investigation must be postponed. Another problem is presented by the numerous young women who are pretty rather than beautiful: the distinction between prettiness and beauty lying in a triviality of visual effect and a lack (which may have other compensations) of dignity. To some tastes, no doubt, many 'pretty' girls should be classified among the beautiful, in the piquant category. But not all pretty faces are piquant. What I have in mind are faces made attractive by youth, coloring, and complexion—all perishable commodities. It is pretty girls, rather than beautiful women, who attract young men and some older men undergoing an Indian summer of sentiment or eroticism. In this way the pretty feminine face corresponds, as a ready-made ideal of desirability, to the handsome Hollywood man's face which is put on the world market presumably to meet a demand. Here is some justification for calling beauty 'skin-deep,' but, if my argument is valid, it is not beauty at all which creates the attraction here, not even physical beauty untouched by the qualities of the mind (as it should not be in adults), but solely youth and health.

From this conclusion another question inevitably arises: by whose aspirations and desires is each standard of beauty set? By men for women and women for men, or by each sex for itself? Most people have learned to doubt the old, glib formula which held that women make themselves beautiful solely to please men. A little intelligent observation, and listening, will show that women dress their bodies and prepare their faces to a large extent in conformity with conventions observed by other women and to satisfy other women's critical standards. Yet it is also true that a woman will esteem admiration far more highly from a man than if it comes from a woman, though she knows it is easier to get. In matters of personal appearance women are much more analytic; many a man, head over heels in love with a woman, if interrogated would be unable to give any detailed description of her appearance. As likely as not he could only guess at the color of her eyes. What a man receives into his mind and his emotions from a beautiful woman's face is a general effect of pleasure; but almost every woman, seeing a face for the first time, if she is at all interested, will in a few moments mentally catalogue its composition into what she judges to be its good and bad 'points.' Women certainly have an instinct to arouse the admiration of men for their beauty, but it is not a simple, overriding instinct. They respect each other's criticisms as well, and are profoundly influenced by them.

With men also there should be no facile answer to this question. In dress and toilet, as in social behavior, they are bound by stricter conventions than women, and those conventions change less rapidly;

when a community makes an attempt to break away, like the Chelsea and Bloomsbury young men who in the 'twenties took to bright-colored shirts and ties and broad-brimmed hats, supplemented a decade later by corduroy trousers, the revolutionary costume quickly hardens into a new convention. With few exceptions, men try to make their appearance conform closely to the prevailing customs of their environment: the 'novelties' produced seasonally by tailors and outfitters are very timid experiments indeed. And in choosing his clothes no man has the variety of shape, color, and material to select from that women obtain. This tendency to emulate the house-sparrow instead of the cock and the bird of paradise is modern, and, despite all the recent relaxations of Victorian formality, still powerful. When he does wear bright colors the average man takes care that they shall be a uniform, a blazer, a tie or a football shirt worn by other members of the same club. And so with the way he presents his face to the world. In general, it seems that he does not wish to draw attention to his personal appearance. A tiny mark of distinction here and there will satisfy his aspirations toward individuality; for the rest he is more than content, he is eager, to merge himself in the herd. Correctness is his guiding light. Apart from achieving correctness, he does not think it proper to devote (or seem to devote) much time or thought to his appearance, except perhaps during two stages of his development: in adolescence, when he first becomes acutely aware of his own sexual emotions, and a little later when he first experiences the ardors and agonies of falling in love. But even in the grip of these biological urges the average young man poses in front of his mirror without for more than a moment contemplating any departure from the current mode.

The reason for this timidity lies in a complex which has tangled itself deep in the masculine mind around the conception of the handsome man. It is not wholly irrational, and not wholly puritan. But it is based on three dogmatic assumptions: that beauty (which is often identified with art) is of its own nature feminine, and therefore a man can concern himself with it—particularly if it be in his own face and body and dress—only by imperiling his virility; that the things of the mind (and by this character or will power in everyday action is meant, rather than intellect and imagination) are more important and valuable than things of the flesh; and that, anyhow, handsome men are usually bounders, outsiders, cads. Of these three arbitrary judgments it can be said that the first, which makes beauty the prerogative of women, is fast perishing in other manifestations, to judge by the greatly increased interest, common to both men and women, in all the arts. The second judgment, exalting mind over the flesh, is puritanic only when carried to the excessive stage of despising the life of the body: and in activities other than those connected with their personal appearance, men, who show no lack of interest in food, drink, sport and sexual intercourse, are far from falling into the puritanic fallacy. The third assumption involved in the masculine complex needs more detailed examination.

The handsome man is likely to be a cad: this proposition may be regarded as suspect from the start. It has all the appearance of a violent jerk in the mind, made to appease the pangs of envy. It looks like a defensive mechanism set up by the ego to compensate for lack of success in amorous exploits. But it is notorious—at least, to the observant—that men who are plain or even ugly are often highly attractive to women. However, this is the sort of knowledge which comes to a man only when he is mature, when he has acquired and digested some experience of the world. It would not therefore prevent the formation of a compensatory complex directed against handsome men at the period when complexes are most easily developed—in adolescence. Many writers have lamented that men hate cads far more intensely and passionately than women do— a cad being a man who breaks the rules, who for his own immediate profit is ready to defy the conventions that other men subscribe to. The fact that the cad may dress and adorn himself in what is commonly condemned as bad taste (a Paris outfitter is said to have once labeled a particularly 'natty' suit in his shop-window as "Très chic, très sporting, presque cad") is only a crude and external manifestation of his disregard of the conventions of masculine behavior. The particular odium of the cad is that women run after him; he achieves in this world the Moslem paradise filled with acquiescent houris which, in some part of their subconscious, most men at times yearn for. The cad is not hindered by the scruples which in day-to-day life hold others back. Therefore the average masculine mind, in those regions which lie below the levels of conscious reason, argues that the cad owes his success partly to his violation of the rules, and partly to taking advantage of the susceptibility which women exhibit in the presence of good-looking men. Whether or not he is in fact good-looking, the cad is therefore identified with the handsome man, the man whose appeal lies in his physical attributes. And most men take care not to do anything which would induce others to consider them more beautiful than the average.

Men's distrust of the cad is not utterly without reason, although a steadier observation of the world might lead them to identify him less often with the handsome man: for a handsome face, because it is so readily classified as a type, does not readily express character. The handsome man, like the handsome woman, is apt to look insipid after a few glances. Besides, he is quite often stupid—though whether this mental inadequacy is a natural accompaniment of neat and symmetrical features or is a stupefaction produced by prolonged flattery I cannot tell. Handsome or not, the cad is certainly attractive to many women. He is Don Juan, Gay Lothario, Casanova reincarnated, the eternal lady-killer, and by impertinence, irresponsibility, shamelessness, calculated disrespect, he disentangles himself rapidly though superficially from the herd. Neither a bad reputation nor bad manners are any handicap to him: his aim is not love or even philandering, but amour. He does in actuality what other men only dream of; and if for his temerity he is despised by other men there are always plenty of women ready to console him. It is true that these are usually young women and of no very great intelligence, unless the cad turns gigolo and sets out professionally to capture older and well-to-do women; even so, he will as likely as not be able to attach himself to at least one girl in her teens or twenties. Rationally, women who become the prey of cads can be dismissed from the field of pity, as brainless flibberty-gibbets. But they are usually young, sometimes beautiful, more often pretty, and therefore desirable to young men who are not cads. It is not difficult to see how the masculine complex is set up.

Finally, it should be noted that the ideals of manly beauty cherished by large numbers of women are held in abhorrence by the great majority of men, who quite honestly, and without any undue pressure from the masculine complex, would not wish to look like these heroes even if they could. There is, it seems, a wide discrepancy between the sexes in their idealization of manly beauty. All too often woman's meat is man's poison. Yet it is only fair to point out that lots of women probably despise in their hearts the sort of pretty girls whose pictures young men pin up on the walls of camp huts and billets. In each case the faulty idealization arises from lack of knowledge and thought, and from the intrusion of sensual desire into æsthetic judgment.

Not all children are beautiful, but almost all are attractive because of their youth and because their promise has not yet had the opportunity to disappoint. Some beautiful children lose their looks as they grow up; others develop as adults a loveliness hitherto unsuspected. The charm of a baby's face arises only in part from its roundness and its comparatively large size—all the proportions of the body are different in infancy; the hair has a silky fineness, and the skin a transparency never seen at later stages of growth. The baby, even when it is old enough to toddle and to speak, has a face compact of plump, soft curves, and from these emerge vivid expressions, unmixed with shame or self-consciousness, of all the elementary emotions of humanity: desire, gratification, anger, indignation, affection, surprise, and amusement. There is no solemnity so absolute as a baby's: it can stare down any royal or ecclesiastic dignity invested with the purple or crimson-and-gold trappings of splendor. Similarly, mirth is never so pure or so spontaneous as in a baby's face. It is a mirth utterly innocent, and innocence is a quality to which even the most vicious pay tribute, if only by jealousy and hatred. It may be that the innocence of children is no longer beyond criticism, since Freud began to delve with surmises and theories into the private lives of the very young. But the baby at least is, willy-nilly, an innocent creature, poignantly innocent as in the Mervyn Peake drawing (Plate V, page 27), because it lacks the power to lay hands on the world around it (unless the rough handling of toys be included) and give effect to malice.

Towards babies, except when screaming fits shatter the nerves, everyone feels tender; only the brutalized, the insane, or the degenerate can feel otherwise, for the baby is helpless. It is in every sense a soft-shelled animal, and all the expressions of its plump face call forth the protective instinct. When we look at a representation by a great artist of mother and child many psychologists will tell us that we are moved to some extent because our own personal memories, lost to direct recall, are touched: we are said to identify our past infant selves with the child portrayed in its mother's arms. I have no reason to doubt the truth of this suggestion, but surely the identification does not stop there? Surely what is called the mother instinct is not confined to women who are or have been mothers, or even to one sex? The baby's face is blank as a record of experience: it knows only the present, and hardly glimpses even its own immediate future. And the range, though not the intensity and purity of its expressions, is in consequence severely limited. But by reason of its helplessness the baby's is the most powerful of all varieties of the human face in its appeal to others.

After infancy the face changes frequently and sometimes rapidly, losing and regaining chubbiness and acquiring its stable adult form only when adolescence is over. The changes are perhaps more noticeable in girls, apart from the disorders of the complexion which may accompany puberty, for as late as the early twenties many girls put on excess flesh which not only makes their bodies clumsy in movement and sedative in repose, but transforms their faces by half obliterating the features in a general plumpness. Girls differ from boys in figure long before what physiologists love to call the secondary sexual characteristics are developed: but not in face. The approximation to a standard of structure and delineation common to both sexes is even more marked before adolescence, when complexion and skin texture are hardly differentiated. The Gainsborough drawing of an adolescent girl (Plate XI, page 91) might, if the head alone is considered, pass for a sketch of a boy, and neither sex need be affronted by the misattribution. Similarly, Eric Kennington's pensive but not unmischievous little girl (Plate X, page 90) might, with short hair and a collar and tie, easily be a schoolboy. Shakespeare's heroines, in his own lifetime, were always played by boys. And we do not know for certain whether the painters of the Renaissance used girls as well as boys as models for their devotional pictures, which is perhaps one reason why there has been so much argument over the sex of angels. The similitude can be taken as one more cautionary sign to remind us that far more of that extensive subject, human nature, is covered by behavior in which both male and female have equal shares than by characteristics peculiar to one sex.

Still confining the discussion to the physical, and turning to middle age and old age, it must be noted at once that much that is judged to be beauty in youth does not long survive. The skin, as the years pass, grows tougher and often less transparent: what passes for a fresh complexion on an old face would seem crude on a young one. Those people continue to be beautiful—physically beautiful— who are blessed with a pleasing structure to the face. But as the hair turns gray or white, and perhaps sparser, as the skin shrinks and rearranges itself into folds and wrinkles, as first the brow and then the throat and at last the cheeks are seared with a network of engraved lines, another and more complicated form of facial beauty becomes possible. But because age which has neither absorbed experience nor wrought a firm character for itself forms a mask of undignified failure, it is much more difficult to separate in an old face the physical from the spiritual attributes. By the time full maturity is reached the spirit ought to have written its record clear and deep in the flesh.

Between the front and the profile there is the three-quarters aspect of the face, but this, bringing one ear and the back of the head into sight and foreshortening the further side of the face, still exhibits both eyes. The profile is therefore the one distinctive secondary aspect of the face. It is distinctive because of its sharp delineation from brow to throat, and because it substitutes for the enclosed oval or near-oval of the full face a more complicated and asymmetrical outline, the back of the head remaining blank and expressionless, while the silhouetted face is vividly drawn in a line delicate or coarse, droll, majestic, or aggressive. Normally the profile falls vertical or nearly vertical down the brow, then from an indentation reaches forward along the nose, and regains the vertical or a receding slope from the upper lip to the point of the chin. This continuous line is susceptible of endless variations of exquisite beauty. If, however, it approximates to an angle, with the apex at the tip of the nose, or if the chin lies directly under the brow or even in advance of it, the profile may be grotesque. Some faces come to an apex not only from brow and chin, but from each side, along temples, cheeks, and jaw; they are constructed like a ship's prow, blunt or sharp. In others the features are embossed in low relief, as on a platter. Both James Joyce and Hugh Walpole—as men and as writers poles apart —had faces of this kind, and Walpole's complexion remained a flowery pink to the end of his life. Sometimes the platter face is shaped like an inverted shovel, the full round jaw representing the shoulders and a square brow the sharpened edge of the blade—as in most of the Velasquez portraits of the seventeenth-century Haps- burgs. This converging or flattening of the facial planes affects the profile, which may vary plastically, though not in outline, as it is viewed from one side or the other: for it is said that no human face is perfectly symmetrical, that the right half is never identical to the last measurement with the left half.

85

In some faces the profile seems to have a character of its own, quite distinct from that of the full face, and often one is conscious of being startled as a person turns away and a profile is revealed of which the front view gave no hint. Seen from the front, a prominent or high-arched nose, or a nose with an undulating ridge, is subordinated by perspective, and rarely becomes the dominating feature of a face except when it is turned aside. In the drawing attributed to the school of Rubens (Plate XXII, page 218) a face of considerable delicacy and refinement is dominated by a high forehead and a prominent nose; but the draftsman has realized that some of this effect might be lost in a direct front view, and so the head is turned slightly to throw the line of the nose into profile. The full profile of any face does not depend only on the line from brow to chin, although this delineation is the sharpest and most striking. The formation of the eye also is thrown into profile, the lids opening into a V-shape, the upper lid hanging like a blind or shutter above the eyeball. In the side view of the eye, beauty is easily spoiled, for large and protuberant eyeballs become more noticeable, deep-pitted eyes are almost lost to sight, and the upper lids of eyes set too far forward may obscure the bridge of the nose. In some faces, particularly in mature faces where the flesh has settled into folds, there is visible a secondary profile: a crease from the upper cheek, just below the eyes, to the corner of the mouth and even lower. This crease may describe a single or double curve or may fall almost straight; either way, it has the effect of shortening the space behind the true profile from brow to throat, and if the profile is angled sharply to the nose, or if it thrusts forward or slides back at the chin, the fantasy of the outline is strongly emphasized.

So far the face has been considered in repose. Speech, laughter, and all the slow or swift variations of expression transform the outer shape and its surface planes. This interior mobility of the features, the opening, closing, half-closing of the eyes, the wrinkling of the forehead, the pinching or expansion of the nostrils, the pursing, broadening, and parting of the lips with the attendant creasing of

86

the cheeks, as well as the independent freedom of the lower jaw, provide infinite combinations of visible effect, an endless series of moving pictures, all the more vivid for their evanescence. One of the stiffest problems art has to tackle is the suggestion of movement of any kind. The violence or grace of bodily action can be precisely recorded, and an extension of space suggested by using the frame as an abrupt boundary, against which incomplete figures thrust and strain; but, because the picture is itself a still object, there is always a sense of artifice, and the observer may be left with an ache in his mind, a dissatisfied feeling that this depicted moment cannot exist by itself, that movement has been aborted by the insufficiency of the dimensions. And so with the expressive mutability of the face: repose is not only easier but more satisfactory to portray.

The more lively a face, the more it is transformed by the mutability of its expressions. Here two examples may be taken from the cinema. The face of Anna Neagle, though not modeled on the classic oval, has in repose something akin to a classic beauty, owing to the exquisite shaping of the features. It is a face of considerable beauty and dignity, and its piquant potentialities, of fun and mischief, are held in reserve while it preserves its repose. But when Anna Neagle laughs (and her laughter is unforgettable—a brisk, full-throated peal) her head tilts back on the column of her throat, and the face is transformed, as if a remote goddess had elected to become human. And again, it will be remembered for how many years Greta Garbo, by choice or direction, was shown to the world, in film after romantic film, with never more than a faint smile disturbing the serenity of her face—a face which seized the popular imagination of the nineteen-twenties and 'thirties as powerfully as Helen of Troy's "classic face" dominated the smaller Ancient World. Then Miss Garbo appeared in comedy. She laughed. And (although the susceptibilities of some romantics were wounded) a new face was added to the store of popular beauty; yet it had been available all the time. Both laughter and smiles are human prerogatives, in which other creatures have no share. Amusement transforms the face. As Mr A. S. J. Tessimond describes it in his sonnet *Saving Grace:*

cheekline gently

Creases; the mouth wide-flowers; the stiff mask softens;
And Man bestows his simple, unambitious,
Unservile, unselfseeking, undeceptive,
Uncorrupt gift, the grace-note of a smile.

The expressiveness of the face is a richness, an endless resource, as distinctive a human attribute as the faculty of communication by speech. It is sometimes, however, held deliberately in check by occupational necessity. The face can be smoothed into decorum or impersonality, by soldiers on parade, by mourners at funeral ceremonies, by judges charged with the burden of rendering impartial justice. It can be blanked into a two-way barrier, against the revelation of thought and emotion and against the inquisitions of other people, by police officers interrogating suspects, by bidders at auction sales, and by those who play poker. Or again, the face may abrogate its powers of expression on all occasions, public or private, as in the perhaps mythical impassivity of Orientals or in the eighteenth-century ideal of the gentleman which prompted Lord Chesterfield to denounce laughter as unbecoming to the well-bred.

There is, however, another kind of beauty, so far left out of consideration. It is visible enough in many faces, if only on occasion, but it does not reside in shape, texture, or color. So far as we know, it is inseparable from humanity and humanity's conceptions of its originator. It hardly exists in the physical world, although human beings, gazing at skies and seas and landscapes, may be stimulated to read this other order of beauty into their sensuous perceptions. Its nature is transcendent and pervasive. It is a beauty which speaks through the eyes (though how is not explicable) to the heart and the mind; we may assume, therefore, that it is from the heart and the mind that it is derived. For lack of a better epithet, it can be called spiritual beauty. It is akin to what we call character in the face, but it is not the same thing: for character may be evil or weak. Another necessary discrimination must be made: spiritual beauty is not to be conceived as in conflict with physical beauty—the two can get on very well together in the same face. Indeed, while sensualists take pleasure in beautiful or, more likely, pretty faces, the appreciation of physical beauty is not in itself gross or corrupting, not what St Paul calls an "inordinate appetite." To observe, to study, and to delight in the physical beauty of human faces may well be an experience so keen and exalted that it can hardly be denied the highest attributes of human activity. The Puritan who fears and hates the senses wanders as extravagantly from sanity as the voluptuary who makes the senses unhealthy by gorging them. And there is something to be said for the licentious lover. He is confused and inconsistent in his aim, for if he desired only what he believes he desires—the gratification of his sexual powers—he would be content to go to bed with any woman possessed of a beautiful body, no matter how ugly her face. But this is what no sensualist, unless he suffers from some fantastic perversion, will consent to do. His paramours must be at least pretty and, as the individualization of the human body is concentrated in the face, this anomalous preference may be taken as the sensualist's confession that he too, in his blundering way, is seeking more than a physical experience. Casanova, indeed, said as much.

But if spiritual beauty is not the equivalent of character or physical beauty, what is it? How is it to be defined? Only, I fancy, as a force emanated from the lonely and intangible individual caught up within the flesh for the term of human life. If a parallel must be found let it be with light, as force of character can be compared to electric power. Spiritual beauty is an energy which may be emanated violently or gently, and is more easily apparent when the emotions are active. It is readily traceable when it operates between two or more persons: in solitude it expends itself upon inward contemplation of ideas. In personal relationships spiritual beauty is manifested in many ways: by choice of words in speech, by their intonation, by gestures—most luminously of all by the expressions of the face, to whose physical variations it adds its own glowing patina. Spiritual beauty is to be seen in mothers with their children, and sometimes in the faces of the children too. It looks out more guardedly from the faces of fathers. It can transform, by its avowals for the future, the still callow faces of young lovers. It is the radiant power which, defying all the laws of æsthetics, makes the beloved face, for the lover, "the most beautiful in the world," and which, in fact, does invest the faces of those who are loved with a visible new attribute. It eclipses what, without it, would be ugliness, and it transfigures the bleachings and shrinkings of old age. It is the immaculate child of all true affection. It is compassion's golden robe. It is the majesty enveloping the humility of prayer. It is the candid illumination of honest friendship and the unsuspected reward of all selfless endeavor. It eludes description, but it can always be recognized at sight.

PLATE X: PORTRAIT OF A CHILD, *by* ERIC KENNINGTON

PLATE XI: SKETCH OF A GIRL, *by* THOMAS GAINSBOROUGH

Author's Collection

CHAPTER FIVE

❦

THE MARKS OF TIME

THE importance of the face in human life is indicated by the fact that any but the most superficial consideration quickly brings the inquiring mind knocking up against the prime abstracts, such illimitable and elusive conceptions as beauty, goodness, taste—and now, time. Lately time has become a playground for writers. Skillfully or not so skillfully they jumble up its sequences, and produce elaborate theories, with the solemnity of metaphysical conjurers, to account for adventures of the mind which lift past and future into the present. There were the ladies who saw the Versailles of the eighteenth century; there was Barrie's forest of lost opportunities in *Dear Brutus,* and Mr Priestley's Conway family. I find these speculations interesting and justifiable in so far as they enable works of art to be created. But for sober, everyday use they are, to my mind, flimsy and superfluous. If it were true that we have the power to enter the past and the future, as actors in their events, by jumping a few spaces on a kind of cribbage-board, then it seems to me we should be impotent creatures caught up in a machinery of determinism. All our struggles would be futile, and free will a monstrous delusion. But this is not so. We may not be absolute masters of our fate, but at least we are subalterns of our souls. Every minute of every day we have a limited choice of action set before us, and according to the choices we all make as individuals, so the record of the present is inscribed in the chronicles of the past, and so in turn it influences the choices which will be set before us in the future, approaching neither faster nor slower than it approached our fore-fathers. We live in an apparently endless series of dissolving present moments, no sooner realized than replaced; and our power to enter the past and the future is a power of the intellect and the imagination.

Time, however, has a twofold existence for every human being. It is an external environment, the "ever-rolling stream" of the old hymn which, without deviation or alteration of pace, carries each one of us from the cradle to the grave, and so completes the cycle of individual existence. But time also exists within the mind, as a free and yet a practical concept. Memory enables us to achieve a panoramic view, a continuity, of our own experience, and by comparing what we have done and undergone with the communications of other people and the surviving records of those who are long since dead, we are able to create in our minds another panorama, of history. From this we project, by a logic of possibilities, an expectation of the future, in the light of which we plan and order our present movements as they slide towards and then recede into the past. And thus we live a larger life. We interpret past or future, in the last resort, from the crib put in our hands by memory, just as we interpret another person's motives by our own, noting similarities, distinctions, and contrasts.

In both these aspects time profoundly affects the human face. The longer a civilization lasts, the more subtle, refined, and various become the expressions of the individuals who live in it. The faces to be seen in Great Britain today would be different had they a different national history behind them. To one degree or another (for all are not equally responsive) they record, dimly, the long, slow intermingling of Celt, Saxon, and Norman, the rigid social orders of feudalism, the poetic excitements of the Renaissance and the empire-building period, the painfully achieved compromises of the established Church and the limited monarchy. More accessible in the British face are the traces left by the evolution of democracy, from its remote and tentative origins in Magna Carta and Habeas Corpus, to the wide tolerances, combined with strong opinions, of present-day politics, and the realized ideal of an Empire transformed into a Commonwealth of self-governing states. Besides this, British faces record the communal experience of industrialism slowly brought under some sort of control, the protracted avoidance of civil war, the idealisms and the realisms of two world wars against German tyranny. Most vivid and recent of all are the marks left by the privations and sufferings of standing up alone, without allies, against the Nazi power dominant only twenty miles away. More than a thousand years of civilization is written in the faces of the British people. You will find Roman law there, and Shakespeare, even in the faces of those who have neither seen nor read his plays, for Shakespeare has made his way into the rhythms of British thought. The Bible, also—the Authorized Version: those who no longer read it still inherit subconsciously the intimate knowledge of their forefathers—and Biblical ideas and phrases are trenched deep in all our minds.

Time sprawls its larger records across all faces, and much that it writes is foreordained before the baby is born. Some American faces bear a close resemblance to British; others are very different. What history has written on American faces is to a large extent of European origin, for even the descendants of pioneering families take from their ancestors the obstinate valuations of seventeenth-century Dutch and English. There is puritanism and frontier lawlessness to be seen in certain American faces, as well as the confused idealism and self-interest of the War of Independence and the Civil War. A later record comes from the era of expansion and prosperity, cross-cut by the doubts and disappointments of economic slumps. In other American faces—those of immigrants or children of immigrants—the groundwork is all European, and if the form of the face is peasant this is often overwritten by an excessive, if understandable, materialism, a boisterous delight in cheap and plentiful food, clothes, furniture, entertainment, as well as by a recent reaction against puritanism into promiscuous sensuality and drunkenness. However, time has an infinite vocabulary to draw on, and there is another characteristic American face in process of evolution, without the spoiled-child mouth, the plump jowls, and the self-assertive, undisciplined eyes which everyone will hope are only intermediate manifestations of one aspect of 'the American way of life.'

Time deals no less strictly with the individual, as an animal born helpless, demanding nurture and training, due to expend its energies for a long period in supporting its own life, and ultimately doomed to death by disease, violence, or the exhaustion of the body. This is the fate—and it is not on the whole an unkindly fate—of every one of us. Its prophecy is written in our faces. The new-born infant does not at once acquire that smooth-skinned placid appearance, like an unbruised fruit, which awakes ready rhapsodies. It comes into the world red-faced after its struggle to emerge from the womb, and signals its achievement of a separate existence with a shout which might pass for a lament or a remonstrance. For a day or more its face is not only suffused with an excess of blood but wrinkled and shriveled in a similitude of old age. At this time its appearance is often triumphantly acclaimed as proof of its legitimate fathering. Some days pass before the baby dares to open its eyes on the world, and then they are invariably and disarmingly blue. If they change color in the next few weeks the mother will no doubt be disappointed, but the change will hold good for the rest of the baby's life. Meanwhile, its ruddy complexion subsides to pink and white or gold, and the face smoothes out to the familiar plump contours. Compared with adult proportions, its limbs are too short and its head too big for its body, and the structure of the unhardened skull is clearly evident. This distinction is manifest, though subordinated to the maternal relationship, in John Wheatley's gracious drawing (Plate XIII, page 107). The painful cutting of the teeth makes it quite clear to the newcomer that life is not going to be all milk and dandling, that whatever it acquires will be bought at a price, and luck will be needed to strike any reasonable bargains with the outward world. Thenceforward the face, more than any other part of the body, becomes a score-sheet for time, which works so minutely on the surface, however, that the record advances with no such steady monotonous beat as time itself, but in sudden and disconcerting leaps, marking with a rapid imperious gesture a period ended, a period begun. There is a day when little Tommy is no longer a child but a shambling youth in need of a razor; a day when Betty Mary can no longer be treated as a schoolgirl, at least in front of other people; and another day when they both abruptly achieve the status of adults. Then life lets them out on a long leash: perhaps they marry, and little red-faced, squalling babies are born for them to adore and worry over; but their responsibilities cannot blind them forever to the witness of their mirrors. Youth relaxes out of their faces in an unwanted sag here, a tautening or a roughness of the skin there; and soon there is a white hair or two showing. Before they have grown used to the silent echoing note of their own inward dismay they find a new generation of young men and women regarding them as middle-aged. Custom consoles them—for how long? Perhaps twenty years: time has its generosities, though every mortgage is foreclosed in the end. One day they discover they are elderly; then that they are old. And one of them must die before the other.

There is a tragedy in the aging of the human face, because it is inevitable. The plot works itself out; and there is no escape for anyone. The consolations are numerous, and the run of the play may be long, longer than the Biblical threescore years and ten. But the tide of time flows only one way, and of the sea which the weary river attains at last we know only that it is what we call death: that it is a sea of separation, casting up on its shores the derelict cold body and bearing away the spirit, we know not where. I am one of those who find it impossible to believe that death is a final extinction, but I am told by my more philosophic friends that this is no more than an urgency of the wish to survive, a characteristic of what is called a sanguine disposition, a projection of my own vitality. To that I can answer only that, for me, vitality is the decisive evidence against the absolute verdict of death. Perhaps oblivion awaits me this year or next year, though I rather suspect I shall live to see eighty at least. Before then I may be overtaken with a Swinburnian weariness, and death—the state of being dead, not the act of dying—will not seem so terrible. But at present I cannot imagine not being alive and not enjoying life.

Better, till death comes close, to confine one's courage to the more immediate problem of growing old. It is a problem of reconciliation, because the body, and especially the face, ages more rapidly than the mind. The two machines are out of gear. Many conclusions are drawn from the observation of the face; it is the perpetual reference from which personal judgments are made. And among these conclusions is the assortment of people into age groups. But the person who dwells, more secluded than any hermit-crab, behind the face does not see it, except occasionally by reflection in a mirror, or projected in a photograph or a portrait. His conception of his own face is different from other people's, more indulgent, less detached, and almost certainly he will assign it to a different age group. For a face to its owner is part of his ego. It is doubtful if at any stage of human development the subjective and objective views of anyone's age coincide. The exception perhaps is the young child, who, being treated as a child, accepts the valuation as it accepts, pragmatically, the whole world that it explores, pioneer fashion. But the young child, one has to remember, hardly identifies grown-up people as the sort of creature it will itself eventually become: they are beings of another order, distinguishable from elephants and motorcars by their shape and the personal interest they take in the egoistic child.

A little later, however, this blithe content disappears. The growing child becomes intensely concerned with age classifications among its own young acquaintance: it will envy those a year or even six months older than itself, for the privileges and enlarged activities they possess, and it will patronize and perhaps bully those younger than itself. Moreover, childhood maintains a delicate inner balance: it clings to certain customs of an earlier stage, fervently if secretly, in the form perhaps of a worn-out teddy-bear or rag doll taken every evening to the bed that has long replaced a cot. At the same time it is always reaching out—as we say, precociously—to worlds of knowledge beyond the scope thoughtfully marked out for it by educationists. The same child may be found on the same day enjoying both *The Wind in the Willows* and *The Intelligent Woman's Guide to Socialism*. Childhood is essentially an existence conducted on many different levels of progress, and it is the child's power of self-absorption, its ability to forget what it was doing just now in the interests of its present sensations, which enables it to move so rapidly and so sure-footedly forward in a private world of increasing size and complexity.

With adolescence, this exquisite balance comes to an end. Life becomes a bewildering alternation of ecstasies and abysmal depressions. The body changes its interior economy so rapidly that it creates a chaos in the mind and the emotions; and this chaos parallels, but not neatly, all the sloughings and cellular renovations of the flesh. The adolescent can attain no stable view of the outer world because his point of vantage—his own nature—is forever pitching and tossing like a tiny boat in a stormy sea. Can it be wondered at that he longs, fiercely, solemnly, with a pathetic, absurd dignity, to attain the apparent certainties of adult status? Lacking confidence in himself, he looks for assurance to other people, and to make certain of it he strives earnestly to ape the outward semblance of adults. Yet he has only just begun a new existence, into which he ventures almost as ignorant and inexperienced as the new-born baby. He can never hit the happy medium: if he is not introspectively moping, he wants to sing and shout at inappropriate times. His limbs and his voice shame him by responding unfaithfully to his commands. The drastic adaptations of his glands poison his blood, the blood which feeds his heart and his brain. In despair, he concentrates his attention on the superficialities of life. For the first time he becomes keenly aware of his own appearance, just when it is least prepossessing. He seeks assurance in correctness and conformity; he longs to look exactly like young men a little older than himself, to stand and walk and talk as they do, to wear the same sort of shirt and tie, to manage his cigarette or pipe in the same way. And he cannot. He discusses, with an affectation of expert knowledge, sport, girls, clothes, even razors and hair-creams, hardly guessing that the over-intensity of his interest betrays his inexperience. He examines his face in the mirror several times a day, fretting over the technique of a not altogether necessary shave, depressed by pimples and boils and the chubbiness of boyhood which will not yet be compressed out of the shape of his cheeks and his chin. And at the same time the poor creature is probably infatuated with some girl as dizzily perplexed as himself by the switchback ascents and descents of the adolescent temperament.

Children commonly wish to be taken for a little older than they really are because they associate the progress of the years with the graduated acquisition of extra privileges. Responsibilities and cares, loaded on the back along with the privileges, are hardly felt till the weight of them settles into place. Adolescents desire to pass as adult because of impatience and the urges of emulation. And so begins a life-long process of incomplete adjustment to the outer world. The young man and woman may glory in their new-found combination of youth, maturity, and independence, yet they are always noting, with a mixture of jealousy and humility, the superior *savoir-faire* of those in the thirties, and will be flattered if they are admitted on equal terms to the counsels of their elders. Then there comes a time when they are best pleased if opinion credits them with more wisdom and experience than their years and—simultaneously—with looking younger than they really are. This is the topmost ridge of their careers. After this they have done with imitating the behavior of their elders, and a new younger generation, thrusting upward, is all too ready to point out that the bloom is off their youth. Flattery can reach them only by imputing freshness to their appearance. And so for the second half of adult life each of us lives behind a mask which, he feels, belies the truth: our faces look wiser and more staid than we know we are. We can get along very well with our contemporaries, crack our little jokes, play the fool when the mood is on us, kick up our mental heels. Those who are of an age with us understand: they have perforce to be tolerant, knowing that behind their own aging faces the spirit is still impenitently youthful. But in the presence of our juniors we must behave more decorously. If they respect us it shows they acknowledge our superior experience, of which we are, illogically, just as proud as of our mental sprightliness: lest we sink in their opinion, and conduct ourselves ridiculously like sheep gamboling among the lambs, we respond to the expectation of our juniors: we become outwardly grave and reverend. And if they fail to show the respect due to us we turn severe: we visit them with our displeasure; for, behind our matured faces, we are still touchy with the vanity of youth.

I am forty-five: middle-aged. I do not yet know what it is to feel old. Physically I am strong and healthy, though perhaps somewhat short of exercise. When I look in the mirror I see white hairs above my ears: a damnable injustice, for I know plenty of men of my own age without any. My face is still fresh-complexioned, and not so plump as it was a few years back. But I cannot deny that it is the face of a man—how do they call it in magazine stories?—no longer in the first flush of youth. These are indisputable facts. They ought to be deeply impressed in my consciousness. But they are not. Unless I bend my mind to it, I think of myself still as a youngster. In my casual assumptions I class myself with men round about thirty. I think of them as contemporaries. I talk to them as to contemporaries. Against the background of most of my thoughts, forty-five is a venerable age, and remote from me. It is not I who have attained that undesirable beacon, but my face and my silly white hairs. If I could disown them I would.

Thus it is, I believe, with most people. Time marches on across the face, digging in its heels as it goes, but it cannot drag the mind and the spirit at such a headlong pace. Past the milestone of maturity, we all feel younger than we look. Vitality is a rebel within the crumbling fortifications of the body: and no man is beaten till he has lost the will to fight. I am convinced that many an old man and woman dies young, and reluctant, and surprised. Find the secret of renewing physical youth, and the mind, whatever load of experience and disillusionment it may carry, will have no trouble in matching the vigor of the body. Meanwhile, it would make for happiness all round if the young would occasionally remember that their seniors, behind their time-betrayed faces, feel much the same as they did ten, twenty, thirty, or even the full forty Harrovian years ago, and that the irony of misrepresentation lies in comprehensive ambush waiting for those whose only care today is that they should seem more adult than they are. But then, if the young realized that, they would no longer be young. Time is a schoolmaster who will not let the brightest pupil skip a class or two.

If the body—and particularly the face—ages before the mind, the mind is, in another sense, very strictly subordinated to the influence of time. The date of our birth destines us to grow up and work out our individual lives in an historical period which, however it may be judged by later generations, will probably seem, to those living in it, an age of transition. All periods progress, backward, forward or sideways, in some confusion and very rarely with a clear, sustained view of whither they are moving: the difference between a 'settled' and a 'restless' period is one of pace and unanimity of outlook. It is a matter for dispute whether it is a happier fate to live in a sedative or a feverish period, and to me the answer seems to depend on the temperament of the individual and his responses to mental stimulants or bromides. Many people nowadays will openly declare their longing to have lived in the eighteenth century, and some, endowed with a private income and a secure social position, would doubtless have been happy in that age. But I wonder if William Blake would have agreed with this preference? Or Christopher Smart, who scrawled his one great poem, the *Song to David*, with a key on the walls of a cell in a lunatic asylum? Or Chatterton, the medievalist poet turned forger, who committed suicide before he was eighteen? It is therefore also a matter for dispute whether a man of outstanding ability does well to be in harmony or at odds with the period he lives in. Was Shakespeare a characteristic Elizabethan? Or has the best of him become visible only since he died? Was Thackeray a true Victorian? On the other hand, would Sir Walter Scott rank (with so many literary historians, at least) as a great novelist had he not flourished on the first awakening of interest in the picturesque details of the Gothic past? Would D. H. Lawrence have been idolized except in a postwar period?

But some composition must be made, if only with drawn daggers, between ourselves and the age we are pitched into by the accidents of birth. Each period has its own mental climate, and those who live in it are to one degree or another affected by the tastes, opinions, interests, and activities pervading their environment. Even the rebel is modified by the act of rebellion: he becomes the naughty child of his age, and if he pulls faces and puts out his tongue we ought to remember that, born at another time, he might have been content to say his piece in the drawing room and receive applause in a glow of modest smirkings. One of the important factors in the mental climate of any period is its ideal of feminine beauty. Again it shall be left to others to argue whether these changing ideals are set up by the hazard of some young woman or other achieving favor with influential men and so establishing a fashion, or whether the ideal is implicit in the outlook of the age, so that certain young women, in or out of 'Society,' become popular because their appearance embodies the ideal. To take a ready example: when the eighteenth century was giving place to the nineteenth did Emily Lyon captivate Sir Harry Featherstonhaugh, Charles Greville, William Hamilton, and eventually Horatio Nelson because she would in any age have been judged beautiful and charming, or because the time was ripe for the apotheosis of her particular style of soft-featured, melting-eyed, high-complexioned beauty? Leaving morals temporarily out of the question, would she have had the same appeal for

Sir Francis Drake or Admiral Beatty? Emma Hamilton is dead, and in any case lost her beauty, her popularity, and her luck before she died. Nothing survives but memoirs, contemporary comments, kind or unkind, and the numerous portraits, most of them by Romney. And Romney is not everybody's cup of tea: he is not mine, for example. Like Greuze across the Channel, he does not appear to have seen his sitters plain: he viewed them through an almost physical mist of acute romantic sensibility, blurring the outlines, turning gestures into poses, and imparting sentimentality even to the draperies of a gown. What do we see in Romney's portraits: Emma Hamilton as she was, or as Romney (and probably Nelson) credulously longed to see her? There can be no certain answer to these questions. Each age lives swathed in its own illusions, and although, comfortably detached by the passage of time, we may recognize the illusions of the past for what they are, and analyze them, we cannot do more than guess at their extent or define the precise point where illusion stopped and reality began. One final speculation on this problem: suppose Romney had painted Jane Austen, should we recognize Jane's acid under the painter's golden syrup?

Each age has its own ideal of woman's beauty. What these were in more primitive civilizations remains obscure: the surviving art (although it is one of the illusions of this age to bow the head before the primitive) is too scarce and too crude, and there is too little evidence to show us what was admired and what was recorded for other reasons. I do not think we can even be sure whether Nefertiti (who, as an excavated sculpture copied by mass production, became almost deified in the twentieth century) was important to her contemporaries in Egypt as a great beauty or merely as royalty. The known record of ideal beauty begins, so far as the face is concerned, with the classic oval of the Greeks and, in a rather coarser form, the Romans. It was revived, and modified, by the Italian Renaissance. But before that there had been other ideals. From the formal, half-abstract murals of the Byzantine Empire (whose artists tried to depict a symbolic type rather than a representation of individual humanity) Western Europe seems to have taken, in the late Middle Ages, a fashion for rather heavy, dark eyebrows, formed in a full curve, and of equal thickness from one end to the other. Later— in Italy and the Low Countries at least—this fashion gave way to thin eyebrows, perhaps shaved or plucked, and a high forehead, artificially heightened by plucking away head hair. This medieval or early Renaissance forehead was usually protuberant. It was a dome. In fact, it was bumpy. And it is odd that this bumpy forehead (the High Renaissance brought back the classical brow, twice as broad as high, but flattened it a little) reappears in the nineteen-twenties, as photographs and Augustus John's drawings show, in James Joyce: and Joyce was almost as much the wayward, rebellious child of St Thomas Aquinas and the Middle Ages as he was of Edwardian Dublin.

The High Renaissance subtilized and Christianized the classic oval, and thereby transformed it. With Rubens and other Flemish and Dutch portrait-painters the Renaissance face often (not always) was plumped out into jolly or sensual curves—and the figure with it. Rubens was, in the social sense of the time, a gentleman. He was knighted in England; he became a diplomat. But he was a child of his age, and his age was dominated by a *nouveau riche* aristocracy. It is hardly stretching a point to see him akin to the other painters of the Low Countries, set free from the tight restrictions of feudal patronage and reveling in a new-found prosperity. Food was plentiful and cheap; so was wine; fruits were imported from distant countries, and with them spices. Good furniture, flowers, tapestries, carpets, curtains, were now to be found in bourgeois homes as well as in castles and manors. All these things Pieter de Hooch, Jordæns, Vermeer, Mæs, Os, Snyders, and Steen painted with loving verisimilitude, for burgher clients, delighting in the shape and solidity and color of their possessions. Rubens often let other painters or even apprentices fill in details of the backgrounds to many of his pictures. For himself he took his pleasure in painting well-fed women, clothed or naked, thus celebrating the ample provender of his time through its effect on human flesh. It is doubtful if among all his thousands of pictures there is one which portrays a thin woman. Practicing his art in the nineteen-twenties, he might have starved for lack of models and appreciation. From all this it is not to be deduced that Rubens was anything less than a very great painter, and his drawings are among the very finest ever made. But his taste, and the taste of his time (except perhaps in Spain, where Velasquez and Greco were recording austerities, and in England and France, where Holbein and Clouet recorded numbers of comparatively thin-faced women) were different from ours. His drawing of his first wife, Isabella (or Elizabeth) Brandt (Plate VIII, page 74), shows a face less plentifully fleshed than those of most of his goddesses and saints, less plump than it afterwards became, and less plump too than the face of his second wife, Helen Fourment, whom he painted still more frequently. Isabella Brandt does not look thin to our eyes, but it is not difficult to imagine her husband (they were a devoted and happy couple) fretting over her health and encouraging her to eat more.

By the middle seventeenth century the swollen cheek, the fat neck, and the double or triple chin were no defects in an English-woman's face. Contours could hardly be too rounded, and the beautiful woman had her face, as well as her body, cushioned with fat. Sir Peter Lely's large canvas of Nell Gwynn in the National Portrait Gallery, it is true, shows her no more than youthfully plump, but there are several other portraits and engravings to indicate that the menus provided for a royal mistress soon put that right. Charles II, indeed, like Louis XIV in France, seems to have had an Oriental liking for full-fleshed women, and as he gave titles to so many of them, thereby founding many of the noble families of England and Scotland, I find it ironic that their present-day descendants, to judge from prewar Ascots and Levees, should on the whole be a skinny lot. It is not possible, because of his known debauchery, to assume that Charles's friend, Rochester, was moved by righteous indignation when he wrote his satiric and obscene poems against the King and his mistresses, the Duchess of Cleveland, the Duchess of Portsmouth, and especially poor Nell Gwynn, who never got a title for herself, and whom Rochester delighted to address as "Madam Nelly"—the familiar diminutive providing him with the sort of rhyme which appealed to his sense of humor. And as Rochester was in no position to denounce Charles for immorality, I have been tempted more than once to see him as a man whose taste was at odds with his times, a man who did not think fat faces beautiful. On reflection, however, I am afraid this theory will not hold. Rochester was as much a pasha as any of his contemporaries, and also carnivorous in his love of flesh. The motives behind his denunciatory poems are jealousy and snobbery. He was not only an earl but the son of an earl, and having entered an exclusive society by inheritance, he disliked seeing others admitted by favor. Nell Gwynn, in particular, offended his sense of caste, and what he chose out of the record to insult her with was not so much lack of virtue as lack of breeding: she had sold apples and oranges to theater audiences, acted on the stage, and—most despicable of all, in Rochester's eyes—she had been a maidservant when part of her job was to rake out the household fires. Rochester calls her "Cinder Nell"—a nickname which, if it became or was already popular, may be one reason for the later popularity of Perrault's fairy story, *Cinderella*. So, if there is any substance to this speculation of mine, Eleanor Gwynn of Drury Lane survives on the English stage, year after year, in the bowdlerized and hacked-out allegory of pantomime, with Charles Stewart prettified as Prince Charming, and her titled rivals, presumably, cast as the Ugly Sisters.

The full-fleshed face, often dimpled and with a pronounced or hinted double chin, maintained its popularity in high society for a century and a half. It is to be traced intermittently in the works of many fashionable portrait-painters—Lely, Van Dyck, Hoppner, Boucher, Watteau, Fragonard, Nattier, Kneller—and begins to lose favor only with Hogarth, Gainsborough, Lawrence, and Alan Ramsay. At the end of the eighteenth century full curves are giving way to a leaner version of classic oval, but the face is becoming less maternal, almost boyish. In the nineteenth century the oval is emphasized by the style in which the hair is dressed, plastered flat over the crown of the head and sometimes over the temples from a center parting; the chin is narrowed, but rarely squared, and in the portraits of Ingres and Winterhalter (who was as much in demand in France and England as in Germany) the oval face is flattened till eyes, nose, and mouth seem to be presented on a single plane, and the complexion is so smooth that the face might almost be carved out of tinted soap. This was the mid-Victorian ideal, not confined to England by any means; and portraits engraved for reproduction in magazines and keepsakes show this oval platter superimposed, as it were, on faces as various as those of Queen Victoria, Mrs Lincoln, the Empress Eugénie, and George Eliot.

It is at the end of the nineteenth century that young women begin to be known as girls. The Du Maurier girl, the Grosvenor Gallery (or Æsthetic) girl, the Gibson girl, were types and ideals made familiar to millions by photographs and colored drawings in the weekly, monthly, and annual press. When musical comedy was invented, blending waltz tunes more or less Viennese with plots from Palais Royal farce, it quickly caught the new fashion in such titles as *The Quaker Girl, A Gaiety Girl, A Country Girl, The Cabaret Girl, The Girl in the Taxi.* About 1930 the United States achieved a new development of this idiomatic euphemism, with the term (also used as a musical-comedy title) Girl Friend: a term used to indicate any relationship from comradeliness to a casual or permanent amour. And just before the Hitler war began America exported yet another fancy name for a phenomenon not so new. This was Pin-up Girl, one whose picture is fastened to the wall of a bedroom or study by some love-stricken youth to console him for her absence in the flesh. The pinned-up picture may be a photograph, obtained by free gift from the girl herself, but is more likely to be a colored drawing torn out of a magazine. In essentials, the Pin-up Girl has been with us ever since mechanical processes of reproduction became comparatively cheap, easy, and rapid. During the 1914–18 war Army officers

PLATE XII: PORTRAIT OF A MAN, *by* ALBRECHT DÜRER

PLATE XIII: WOMAN AND CHILD, *by* JOHN WHEATLEY

Author's Collection

of frivolous disposition displayed on their dug-out and mess-room walls colored pages or postcards by a French artist with a German-sounding name, Kirchner; the girls he depicted were usually of a Southern French or Latin type, but their scanty clothing and their fetching attitudes were Parisian of the Paris which caters for the foreign visitor on the loose. The men in the ranks on the whole preferred more decorous pictures, usually portrait-heads by Harrison Fisher or Barribal. And there were still to be had plenty of extremely glossy postcards of musical-comedy actresses and Society women, although the vogue for the 'Postcard Beauty' had reached its height during the reign of Edward VII. These glossy postcards, sold at twopence each, had little of the cinema 'still' and arc-lighted chiaroscuro which is commonplace nowadays. The beauty struck a fetching pose and almost invariably smiled to reveal two rows of extremely even and white teeth. The piled-up hair, the flower-fruit-and-bird encrusted hats, the ropes of pearls, the lacy-bosomed frocks or blouses would look more fantastic than fascinating nowadays. But to millions of youths, and even to young men, the Postcard Beauties gave a prolonged and innocent, if vicarious, pleasure. I had a collection of glossy postcards myself in my schooldays, among which my favorites were Lily Elsie (had I not played truant to watch her from the gallery rails in *The Merry Widow?*), Zena Dare, Gertie Millar, Gabrielle Ray, and Gladys Cooper. At the same time schoolgirls and young women were propping upon their mantelpieces photographs of romantically handsome actors, often known as Matinee Idols: George Alexander, Lewis Waller, Forbes-Robertson, Gerald du Maurier, Austin Melford, and many others.

The Postcard Beauty differed from the Pin-up Girl of today in that she was rarely portrayed in color and never with any more of her body exposed than the shoulders and arms. I would not claim that the youths of my time were cleaner-minded than those of today, although most of them were more ignorant. But their sexual desires were less continually under stimulus; semi-pornography was not offered to them on every other bookstall: if it was wanted it had to be sought in the side-streets. And depictions of alluring female bodies were not thrown at their eyes day and night from billboards, magazines, and cinema screens. In consequence they tended to concentrate their ideal of feminine beauty in the face, and it was to supply this modest demand that the glossy postcards were produced. The mental climate of the two periods is different: and while the earlier one can be accused of encouraging hypocrisy, sniggering, and furtiveness, I sometimes feel that present-day manners are blunting the senses of the young with an overwhelming excess of stimulation. In one way the Pin-up Girl is a reversion to the classic conception of beauty: the face is subordinated; it is seen simply as a detail of structure and color at the upper extremity of a virtually naked body; it is of far less erotic value than bosom and thighs. Considering the kind of face with which Nature and the make-up man has endowed most Pin-up Girls, this is perhaps inevitable. But it marks her as a sensual mechanism rather than an individual. She is a manufactured product, a popular aphrodisiac, put on the market by her owners; and as soon as the demand falls off she is scrapped and a new model brought out. No woman of character and ability is likely to let herself become a Pin-up Girl. The very name has a derogatory ring to it.

It would be misleading, however, to conclude that the present is a degeneration from the past. From the Renaissance onward painters have been employed to provide depictions of beautiful women, which were displayed in the homes of wealthy men, and often fulfilled the same function as colorplates torn out of magazines today. No doubt many great nobles were men of taste and discrimination, but others almost certainly rewarded the painters they employed for their power of erotic suggestion rather than their artistic skill. Coincidence cannot explain the fact that in so many old palaces and mansions the rooms formerly used as bedchambers will be found hung with pictures of nude women. The French aristocracy under the *ancien régime* was a great patron of aphrodisiac painting, as well as literature, and it is alleged that Louis XV commissioned Boucher's portrait of Mlle O'Morphi, or Murphy, *Le Reveil* (which exhibits her buttocks more prominently and plumply than her face), in order that he might be able on suitable occasions to revive his faltering sexual powers. Pictorial aphrodisiacs are by no means new, but vices which were in the past confined to a small, privileged, and wealthy class have now, as an unregulated by-product of democracy, popular education and mass production, become available to everyone. To determine the extent to which the community, in its public life, should be exposed to erotic stimulus, is a neglected problem, immensely complicated by urbanization and industrialism. It would be a mistake, however, to suppose that the present generation is the licentious offspring of invariably chaste forebears: the peasants and artisans of the past, like their social 'betters,' often took their morals from the farmyard. But—again there is another period difference of mental climate—illicit couplings in fields and hedgerows during spring and summer, however reprehensible, are natural phenomena compared with the day-long, year-in-and-year-out, short-circuited excitements aroused by so many aspects of contemporary entertainment and advertising. The flow of time is presenting us with powers which intoxicate our imaginations but evade our control; we live in the age of the airplane, the radio, the flying bomb, the rocket bomb, the atomic bomb—and also in the age when that essentially private affair, sex, has developed an insatiable appetite for publicity: the age of the half-naked Pin-up Girl.

Thus to the people of any period time presents certain inescapable and influential conditions, both within their minds and pervading their environment. Between these inner and outer pressures character is formed. But in every case the maturing and outwearing of the individual body follows its ordained course, and the last operation of time on the face is performed at the moment of dying. Death may come slow or quick, armed with pain or violence, or stalking mercifully behind unconsciousness. It may leave the face mutilated by wounds, swollen, emaciated, or discolored by disease, or it may compose it to serenity as if by an exaggeration of sleep.

The spectacle of the dying and of the dead is moving, repugnant, and startling, an ordeal to the onlooker only less than the ordeal of the one who dies. The faces of dead children and young people look especially pitiful: the obvious reflection that they are unfortunate in being deprived of the normal number of years is an oblique confession that, despite all its disappointments and endurances, life is a thing commonly valued as good in itself. The dead face differs from the living in its loss of mobility, its fixed expression; in the coldness of the flesh which is apparent, by a transference of sympathy between the senses, to the eye; and almost invariably in the pallor of the complexion and the lips, due to the stoppage of the blood's circulation. A dead face may be made grotesque by the last agony, or it may be stilled into what would otherwise be a ludicrous expression of surprise. The muscles no longer having the power to clench the jaw, the mouth may drop open, and the eyes may stare blankly, the most vivid sign that the body has lost its animation: there is a traditional office of nurses and watchers of the dead to remedy these gapings with bandages and heavy coins.

Peaceful or violent, with or without facial distortions, death imparts its own peculiar dignity to the face. An act of finality, which can neither be questioned nor altered, leaves its record most plainly in the face. The living have to accept the fact that one human relationship has come to an end. If there has been affection between the dead and the survivors, the sight of the familiar face transformed by death may seem an intolerable prolongation of anguish, and mourners all over the world are glad to take refuge in traditional rites to conduct them through the bleak days of immediate mourning back to the superficialities of a normal routine. The death of any one person is a sharp reminder to others that their tenure of life also is limited; the nervous system quivers under the shock, and seeks relief in the very contradiction of grief, as in the stylized revelry of Irish wakes or the exchange of anecdotes and genteel jests over port or sherry at the conclusion of an English funeral.

Death is a thief, a taker-away of what is most valued. It evicts from the face the spirit which made it individual, and leaves only a perishable, cold monument. Death is common to all, as so many poets have remarked. But whether anything so powerful, so subtle, so strong and so delicate, so universal and yet so individual in each manifestation as the life in the body can itself be brought to naught when it is sundered from the flesh—that is a question to be answered only by speculation and belief. For a lease of years the spirit agitates a structure of chemical matter and sets it in motion, walking, talking, laughing, and weeping, upon the surface of the earth, endowing it with a consciousness of its own thoughts and emotions, and giving to its face potentialities of the most various and expressive beauty; at the end of the lease, is all this power snuffed out, like a flame? Science can do no more than affirm agnosticism, for between question and answer lies the obstructive separation of death.

The faces of the dead stare at us, blank and unseeing. Is the blankness evidence of annihilation or, negatively, a sign that the vitality which once informed the body has moved elsewhere? Physiology makes man an animal: his superior status is delimited by the fact of death, which, like so many other physical conditions, he shares with other living creatures, with trees and herbs, protoplasms and reptiles, as well as animals. It seems impossible that all these should have a continuous immortal existence beyond the scope of their material form. And if they perish, why not man? Is he merely tormented, or does he, in the foolishness which always peeps through his hard-won wisdom, torment himself by his aspiring longings towards immortality? Or should he chasten himself with the austere consolation that while individuals perish, the race survives? It is hard to conceive any perplexity more fundamental than that which poses these unanswerable questions. Human life is no more than a minor activity on the surface of the earth, which is itself but one little sphere whirling about in space among millions. Viewed like that, the problem of immortality shrinks in perspective. But then, so far as we can tell, except among human beings there is no awareness anywhere of the earth, the sun, the moon, space, the whole vast multiplicity of the universe. There are the minds of men, we know, and they are akin to one another. They have their systems of intercommunication. And in the minds of men exists, almost universally and as far back as history goes, the idea of a God, a greater, all-enveloping, all-pervading mind. It is a commonplace that men make their conceptions of God, clumsily or deftly, in their own image. But in this diffusion of imaginative light is man the sun, the sole emitting force? Or is he the moon, which reflects back the image-creating power of God? It is difficult to perceive how we can make sense of anything and everything unless we postulate a consciousness exterior to man, exterior to the physical universe. And I marvel that any dare to deny that the postulate may prove to be a true one, although its confirmation, like the answer to so many questions, must still lie on the far side of death.

CHAPTER SIX

ART AND THE FACE

PORTRAITURE—in its remote origins, at least—is bound up with human vanity and the desire to outwit the oblivion of death. In primitive cultures the elders of the tribe see to it that they are reverenced; under their skulls is accumulated experience, knowledge, and wisdom of value to the whole community. From this it is but a step to the making of effigies and portraits of leaders, and so to ancestor worship. The great man is not wholly or truly dead while the living can gaze at a representation of him on the wall of a cave or tomb or temple. Portrait-making as we know it today, however, is hardly an ancient art: the desire or the ability to create a faithful likeness goes back only to the early Renaissance, to the fourteenth century in Italy, and rather later in Northern Europe.

Various reasons may be suggested for this, and probably all are valid to one degree or another. First I should put lack of skill in the artist. It is true that there are pictures of deer and fish and bison which were engraved or painted on the rock walls of caves in Spain and Africa and elsewhere perhaps as long as fifty thousand years ago, and these reveal a precision of observation and a mastery of design which contemporary artists are content to admire—and to study—wholeheartedly. But skill once acquired does not persist of its own accord: it needs to be maintained diligently from generation to generation. Only at long intervals, and for brief periods in certain countries, since the palæolithic cave pictures were made, has a comparable standard of craftsmanship been achieved. Traditions of high technical accomplishment, which to those who are seeking to overthrow them seem as solid and immovable as the Pyramids, are in fact brittle, precarious, transient.

A second reason for the comparative modernity of portraiture may be the old insoluble conflict of aim which overcasts all artistic effort: the conflict between, as Sickert put it, the design and the sketch. Should the objects depicted be represented as they are, or should their appearance on canvas or panel or wall be adapted to fit into a decorative scheme? In practice, nothing can be represented with complete faithfulness, except by creating a duplicate, which is another matter altogether. Even a photograph omits or falsifies color, and, like every other flat picture, can suggest the third dimension only by linear perspective and the interplay of light and shadow. The conflict centers on the degree to which shape and color are to be distorted in order to create a pleasing and distinctive design. And, to judge from what is called "peasant art," the less sophisticated men are, the more they value decoration at the expense of lifelikeness. Thus the portraiture of Ancient Egyptian temples, Greek vases, American Indian and African Negro carvings, is hardly recognizable to us as portraiture at all: the likeness is subordinated to the decorative convention.

And, third, the influence of religion has often been hostile to portraiture. In reaction against the idolatry of other nations, the Old Testament Jews were prohibited from making 'graven images,' while Mahomet forbade his followers the indulgence of any kind of representational art. His command was not always obeyed, as Persian and Indian pictures show, but to this day mosques are decorated only with calligraphic inscriptions and abstract designs of the kind known as arabesques, and the thoroughly devout minority of Moslems will not allow themselves to be photographed. Portraiture in ancient Greece may have begun with silhouettes: there is a story of a Greek girl tracing the outline of the shadow of her lover thrown on a wall, and the old Egyptians maintained a convention of depicting human beings in a not very naturalistic profile. Two thousand years before Christ, Minoan women were portrayed in beautiful colored statuettes. The Greeks developed the carved portrait-bust, and the Romans, great looters of works of art, who at an earlier stage had erected in their temples wax molds of the faces of their ancestors, took this craft over. But when the Roman Empire became Christianized and then fell into the hands of barbarians from the north and the east, portraiture, and indeed all the arts except music, came into disrepute. The salvation of the soul by belief in Christ was interpreted as involving contempt for the body, of which the face was still reckoned only a subordinate part of no special importance. Thus there is no record of the personal appearance of Christ, of the Apostles and disciples, or of the early Fathers of the Church. When pictures came back into favor, about the fifth century, they were dominated by a Byzantine (ultimately an Oriental) influence: that is to say, they were conceived as decorations, and very ascetic decorations at that, and insofar as they depict human beings they seek to show not outward but inward reality. They are semiabstract and heavily conventionalized, pictures of mental conceptions rather than of persons. In the eighth and ninth centuries art underwent another eclipse, when a puritanical excess set fanatics to work all over Europe destroying pictures whose very existence they held to be an insult to God. This iconoclasm was more violent and comprehensive than that in Cromwellian England nearly a thousand years later, for the Lord Protector's men turned their destructiveness chiefly on the monuments and stained glass of the churches, and Cromwell was cunning enough to sell off most of the valuable pictures in Charles I's collection (for £118,080 10s. 2d.) to foreign bidders.

Painting did not revive till the thirteenth century, with Cimabue and Giotto. It was under the almost exclusive patronage of the Church, and for a long time confined itself to devotional subjects. Landscapes were introduced first as backgrounds and glimpses through windows, and portraiture came in sideways, when the man who was to pay the artist and present the finished picture to a church or monastery had himself depicted, praying, sometimes with his wife and children, on the side-panel of an altarpiece. Then in the fourteenth century Ghirlandhaio began the practice of including members of important Florentine families among crowd scenes in his frescoes. A little later, as interest in the classical past increased, art shook itself free from the exclusive patronage of the Church: mythological scenes from Græco-Roman history, literature, and legend were painted, on commission, to be displayed in the palaces and mansions of great noblemen. From this developed in due time the separate practices of landscape and seascape, figure studies, still-life, and *genre,* all of which were originally elements embodied in the sacred or profane pictures of the Renaissance. Abstract, or non-representational, painting is part of the modern reversion to the primitive.

But there was one other direction in which painting and sculpture moved when it gained its Renaissance freedom from Church domination. This was portraiture conceived as an end in itself. After a time the patron was no longer content to be recorded for posterity, in tempera or oils, as a subordinate figure in a religious composition. He wished to be portrayed, as a single figure or with his wife or his family or his mistress; and he wished to possess the finished picture, to hang in his own house and to hand down to his heirs. The primeval desire to outwit death had returned in full force. Portrait-painting was established, with the portrait head, necessarily concentrating attention on the face, preferred to the full- or three-quarter-length figure, which Titian first made fashionable. By the seventeenth century the profession of portrait-painter was fully recognized, and ever since it has been, at least for the artist of modest talents and flexible conscience, a lucrative profession, probably because wealthy men are highly susceptible both to flattery and the fear of oblivion.

Since the Renaissance also there have been professional models, men and women, young and old. Modeling is not a well-paid occupation, and it may be very arduous. The model, unlike a sitter who commissions a portrait or who is chosen because of eminence and 'publicity value' by an artist, must possess physical attributes of interest, although beauty of an obvious kind is not essential. There are two ways of painting from the model. A pose and a background may be arranged in the studio or, more rarely, in the open air, and a picture made, with or without preliminary experiments, from what the artist has in front of his eyes while he paints. Or one or more models may be used for sketches and designs, in pencil, charcoal, or brushwork, which are afterwards kept at hand for reference when an elaborate composition is created; the models may also be called in again when the picture achieves its later stages, so that a kind of direct portraiture is included in the composition. Sculptors similarly make miniature or full-size studies in clay, or drawings on paper, from which they proceed to the final modeling or chiseling, although it is rare for a sculptor to work from first to last with a model in front of him. Except for 'Society' portrait-painters, artists use the physical presence of models as a springboard for the imagination: their aim is not to copy the natural appearance but to modify it in accordance with some private vision of their own which, however, to one extent or another arises from the experience of the eyes.

The personal relationship between the male artist and the young female model has long been a matter for ribald or condemnatory suspicion by the general public. The suspicion is somewhat in abeyance just now because two great wars have made a hash of bourgeois sexual morality. But in general the lay view seems to be that if a moderately personable man and a young woman who has been selected for her attractive appearance (the model, like the chorus girl, is held, despite plentiful evidence to the contrary, to be *ipso facto* an outstanding beauty) are shut up together in a room, hour after hour, day after day, with the man continually staring at the young woman, an amorous relationship will inevitably ensue. The bohemianism of the artist, in fact, is commonly interpreted as a defiance of the moral code, with sexual promiscuity as one perquisite of an easy and romantic profession. The artist is regarded either as an enemy of society or a lucky devil who gets away in his daily routine with what the poor hard-working businessman can glimpse only in fiction, the theater, or the cinema. This attitude of the layman, not so freely expressed as it used to be, is still to be found in many places; it is a leftover from the neuroses of Victorian respectability, when Paris was thought of as a city of dazzling sin, and when, indeed, most artists of genuine ability made their way to Paris. It is a kind of communal memory of the garret and studio life, complete with velvet suits and long hair, of Murger's *Scènes de la vie de bohème*.

Confronted with such arguments or insinuations, most artists of today will seek to refute them by pointing to the respectability of their own lives and the lives of their colleagues. They are married, they say, and happily married: they rear families, they pay rent and taxes, they perform all the duties of the good citizen. To this the layman replies, "Ah, but before you were married! What revelings! What orgies! What goings-on! Besides, there are other artists not at all like you." The painter or sculptor (as likely as not he turns out abstracts or still-lifes) to whom this is said will probably smirk a little over the suggestion that he has been the devil of a fellow in his time (this kind of vanity is everybody's weakness), but if he is put to it he will argue that most models are highly respectable, and that in the nature of his job the artist must look at them with the utmost detachment, not as women, not even as human beings, but as arrangements of shape and color. The study of the model for the artist, the argument continues, is a function of the mind at a far remove from the personal and sensuous interest of desire. The one cancels out the other, and the last person an artist is likely to fall in love with is a young woman whose appearance he has minutely examined for whatever artistic profit he can derive from it with brush or chisel. If he seeks a comparison for his relationship to his model it will be with the doctor's attitude to his patient. Each represents a job of work, a professional problem, and the necessary detachment acts as an antiseptic against any infection of the emotions.

Undoubtedly such an explanation is valid for the majority of artists and the majority of models, and the layman probably fails to point out the essential difference between the task of the artist and that of the doctor: the artist's model is unlikely to have her attraction marred by varicose veins, rheumatism, skin diseases, or even a hacking cough, and the artist's interest in her is not scientific but æsthetic. It is true that his conception of beauty may not be the same as the layman's, but, whatever he calls it, it is beauty he is in search of, and if a young woman stimulates him creatively there is at least the potentiality of the stimulus being transferred to his emotions. The fact that thousands of artists and young women models take no great personal interest in each other should be recorded on one side of the ledger, and no doubt these entries will overbalance the others. But the others exist today, and have existed in the past. No artist can dispense with technical skill except to his own loss, but technical skill alone can produce only craftsmanship, not art. To create a work of art the artist must have been deeply moved. Often he has been moved by emotions of desire and affection towards his model, and sometimes—not always—he has been her lover. Whistler had his Joanna Heffernan, and Rossetti his Fanny Hughes, and over in Paris many of the Impressionists were painting women with whom they lived. Manet, it is true, married the girl who sat to him in the nude for *Le déjeuner sur l'herbe,* but he had mistresses also, though it is difficult to tell what precisely were his relations with Victorine Meurend, the model for *Olympia* and perhaps for the boy in *The Fifer.* But when Victorine fell on hard times, after Manet's death, Madame Manet does not seem to have been sympathetic—from which anyone may deduce anything he pleases.

This sort of story is pretty old. Phryne, the model for Praxiteles, was a courtesan, and it is said that Alexander the Great, having commissioned Appeles to paint his Campaspe, found the artist so much in love with her that in a magnanimous mood the tyrant gave her up. The Sistine Madonna and other Madonnas of Raphael are believed to be portraits of his mistress. Considering how much pious devotion has been and is still lavished on these pictures of the mother of Christ (which, in their present state, are notably inferior to the surviving Raphael drawings and cartoons, many of them having been overpainted by later hands), this may seem an affront to religion. Indeed, few of the devout care to remember that real though obscure human beings acted as models for most of the great religious pictures. But the mental climate of the Renaissance made it easy for a somewhat artificial and self-conscious paganism and a highly organized Christianity to exist side by side, and, in fact, to intermingle in almost every human activity. Similarly, the life of the body and the life of the mind and spirit rarely trod on each other's toes. The universe was accepted as a whole more enthusiastically than ever since. There can be no absolute certainty that Raphael painted as the Madonna any woman with whom he lived, any more than we can be sure what were Shakespeare's relations with the Dark Woman of the Sonnets or what he meant (if he was responsible for the drafting of the will) by his bequest of his "second-best bed" to his wife. But it is recorded that Raphael, whose popular fame depends on his august and ethereal depictions of holiness, had at least one mistress, and that his love for her interfered with his work.

Here is the account given by Vasari, who knew many who had been Raphael's friends, in his *Lives of the Painters, Sculptors, and Architects:*

> He was much disposed to the gentler affections and delighted in the society of woman, for whom he was ever ready to perform acts of service. But he also let himself be absorbed overmuch in the pleasures of life, in this unduly encouraged by his friends and admirers. A story is told that when his close friend, Agostino Chigi, commissioned him to decorate the first floor of his palace, Raphael was so bound up with his love for the lady of his choice that he could not give proper attention to the work. Agostino despaired of seeing the job finished, and having made many vain efforts directly and through his friends, at last persuaded the lady to move into his own house [the Villa Farnesina]. He installed her in a suite of rooms near those where Raphael was painting, and in this way the commission was at last executed.

The story is also told rather differently by Fabio Chigi, a seventeenth-century Cardinal who later became Pope as Alexander VII. The Cardinal relates how his ancestor, a successful financier, named Agostino Chigi, and the Pope of the time, Leo X, were perturbed because Raphael, employed at the Vatican and on Chigi's private commissions, was neglecting his work. They decided his slackness was due to infatuation with his mistress, and Agostino Chigi had the girl kidnaped. Raphael was very upset, and Chigi promised to find the lost mistress, on condition that the painter resume work on some frescoes at Chigi's palace which he had started and laid aside, and also on the 'Sibyls' in the Church of Santa Maria della Pace. Like a good boy, Raphael promised, and worked hard for a time. Then, the girl not turning up, he again began to neglect his work. Chigi woke him out of his moping mood by forging letters which promised the girl's return in the near future, but ultimately he had to fake a rescue and bring her to Raphael. What the girl thought about it all we are not told.

We do not know her name either, nor can we even be sure of her identity. Informed opinion goes more cautiously now than in the past, and, so far as it ventures at all, it identifies the lost mistress with the model for the portrait in the Pitti Gallery called the *Dona Velata*, or Veiled Lady. The veil is rather a mantle or scarf thrown over the top of the head and flowing wide below the shoulders, so that the face remains quite unobscured. It is a classic oval face, young and moderately plump, gracious but little characterized, with all the golden-skinned Italian comeliness and extremely simple spirituality with which Raphael's name is invariably associated. If this unknown lady was the painter's inamorata, then almost certainly she was the model for the more famous Sistine Madonna, at Dresden, for the Magdalen in an altarpiece at Bologna (the resemblance is clear enough), and probably for others of his later paintings.

But there is another picture, in the Barberini Gallery in Rome, which, until comparatively recently, was more closely identified as a portrait of Raphael's mistress. This is referred to by Vasari as a portrait of Beatrice of Ferrara, while others have seen in it the features of Vittoria Colonna (to whom Michelangelo was platonically devoted), and its popular name is *La Fornarina,* which might mean the wife or daughter of a baker. It is not even certain that it is the work of Raphael. Dr Bode of Berlin (whose opinion carries authority despite his ludicrous error over the 'Leonardo' wax bust of Flora) attributed it to Raphael, but other experts have suggested Giorgione and Sebastiano del Piombo, and Bryan's *Dictionary of Painters,* which describes the portrait as "coarse and vulgar," gives its authorship to Giulio Romano, one of Raphael's pupils and imitators. Fabio Chigi, writing a century later but presumably relying on family documents and traditions, was the first to identify the sitter for this portrait as Raphael's mistress.

What is the ordinary man to conclude when experts differ so extravagantly? It would be rash to offer any solution dogmatically, but as there is apparently a close physical resemblance between the Veiled Lady, the Sistine Madonna, and *La Fornarina,* and as a painter is just as likely to paint a woman with whom he is in love as a poet is to write poems to and about her, it seems not improbable that all three pictures are representations of the same woman, and that she was Raphael's mistress. As for the third, the "coarse and vulgar" picture, it may not be the work of Raphael, but that would not invalidate it as a portrait of the unknown lady: she may have sat to Giulio Romano, or some other artist, after Raphael's death. Her face may have coarsened, and not only with age. And the popular name given to the picture, *La Fornarina,* might well be a misreading of a manuscript. Both Vasari and Fabio Chigi speak of Raphael's mistress at Agostino's new house, which many years later became known as the Villa Farnesina. Suppose Vasari is right: suppose the girl did live for a time in Agostino Chigi's palace or villa, while Raphael was working there. It is not unlikely then that some might refer to her as "La Farnesina," which might be read as "La Fornarina," and so start on its way the unjustified legend of the baker's wife or daughter. The surmise will not seem so far-fetched when we remember that in Vasari's *Life of Raphael,* whether

PLATE XIV: CHARIOT LADIES, *by* J. J. TISSOT

Author's Collection

122

PLATE XV: AUBURN VICTORIAN, *by* ROBERT GREENHAM

Author's Collection

by the author's error or a printer's misreading of his manuscript, the famous family name of Chigi appears not once but several times as "Chisi."

The end of the story is hardly edifying in the Victorian sense. It is tinged with the flavor of Renaissance worldliness. Another intimate friend of Raphael (he was successful and wealthy) was Bernardo Divizio, Cardinal of Bibbiena, who often urged him to marry, and made him promise to marry someone whom the Cardinal was to choose. Raphael kept on postponing any definite decision, but at last consented to make the Cardinal's niece his wife. Even after this he put off several times any arrangements for a wedding, and in the end he never married at all. Vasari suggests that this was because he expected to be made a Cardinal himself. It seems also that Raphael still kept his mistress, in a separate establishment. One day, says Vasari,

returning to his house from one of these secret visits, he was seized by a violent fever, which being taken for a cold, the physicians inconsiderately caused him to be bled, whereby he found himself exhausted when he had rather required to be strengthened. Thereupon he made his will and, as a good Christian, he sent the object of his attachment from the house [which one is not clear] but left her a sufficient provision with which she might live in decent comfort.

Raphael died, exactly thirty-seven years old to the day, on Good Friday, March 6, 1520, and with him died the secret of his love affair. Perhaps he did not marry his mistress because he was a bit of a snob, and she was lowly born—there may after all be some truth in the bakery legend; or she may have been married already. It seems clear he did not live with her openly. Or again, although no other painter received such advancement in the Church, it is possible that Raphael had some reason to believe he was about to receive a red hat. Whoever she was, the unknown lady's chief misfortune seems to have been that she was not a Cardinal's niece.

About Fra Filippo Lippi, nearly a century earlier, we know less than about Raphael, but the story of his most famous model is quite clear and precise and romantic. The jovial Carmelite friar, whom Browning celebrated in one of his best-known dramatic monologues, at the age of fifty was commissioned by the Convent of Santa Margherita in Florence to paint a picture for the high altar of the church. He fell in love with a young nun of the order, Lucretia Buti, and persuaded the Abbess of the convent that Lucretia was the only possible model for the Madonna he was about to paint. The sittings must have been inadequately chaperoned, despite Fra Lippi's scandalous reputation, for on the day of the Feast of the Holy Girdle the friar ran off with the nun. Lucretia lived with him, and bore a child, who in due time became the painter we know as Filippino Lippi. At first this must have seemed to the Florentine world just another of Lippi's escapades, but presently it was clear that this time he was in earnest. On the intervention of Cosimo de Medici, Pope Pius II absolved the lovers from their monastic vows and declared them man and wife.

It is noteworthy that, long before he met Lucretia Buti, Lippi was painting Madonnas and saints with faces of the same thin-cheeked, high-foreheaded kind, and this is all the more interesting when we remember that Botticelli was apprenticed to Fra Filippo a year or two before the Papal intervention. Out of the Lippi model Botticelli evolved a style of feminine beauty which gradually pervaded almost all his work, and in comparatively recent times has exercised a great influence on the popular imagination. Ruskin, who more or less rediscovered Botticelli, saw in Simonetta Vespucci, a married woman who was the mistress of Giuliano de Medici, the inspiration from which Botticelli derived his most famous pictures, and she has been identified as the Venus in *The Birth of Venus* (Plate XVIII, page 154), as both Flora and Spring in the *Primavera, Abundance* in the drawing at the British Museum, Pallas in *Pallas with the Centaur,* and Truth in *The Calumny of Appelles*. On the other hand, it must be noted that in the *Imaginary Portrait* of Simonetta in the Cook

Collection at Richmond, which is attributed to Botticelli, she appears with a decidedly broader face than in the other pictures.

Florentine painters tended to impress great ladies into their service as models for saints and goddesses, while the Venetians used courtesans for the same purpose. Titian (who is said to have started his career, as a child, by painting a Madonna on the outside wall of his father's house with the juice of flowers or fruit) has left large numbers of pictures of voluptuous women for experts to dispute over, arguing whether or not so-and-so was his mistress in such-and-such a year. He lived to a great age, and toward the end escaped from his earlier dilemmas by making his daughter, Lavinia, his favorite model. Rubens, associated even more intimately than Titian with the painting of womanflesh, seems to have been a serious as well as an industrious man, and as with the unvoluptuous Rembrandt, in his religious and mythical compositions there are to be found over and over again the faces and figures of his two successive wives, Isabella Brandt (see Plate VIII, page 74) and Helen Fourment.

But perhaps the most striking example of a great painter whose work is dominated by one type of face is Leonardo da Vinci. Like the high-minded if quarrelsome Michelangelo, like Shakespeare, like many of the supreme artists whose biographies are full of gaps and dubieties, he has been accused of being a homosexual. And it would be rash to deny that this particular form of perversion is incompatible with artistic ability; among the Greeks of the classical era, although the extent of its physical manifestations is uncertain, the love of young boys by older men was developed into a social convention. On the other hand, I cannot think of any major artist whose homosexuality is fully authenticated: Oscar Wilde may be taken as a characteristic type, a man in whom temperament and conversation, ostentatiously cultivated, far exceeds in importance his output. The homosexual is drawn toward the arts because they are associated with a heightened sensibility, which is again associated with the feminine. The homosexual's nature is confused in itself, and seeks satisfaction in relationships, physical or not, with apparently orthodox members of the same sex: this inward chaos is sufficient to refine the senses and the imagination, and the process is intensified by the consciousness, overshadowed by guilt, of difference from normal humanity. But sensibility is not the same as creative power, and so far as I am able to judge the homosexual is more likely to be an amateur of the arts—particularly of the theater and the ballet—than an original artist. When he is an artist his work is likely to be deficient in creative power: exquisite, perhaps, but minor, substituting the extravagances of egoism for an objective view of life. Consciously or unconsciously aware of this (as he is aware, now in humiliation, now in flamboyant pride, that he is different from other men), he seeks justification for himself by claiming, where there is any tiniest foothold for surmise, that men who are universally acknowledged as great artists have had the same abnormality as himself. Hence the minute and strained analysis of a few Shakespearean sonnets—and the ignoring of Anne Hathaway, the Dark Woman, and the endless evidence scattered throughout the plays that Shakespeare knew a tremendous amount at first hand about the normal relationship between the sexes. Hence the attention paid to Michelangelo's interest in the structure of the male body, and the glossing over of his interest in the female, of his devotion to Vittoria Colonna, and, in particular, the drawing and the lost painting (the one in the National Gallery is a reconstruction from the drawing) of *Leda and the Swan*. Hence the supposition that Leonardo was a homosexual, founded on little more than absence of scandal about women in his private life.

Leonardo, sculptor, engineer, architect, inventor, and something of a speculative philosopher, excelled in draftsmanship, and he seems to have been as interested in depicting animals, material structures, and draperies as the human form. But his greatest paintings are of women, and the interest in these is concentrated in the face. With minor variations it is the same face throughout, akin in its symmetrical comeliness to the classic oval but with additional subtleties which have ever since persistently defied analysis, although they can to some extent be located, physically, in the thinning of the cheeks, the mingling of lusters and darkness in the eyes, and the hint and inception of a smile at the corner of the lips and in the adjacent creasing of the face.

The most famous, though probably not the best, of Leonardo's paintings is the portrait known as *Mona Lisa,* or *La Gioconda,* in the Louvre. The model was Lisa Gherardini, the third wife of Francesco di Bartolomeo di Zenobi del Giocondo. 'Gioconda' means happy, smiling, jocund, and it is odd that the model for this portrait of a woman with a world-famous smile should take her appropriate name from her husband, after two other women had borne it. It is not certain whether the picture was painted for Mona Lisa's husband or for Francis I of France. Vasari tells us that Leonardo employed singers and instrumentalists in an antechamber while he was painting, in order to keep his sitter amused and presumably to retain the incipient smile on her face. This smile, by the way, is confined to the left corner of the mouth, and in this it conforms to one of the social tricks cultivated by Renaissance ladies, who were told by advisers on beauty and deportment that it was an infallible recipe for charming the other sex. Vasari says that Leonardo worked for four years on the portrait, and, unable even then to re-create in paint his own inward vision, left it unfinished. It is clear that the picture fascinated Leonardo's contemporaries. Vasari describes it with a naïve enthusiasm: "The eyes have all the liquid sparkle of nature; the lashes, fringing the lids, are painted with rare delicacy, the curve of the eyebrows, the vermilion of the lips are all exactly reproduced. This is not painting: it is real flesh. You can see the pulse beating in the throat. The enchanting smile is more divine than life itself." A Victorian philistine, smarting under Matthew Arnold's rebukes and driven to visit the Royal Academy in a spirit of hopeful penitence, might thus have taken pleasure in the representational precision of Frith's *Derby Day.* But one who lived his whole life within the reign of Victoria discerned more subtleties in the *Mona*

Lisa than Matthew Arnold could have dreamed of. Walter Pater, a cold, shy Oxford don, immensely revered in his day, now lives chiefly as a figure in the background of biographies of other men, and in the elaborate prose mysticism he wrought about this woman.

> Here is the head upon which all "the ends of the world are come," and the eyelids are a little weary. . . . She is older than the rocks among which she sits; like the vampire she has been dead many times, and learned the secrets of the grave; and has been a diver in deep seas, and keeps their fallen day about her; and trafficked for strange webs with Eastern merchants: and, as Leda, was the mother of Helen of Troy, and, as Saint Anne, the mother of Mary; and all this has been to her but as the sound of lyres and flutes, and lives only in the delicacy with which it has moulded the changing lineaments, and tinged the eyelids and the hands.

It is futile to guess whether or not Leonardo was in love with Lisa Gherardini, nor is it certain that her face was the archetype from which he painted the *Virgin of the Rocks, The Madonna of the Rocks,* and the St Anne. For we find a similar shape and molding of the features, and the same equivocal expression, in his portrait of Ginevra dei Benci, who died in 1473, when Leonardo cannot have been more than twenty-one years old. Moreover, he was at that time working as a pupil in the studios of Verrocchio, and if we look at Verrocchio's Madonnas we see more than one resemblance to the typical Leonardo face, just as Botticelli's women derive to some extent from Fra Filippo Lippi's. The similarity comes closest, perhaps, in the terra-cotta relief known as the Albizzi Madonna, generally attributed to Verrocchio but held by Sir Theodore Cook, after detailed comparisons, to be Leonardo's. And as a final complication, it is fairly certain that Botticelli, toward the end of his apprenticeship, was also strongly influenced by Verrocchio's conception of feminine beauty.

Two questions, then, confront us. How does it come about that the same types of woman's face recur in the masterpieces of some of the greatest painters, notably Lippo Lippi, Raphael, Botticelli, and

Leonardo? And why have these faces impressed themselves on the imagination of so many generations? I do not think even a tentative solution can be found in æsthetic theory and the expertise of art study. The investigation must move into the province of psychology: we are compelled to consider the artists not merely as artists but as human beings. The first question—why is there an immediately recognizable Lippo Lippi, a Raphael, a Botticelli, a Leonardo face?—can be answered out of hand by saying that each painter fell in love with a certain woman, became obsessed with her beauty, and commemorated it in various pictures. But this offers only a superficial solution. Lippo Lippi was fifty when he first met Lucretia Buti. He had been painting Madonnas of her type before she was born. And Leonardo was fifty-one when he began work on *La Gioconda,* although thirty years earlier, in his portrait of Ginevra dei Benci, he was already depicting something very like the Gioconda face and the Gioconda smile. And the Raphael and the Botticelli (and for the matter of that, the Renoir, the Degas, the Rossetti, the Burne-Jones, and the Augustus John) archetypes can be traced, to one degree or another of realization, throughout the careers of these painters.

To understand the how and why we must look into our own minds and our own experience. Facial beauty of every kind commands attention, and may stimulate desire. But a closer consideration will show that each one of us is predisposed to fall in love with a certain kind of beauty. It is to this that we respond as inevitably and unconsciously as a flower turns toward the sun. We still have our free will, our liberty of choice, but we are probably storing up trouble for ourselves—and for other people—if we stray for our love affairs outside the prescribed range. And there is always the double danger that the woman to whom we are naturally attracted will fail to respond, because we are not, as the present idiom has it, her 'type'; or else, not feeling a spontaneous attraction for us, she may persuade herself, out of compassion or loneliness or friendship or any other associated but strictly irrelevant emotion, that she can return our love. This is one reason why thoroughly happy marriages and authentic *grandes passions* are rare: on one side or the other what is no more than a plausible approximation to the psychological type has been accepted.

This theory of a predisposition to fall in love can be tested in several ways. It is not merely a sensual reaction to a prescribed facial form, but an attraction to a temperament expressed by and in a kind of face: the face is always the index to the mind and the emotions. In successful second marriages it will almost always be found that the one who marries again chooses a wife or a husband who closely resembles the first beloved, or else, after a false start, the right type has been found. And where a married man can be observed flirting with a woman not his wife, a discerning eye will see that the other woman personifies the same type as the wife he loves, or, if the marriage is unsatisfactory, the type he might have been wiser to marry. The rule is almost as absolute for women as for men, though it is conditioned by the tendency of many women to be unable to love wholeheartedly until they know they are loved. Similarly, while a man will confess to a romantic and harmless idolization of some woman he knows only on the stage or on the cinema screen, it is not often he understands that his idol reminds him of the wife he has or the wife he would like to have: that, in fact, she represents his 'type.' The Don Juan story can be convincingly interpreted as a quest for an ideal demanded by the most profound instincts; but too much compassion should not be wasted on Juan, who, being a sensualist and an egoist, wants more than he is prepared to give, allows desire to override affection, and consequently is incapable of recognizing his ideal when he meets her. Men and women of this sort make their minds a breeding-ground for the insatiable tapeworms of neurosis, and in their feverish, changeable love affairs there is a recurring pattern of psychological situations, all heading to essentially the same forced and dramatic crisis, which their greedy desires seek to achieve, and, having achieved, to shatter.

The rhythm in the lives of more fortunate people is steadier. Desiring to give more than to receive, they find satisfaction in work they respect (Don Juan is, in essence, a disgruntled idler) and in loving someone of the type which alone can wholly satisfy them. Now, if the predisposition to a type is so important for people without any special creative ability, it must be much more so for artists, and particularly for painters, part of whose job is to depict the human face. Artists can link the intimate aspects of their private lives to their vocation, which is the most strenuous but also the most satisfying open to human beings. And if they are painters they can seek not only to find their predestined type in real life, but to express and perfect it in art. It is not difficult to imagine the excitement which filled the mind of gray-haired Fra Lippo Lippi when he discovered Lucretia Buti in the convent of Santa Margherita and eloped with her, nor why Raphael, his mistress stolen from him, was unable to concentrate on the frescoes for Agostino Chigi's palace. And though we do not know who was the model for Botticelli's Venus and Primavera, nor how much of his predisposition was determined by his youthful admiration for Lippo's and Verrocchio's portraits of women, we can be sure that what he painted was the expression of the ideal toward which his deepest instincts urged him. And similarly with Leonardo's smiling women.

In each of these painters there was an inward vision of a beautiful woman, which probably received both satisfaction and stimulus (there is a rhythmic pattern in these alternations also) from some woman in real life. On this inward vision the painter's imagination was richly nourished. The type became an archetype, and pervaded every emotional experience. In Botticelli's work it is to be seen not only in Venus poised on the sea-borne shell but in the winds and the attendant women in flowing draperies; not only in the *Magnificat* Madonna but in faces of the five angels; not only in Primavera, but in Venus, Flora, and the three Graces. They are all conceptions of Botticelli's mind, the subconscious and the instinctive as well as the rational, and therefore they are all informed with his devotion to his ideal. No human face looks quite the same to any two persons: even if there is no personal relationship to guide the interpretation, each observer brings to the exercise of his eyesight a different personality and a different experience of life. What we see in Botticelli's pictures are not representations of women as they were in fifteenth-century Florence, but our interpretations of Botticelli's interpretations; and he saw what no one else could see. In an earlier chapter I said that if the Greek Phryne could be reincarnated into the present-day world she might not seem to us outstandingly beautiful. Now that the argument is further advanced, I suggest that if Simonetta Vespucci (or whoever served as Botticelli's model) and Lisa Gherardini were presented before us we might very well at first not recognize them as the originals of the *Venus* and the *Gioconda*. In these pictures they are shown metamorphosed by powerful preconceptions in the minds of great artists.

At first we might not recognize them. Yet I fancy it would not be long before our minds began to associate the flesh-and-blood women with the pictures. Then we should, at some remove and imperfectly, be seeing them as the painters saw them. For, as the æsthetes of the eighteen-eighties frequently remarked, nature has a habit of catching up, belatedly, with art. Sunsets have looked more specifically glorious to human eyes since Turner painted them. Venice could not be what it is to us today but for Canaletto and Guardi, or Paris but for Sisley, Monet, and Pissarro. The artist's vision, no doubt diluted and simplified, is imperceptibly absorbed into the mind of the community. Most of the time it lurks passive below the level of consciousness, but when we look at scenes comparable with what has been painted in great pictures the artist's vision becomes resurgent in us; our perception is flooded with memories originated in art galleries and color prints and illustrations in books, and our minds rearrange and illumine what our eyes report. This is one immortality at least which great artists achieve on the surface of the earth in which their bodies moulder.

And so we come nearer to the solution of the second problem:

why have faces depicted in certain famous pictures impressed themselves on the imagination of so many generations? Why are Rembrandt's Saskia, Rubens' Isabella Brandt and Helen Fourment,
Leonardo's Mona Lisa, and Raphael's and Botticelli's Madonnas
more vivid and 'real' to us than hundreds of living women we see
every day? The answer is not that these women are surpassingly
beautiful to the eye: some are no more than comely—Saskia might
be judged downright plain. And so far as amorous responses go,
the old comparison between the bird in the hand and the one in the
bush holds good: no beauty immortalized on canvas can compete
successfully with flesh and blood, and young men meeting their
sweethearts, after the old London tradition, within the spacious echoing chambers of the National Gallery will hardly be aware of what
is hung on the walls. The faces which exist permanently in the
common memory have beauty, though it is not necessarily physical
beauty, but their power over us is due to art, and art in which
technical skill has been fused by an exceptional intensity of emotion.
This emotion does not arise merely from the painter falling in love
with his model. He has found a face to which his instincts tell him
he was predestined. Contemplating this face, studying it, learning
it, transposing it into pictures, he is swept into a fundamental rhythm
of stimulus, satisfaction, and stimulus again. The face fascinates
him: he can never tire of it. It is his obsession, his 'type,' and to
a considerable extent the purpose of his life. Without great technical skill he cannot create memorable pictures at all, but it is this
additional intensity of emotion (simultaneously personal and imper-
sonal in its nature) which lifts the pictures into superlative excel-
lence. The intensity is not to be located in any part or aspect of
the painting: it pervades every brush or pencil stroke, it is the guid-
ance exercised, above and apart from reason, over the whole conception and its execution. And when the work is finished the mysterious power which called it into existence resides thereafter in the
picture. It is a universal power, emitted to subsequent observers,
provided they bring to it a receptive mood, as dependably as elec-

tricity from a magnet or phosphorescence from a moonlit sea in summer. The immortal faces of art seize and occupy our imaginations because they perpetuate an intensity of experience to which all humanity, though weakly and with an infrequent dedication, aspires.

This, it may be argued, is all very well, but in hard, everyday fact the great majority of people, even now when interest in the arts is more general than ever before, continue to live out their lives hardly aware of any pictures except magazine illustrations, photographs, and the projections thrown onto the screen at the local cinema. This objection is not insuperable, for below the levels of consciousness people are highly susceptible to indirect influences which, without their knowing, profoundly affect their lives. Nor are all of these influences primitive and physical. There is a parallel in Christianity. Today the greater part of the population does not attend the churches or subscribe to any specific form of Christian doctrine. People are far more ignorant of the Bible than their grandparents were. The surface of life is a turbulent medley of hedonist, pagan, and materialist beliefs and practices. Yet I would hesitate to say that the adult generations of 1945 are, in the essentials of conduct, less Christian than those of 1845. To me it seems that there is in the people around me less selfishness, less Pharasaic self-righteousness, more eagerness to do good to others than I can trace in the records of the past. And while practice may fall short of intention, as it has always done, the fundamental Christian ethic ("and the greatest of these is charity") has become a common assumption, a motive and an ideal which hardly anyone questions. There is more to religion than ethics, but without conduct religion bombinates in a void: and it is noteworthy that while Christian doctrines are so often rejected, the Christian ethic has triumphed by achieving general acceptance, even though its origin is rarely acknowledged.

So, on another plane, with art. There may be millions who would not recognize the *Sistine Madonna* or the *Primavera* if they saw them. But these humanist achievements are still powerful by a kind of remote control. They influence, however obliquely, the conceptions of all kinds of artists, including those who are known as commercial artists. But for the Renaissance, the pretty girls portrayed in magazines and on poster hoardings and, in prewar days, on the lids of chocolate boxes, would be different from what they are. These are extreme and lowly examples, showing the influence in its most diluted form. There are many others, and the Renaissance is only one form of the influential art of the past. The girl who works in an office or factory does not let these impressions short-circuit within her mind. They prompt her to make herself look, as nearly as possible, like representations of beauty she has seen and admired in advertisements, on the stage, at the cinema. She does not know it, but she is copying inferior and haphazard copies of copies of great pictures: she has felt a tiny, tremulous, almost expended ripple from the intensity of emotion experienced by some painter, long since dead, and of whom she may never have heard.

And occasionally she will come—though still, as likely as not, unconsciously—a little nearer to the source. Fashions in dress, especially women's dress, are always harking back for inspiration to the past. So are faces, ever since reproductions of famous pictures became available to the general public at about the same time as inexpensive cosmetics and 'beauty treatments.' Each period creates not only its own fashions but its own typical faces, and in modern times these creations have often been revivals of the past. Far more flexibly than men, women can transform the appearance of their faces to conform to a mode. And in the nineteen-thirties there were two outstanding examples of this metamorphosis. The bust of Nefertiti (Plate XIX, page 155) began to be reproduced in magazines and advertisements, on postcards and in pottery replicas. It was as if this young lady of the Egyptian blood royal had had to wait more than three thousand years after her death for adequate recognition of her beauty, and the proverbial sincerest form of flattery, for in the course of a single year thousands of modern young women, in England and America at least, did their level best to make themselves look like princesses of the eighteenth dynasty.

Their necks were by some illusion elongated, their heads tilted back, and even more surprisingly they shaped their eyebrows and their eyes, hollowed their cheeks and modified their profiles, to conform to this antique model. Nefertiti lived again in countless reincarnations, not all so dignified as her colored limestone sculpture, and indeed she may still often be seen about the streets of many a town.

And when in 1930 the Exhibition of Italian Art opened at Burlington House in Piccadilly, to supplement its immediate effect on fashions in Renaissance caps, brocades, and hairdressing, the hair-wreathed face of Botticelli's Venus (Plate XVIII, page 154) became more popular, and better known, than that of many a film star. Thousands visited the Exhibition, but those who saw the famous picture reproduced in newspapers and magazines numbered millions. And while many brunettes held faithfully to their Nefertiti ideal, most of the blondes, it seemed, set out to try to pass themselves off as Botticelli beauties. And they succeeded remarkably. The long-tressed, wind-blown hair they could not imitate, nor the nakedness of the body, but the Botticelli face, high and wide of brow, serene, candid in the old and the modern sense, delicately delineated, exquisitely modeled, appeared everywhere, and the glory of Florence walked again in London. Life is short, but art is everlasting, and, even in its most remote manifestations, full of charming surprises.

CHAPTER SEVEN

REMEMBERED FACES

EACH of us conducts, often simultaneously, two different lives. One is private, personal, spinning on the axis of the ego and whirling along with it a flux of sensation, thought, and feeling which never halts except in dreamless sleep. The other life is public, turned outward on the world, a traffic of communications—only a few of them put into words—with other people. There is a sense in which each of us is a solitary, a prisoner in the close confinement of a cell of flesh, able only to peer through the bars and see other prisoners staring out from behind bars not dissimilar to our own. In another way, however, we are all subject one to another, members of a community which exerts its obligations and influences so pervasively that the existence of any one person is—to use the fashionable scientific expression—conditioned by the communal life of all the others, itself the sum total of many similarly conditioned individual lives, each twofold in nature. Moreover, between the private and the communal existence of any one person there is a continual interaction; sometimes they run snugly together, like oiled machinery; sometimes one grates resistingly against the other's impetus; sometimes the private life holds back and contemplates, with irony, indignation, surprise, or mockery, the words and actions performed publicly in the name of its ego. Even the problem of adjustment between the private and the communal existence has a double application. In one aspect it is the age-old problem of religion and philosophy, the never-ended struggle of the individual to understand himself and to attain an active or passive inward peace. In the other aspect, the problem is political, the tug-of-war between the rights of the State and the rights of the citizen.

Consciousness itself is a variable condition. Everyone is a different person alone in solitude, with one other person, among a few people, among many people, in the company of intimates, in the company of new acquaintances, in the company of strangers. The manner, the orientation to the world outside one's own body, changes, insensibly but inevitably, and with the manner the face changes also. It is least troubled and least veiled by self-awareness when we are solitary in a room or with one other person dearly loved. In the company of friends we are candid and unguarded enough, but we have in our minds some conception of how these friends see us, and we are tempted to live up to that expectation. We keep one manner and one face for our family, another for our club, another for our business or profession, another for theater-going, another for sports, another for public festivities, and we shift among fine shades of self-expression more readily and swiftly than we change our clothes. Except in utter solitude, the communal man is always dictating (and is sure of instant obedience) to the private man. But the solitary is the critical one and has the last word. It is he who notes everything his more gregarious brother does, marks the papers good, bad, or fair, and makes the ribald comments in the margin. For while he conforms to orders, he always makes his mental reservations. He may render the face stiff, solemn, dignified, appropriate to some solemn occasion, but none shall stop him dotting in a glinting high-light in a corner of the eye, and although the mind at the moment may be busy answering questions and producing the small talk the communal man considers necessary, the flow of private thought goes on, and afterwards, at the first favorable opportunity, it will be fetched back by memory and its dissenting commentary analyzed and enjoyed all over again.

Faces in mass are not all public faces, for there is almost as austere a loneliness to be felt in a crowd as in the seclusion of a quiet room. But faces gathered in great numbers, swaying slightly like so many flowers upborne on stalks, banked and terraced as in the assemblies which watch sporting encounters, or moving past, orderly in a procession or march, chaotic in a crowded street, do by their very multi-

PLATE XVI: MICHAEL REDGRAVE, *by* AUGUSTUS JOHN

Collection of Michael Redgrave

PLATE XVII: VIVIEN LEIGH (Detail), *by* DIETZ EDZARD

Collection of H. L. Holman

plicity suggest the communal life. It is only when, through recognition or a sudden spirit of interest, one face is selected by the eye from among the mass that the individual, the human being with a private life, a unique personality compact of temperament and character, emerges. As I write I turn in my chair, away from my desk, toward a large oil painting by Tissot (Plate XIV, page 122) which hangs beside the door of my study. It often seems to me to symbolize this distinction between the private personality in conflict with the communal, between the individual who through some telepathic force, however momentary, narrows and intensifies the observer's attention, and the mass of people who, in consequence of this selective act, become more than ever a totality of blurred impressions, no one member more important than another, and all merging into a background for the favored one. Tissot achieves this effect in his *Chariot Ladies* by arranging his picture into three simple planes of perspective. In the foreground, the left half of the picture is dominated by the girl in whom he was interested; the remainder is shared out between two other girls with their horses, the girdered and lamplighted roof of the circus, and the receding tiers of spectators; in the front rows many are, with skillful brush-strokes, given individualized faces, and some of these are recognizable as men and women who occur again and again in Tissot's pictures. It is perhaps evidence of the confusion of his artistic purpose that these distinguishable faces, best viewed from a distance of about two feet, are painted with greater care and detail and liveliness than the pretty but insipid chariot ladies who follow, in the middle plane, his principal figure: I imagine Tissot's argument was that the tiers of spectators, made so small by distance, could not distract the observer's interest, whereas the two other chariot ladies, not so far away and consequently larger to the eye, might compete with his favorite—and so he painted them, deliberately, with as little characterization as he could risk.

The girl driving the first chariot I call the painter's favorite not only because she is obviously the main subject of the picture, but because she bears a close resemblance, especially in her face, to a woman who, at various ages and in various costumes, appears in several of Tissot's paintings. To my eyes she is painted from the same model who appears in the *Portrait of a Lady* in the Tate Gallery (to which *Chariot Ladies* is promised) and may even be the woman tentatively identified by James Laver, in *Vulgar Society,* as Tissot's mistress. The story is tragic and ironic. It was first recorded by Arnold Bennett in his *Journals,* and is traced as fully as possible by Mr Laver. Tissot, it seems, came from Paris to settle in England in 1872, and soon became a fashionable and successful painter. He had a mistress, of whom little is known except that he did not allow her to meet his visitors. She was glimpsed occasionally; her existence was known. The *affaire* went on for some years, and when Tissot resolved to bring it to an end he made a not unprecedented mistake which, in the event, transformed the remainder of his life. He wrote a letter to the girl, or woman as she was by then, breaking off relations in terms as gentle and courteous as he could contrive. To a friend he wrote at the same time, telling of his decision, and saying that he was tired of the *affaire.* He put each letter into the wrong envelope, before posting them. The woman committed suicide, and Tissot, overcome by remorse, spent the last years of his life in painting scenes to illustrate the Bible.

Tissot singles out his chariot girl by bringing her into the enlarging foreground. This standard pictorial device is comparable to the unspatial operation of the mind when, from a crowd of faces, one is instantly and spontaneously selected and a personal relationship is set up which may be the acknowledgment of old acquaintance, curiosity, admiration, a coincidence of mood, or the preliminary inquiries of sexual adventure. The relationship lasts as long as two glances hold together. Its duration may be less than a second, but time, no more than space, is not a dominant dimension here. Normally, to complete the brief relationship, the selective glance should be returned, or at least met, but if there is sufficient intensity in the observer's inquiry the experience may be sharp and profound enough in itself, and may afterwards persist powerfully in the memory for years. Such, we may be sure, were Dante's encounters in the streets of Florence with Beatrice. Such, to one degree or another, are all the brief comminglings of glances which occur in crowds when strangers meet, notice each other, and pass on.

These transient communications, spirit to unknown spirit, through the eyes, may be compared to the prodigality with which nature spawns from its more elementary creatures millions upon millions of ova, among which only a few survive to grow adult. The young man as he goes about on his lawful occasions, in trains and omnibuses and tramcars, in the street, at theaters and cinemas and dances, everywhere that he moves among strangers, catches sight of young women on each of whom in turn he directs a stare, bold or shy, brief or sustained. He stares involuntarily, because one face, at that moment, and, as likely as not, without intention, appeals to him by reason of its beauty or its vivacity. If his glance is not met the chord is unresolved: he is thrown into the same earthly limbo of the unrequited which was all that Dante knew of love, and it is extremely unlikely that he will either care or be able to nourish a lifetime of introspection upon the memory. If his glance is met, potentiality has taken the first step toward realization. If his glance is returned the second and more dangerous step has been achieved. From this may proceed acquaintance, flirtation, courtship, and marriage, an adventure in sensuality, or one of those open or secret *affaires* where two people inflict on each other alternations of rapture and suffering violent enough to justify the name of passion.

But these denouements are one in a million or more. Normally the encounter of strangers face to face, the evanescent amour of the eyes, comes to nothing. It is enjoyed, it stimulates, it does no harm, it is forgotten, if not at once, then after a few hours or days. It is part of nature's overproduction, doomed to the wastes of oblivion. But, while it lasts, each pair of eyes seeing one face alone out of many, this brief, spontaneous intimacy holds vast potential control over the future. The young man sees in the girl, and the girl in the young man, the first sketchy delineation of a mate, a desirable complement to the unsatisfaction of a celibate life. A little older, a man or woman will see in the suddenly attractive face of the chance-met stranger a variation, a what-might-have-been temporarily displacing what-is, or, if real experience has withheld satisfaction, a renewal of hope, and so a renewal of youth. The quality of encounters of the eye varies immensely with time and place and mood, and even more profoundly with the nature of the person who looks out through the inquiring eyes. The encounter may be base, greedy or trivial, depraved or perverted, cynical or brutal; it may be naïvely or sadly romantic, generous, modest, sincere; it may, even in its trivial guises, have charm and grace.

As if by common understanding, wiser and more indulgent than by-laws, there will usually be found in most cities and towns a place by unspoken consent set apart at appropriate times for the exercise of this faculty of optical selection. In its crudest form it is a main street where, on fine evenings and week-end afternoons, the adolescents of the town—or such of them as are not restrained by niceties of breeding—promenade up and down the pavements, the boys and girls separately in twos and threes, until, with giggles and squeals, the groups strike up acquaintance and pair off for a few hours. Even market towns and sizable villages have such recognized places of impromptu rendezvous, and although few who meet there are utter strangers, the parade enlarges the range of choice, and the biological purpose of avoiding inbreeding is indirectly served. In seaside towns an asphalt promenade overlooking the beach is the usual site; in America the university campus and the drug store with its soda fountain serve as auxiliaries, and in Europe there are always the cafés. The principal motive which brings about the street pick-ups of adolescents may be crudely sexual, and broadly comic, even grotesque, in its manifestations. But it is not the only motive. There is an element, large or small, of romance, and one of adventure: acquaintance is to be made, for once free from formality and supervision, with another personality. The race is to be run, without handicaps, from scratch. The sudden cries and exclamations, the raucous laughter, the oafish posturings, the self-conscious gestures of the adolescents creating their own society, tell only the most superficial truth of what goes on chaotically in their minds: there are dreams and aspirations there to which their untutored and unlovely behavior can give no expression.

And not all the communal places of potential acquaintanceship are designed for the ill-bred and the immature. The mingling of eye with stranger's eye may be observed almost anywhere where people gather in numbers: at theaters and concerts, at public festivals, in restaurants—possibly, for all I know, even at Royal Garden Parties. One has to be very old to lose the delight of the hopeful eye: age and experience cannot quench but only guard and restrain its ventures. One learns style, perhaps, and also that to avoid disappointment it is usually better, however promising the response, to let the ocular flirtation become an end in itself. When only the face is known, neither the voice nor the banality of what the voice utters can grate on the nerves: and from the observed face it is possible to evoke imaginatively a character and personality for the owner which, a thousand to one, will be much more in keeping with one's secret dreams than the actuality that a prosecuted acquaintance would reveal. Romance is a private fantasy, to which the outward world conforms only rarely and briefly, and the romantic will be well advised not to air his fancies too frequently on the clotheslines of reality. The winds of the world blow bleak and damp and grime-laden, and a disappointed romantic is easily soured into cynicism.

These places of common resort, where people sit and stroll, observed and observing, and provide by their presence and their awareness of each other all the necessary entertainment, flourish everywhere in spring and summer. They are caricatured grossly and professionally wherever the potentiality of an amorous relationship involves the passing of money, as in the Covent Garden of seventeenth-century London, or Vauxhall a century later, or the Empire promenade in the Edwardian years. They become naïve and noisy where louts and hoydens parade the pavements at nightfall. But at their best such places of perambulation have charm and style. In London there have been, at different periods, the Mall, Rotten Row, and St James's Park; in Paris there is the Champs-Elysées; in Rome the Pincio Gardens; in Vienna the Ring; in Budapest the Corso, facing the Danube, and now destroyed; in Venice the Piazza San Marco. All of them are best remembered as on spring and summer evenings, with the stars and the moon and a little artificial lighting overhead: places where it was possible to sit, alone or with friends, to watch the faces of people passing by and allow oneself to be charmed without being greatly stirred, to let the fancy run free and impute to each and every face whatever personality the mind, in its superficial idleness, chose to invent for its own delectation.

It is often in an idealized compost of such remembered romantic settings that, overtaken by reverie, we recall the faces of those we have known, not intimately, but sharply and joyfully, and now think of with gratitude. These daydreams have nothing to do with memories of those near and dear to us, and are concerned with episodes poignant if only because of their brevity. They are theatrical in the sense that the memories are spectacles, a flow of colored pageantry. The reminiscent reverie is an exercise of the mind which is certainly romantic and may become sentimental, over-sweetened by the syrups of false emotion. Wiser to distil its essences one by one, and as each is yielded, let the mind rove to the next. Not that, if the true nature of the reverie is to be preserved, the mind is a free agent. Rather it is under a spell. In our imaginations there is bodied forth, not too definitely, not too solidly, a never-never and yet a familiar scene, evocative of all the past and present moods of romanticism. The air is warm but not hot. There are ripplings of an evening breeze to cool the face and rustle among the pale green leaves and the blossoms of the trees branching overhead, with the stars glittering mildly through. There are lamps throwing a soft incandescence out and down, and never direct into our eyes. There

144

is the noise of conversation around us, but it is not obtrusive, no more than the music: old thin tunes or gypsy airs heavily rhythmical, from stringed instruments, and it may be a piano tinkling away in the distance. And before the entranced imagination there streams, unceasing, unhurrying, a procession of faces we have seen in the past and now see again, animated, vivid, welcome.

No doubt there are hidden associations and semblances which ordain the sequences of these panoramas of memory, but to trace them link by link would be, though not impossible, an abortive task. They are gossamer stuff, made to be glanced at, not handled. In my own reveries a strange assortment of faces will float past my inward eye, their order of march self-sufficient in itself, though it makes nonsense of time and space. At one moment I will be seeing the face of Zaghlul Pasha, Prime Minister of Egypt, as I watched him, a few yards away, plodding on the hot dusty road out to the English cemetery for the funeral of Sir Lee Stack, the Sirdar, assassinated a few days earlier: the face of an old man, olive-brown tinged with gray, thin, creased, wrinkled, and oddly Chinese under the stiff crimson cylinder of his Turkish tarboush. The next moment I see a young girl on a bog-road in the County Mayo, sitting on an ass-cart, in the light of a morning of sunshine and white sea-mist, with her pale cheeks, her blue eyes, her black hair half hidden under a red shawl, lovely enough to jump the heart into the throat.

Then there are the faces of the dead. The first corpse I ever saw, I saw without foreknowledge, by accident, because, a young boy, I opened the wrong door in a strange house: the face of an old sailor, creased into waxen ridges, not so white as the sheet pulled up to his chin, over which the long beard spread out, gray and neatly brushed, still streaked with yellow nicotine stains round the mouth. The face of a young Jew, plumply jowled, with a two-day beard stubble, who was killed beside me in front of Cambrai, his head shorn clean off, thrown into the bottom of the trench, so that it was the first thing I saw as the dust and smoke of the explosion cleared, and I knew that I was alive although I could still swear that for a few seconds I had been ripped, disincarnate and shocked, out of my body. The face of a man, due to die in a few days' time, who awed me by raising himself from the pillows and pronouncing the Biblical blessing upon me: "The Lord make his face to shine upon thee, and be gracious unto thee: the Lord lift up his countenance upon thee, and give thee peace." The faces of soldiers several days dead, exposed to the wind and the rain and the sun, swollen with corruption, all the features spatulated and discolored to dark purples and livid greens and blues. These are memories which have no rightful place in the romantic panoramas of memory, but as, I suppose, with everyone of my generation who has twice in less than a lifetime suffered from the Germanic love of war, they intrude and will not be kept out.

But the procession moves on. Its only constant quality is inconstancy. There are girls and women with whom I have been, or have fancied myself, momentarily in love; and perhaps I was precocious, for these memories go far back. Was I eight or nine when I found myself obsessed by the white-faced girl with a mop of black hair who lived two houses away from mine? This is a shocking memory, for I was not, and am not, sure that my devotion was disinterested. I used to climb the intervening high walls to meet her in her garden, and perhaps it was the raspberries and red currants there I was really in love with. But a few years later I was more selfless. I fell sick of love for one of my mother's maids, much older than myself. She was Welsh, tall, strong, dark-haired, and gray-eyed, and when she was making pastry she would roll her sleeves to the elbows, and the flour on her plump forearms was not so white as her skin. I saw her once, with bare shoulders, brushing her hair in front of a glass. I was going to the attic where I kept my cricket bats, which I not only oiled but rolled with an old stump, to harden the surface. My mind was full of nothing but cricket, and the smell of linseed oil was in my nostrils, but when I passed Diana's room—Diana is the name I gave her in a story I made up, not so long ago, about a sprig of mistletoe—the door had swung back, and there she was, her back toward the open door, brushing her hair. I stopped in mid-stride, ludicrously unbalanced, staring, aware only that I had never seen anything so lovely as that long black hair, rippling with lusters, and the white shoulders. Then, seeing me in the mirror, she told me, laughing, to be off. But, as you may guess from the fact that I wrote the story thirty years after, those moments have never dimmed in my memory.

The black-haired Welsh girl was mixed up in my mind, even then, with a painting of a black-haired Irishwoman: not, I suppose (for I have not set eyes on it for many years), a good painting. It was very big, and occupied a lot of wall space in the Walker Art Gallery in Liverpool. I believe it was called *Tristram and Iseult*. The scene was set in the well-deck of an antique sailing-ship, with a spread of sail-cloth overhead and rolling billows, green and foam-flecked, visible over the bulwarks in the background. On the deck Tristram and Iseult stood facing each other, having drunk from a jeweled goblet the magic potion which is to make them in love with each other forever. I went in often to look at this picture, than which I could conceive nothing more romantic and moving. To Tristram I paid little attention (no doubt in imagination I filled his place), but Iseult I can see now at any moment I let memory stir in my mind, her arms at her sides, her dark hair flowing loose down her back, a little disordered by the sea-wind, her eyes blue and intense, alight with all the simple avowals of love. She was my 'type,' and I knew it.

Or rather, she was one of my types, one authentic version of that kind of beauty which I am predisposed to find attractive. For there are, I am forced to admit, variations in these objects of the allegiance of my senses and my temperament. The face of this predetermined ideal of mine is usually slightly squared at temples and jaw, or else heart-shaped, with hair black or dark brown, and eyes blue or gray or green: heredity gives me some catholicity of taste here. And often I find in myself the same authentic, unarguable response to a face which is rather longer, narrower, thin-cheeked, and so suggestive of austerity or passion or pathos. The other variation is quite occasional. Sometimes I find myself responding to hair which is dark-red, red-gold, a red so intense it carries tints of purple in its shadows. And when I was a boy at school there were two girls with red hair who caused me infinite joy and anguish. I was turned out—aged, I think, twelve—from a cinema, then called a picture palace, because the lights went up and I was found with my arm round the shoulders of the red-haired girl I had brought with me, while her brother sat unconcernedly on the other side, chewing sweets. The commissionaire clucked his horror at my precocity as he led me out.

The other girl I had never dared to speak to, till we both took part in an amateur performance of a play based on—of all undramatic material—Tennyson's *Idylls of the King*. We were too young to have speaking parts. We helped to fill up the stage for the crowd scenes, and at the dress rehearsal, emboldened by a knight's costume of woolen chain-mail and by the masking effect of the first grease paint I ever wore, I edged my way among the other supers till at last I stood beside my inamorata. Then I sought for something to say, anything which would begin an acquaintance. Several times I opened my mouth and could do nothing but gulp. I was overawed by the close proximity of that red-gold hair, no longer braided into a single thick pigtail but flowing free in its glory, and that serene, classic young face, which glanced indifferently at the producer, at Lancelot, at her elder sister who played Guinevere, at the canvas scenery, at the almost empty hall, never at me. But I had to speak. At last I did. And the words which, horrified, I heard myself bring out were: "This limelight makes you look seasick."

I was more successful—but this was earlier still in my boyhood— with the girl on the joywheel, the only blonde who troubled my emotions until the day my wife came home and bade me turn out to see a film with a new actress in it (and a great one, my wife insisted, despite my scoffing incredulity) called Greta Garbo. The joywheel was a seaside entertainment—a flat circular wooden floor, waxed and polished, which revolved, driven by an engine with hand controls, at first slowly, then fast, then faster still. People, mostly young people, tried to cast themselves on the great disk while it was spinning slowly and then to retain their hold, sitting or sprawling, as the pace increased. The girl on the joywheel (that is how I always think of her) was about my own age, twelve or thirteen. She had two pale golden pigtails, with bows of black ribbon at the end, and a scarlet tam-o'-shanter on her head. She wore thick worsted stockings, too, of a brown color between chocolate and café au lait. All this was commonplace: a million English schoolgirls wore clothes like that. What distinguished her was her ability, as good as my own, to fight a way to the strategic central position on the joywheel and sit there till the man in charge of the engine reluctantly gave us best. At first we simply sat back to back, occasionally grinning at each other over our shoulders, but soon we linked arms at the elbows, still back to back. Like that, we were invincible. Nothing else happened. We were strangers; we achieved a public triumph together, and repeated it several times; and afterwards we ate ice-creams till our money ran out and it was time to go home. I never saw her again, but I have never forgotten her. She had very dark blue eyes and a pointed chin, and when the joywheel was spinning at its fastest she sucked in her cheeks with excitement and her whole face gradually became as scarlet as her tam-o'-shanter.

I am forty-five, and not yet accustomed to the verbal respect which young men in the twenties sometimes think it proper to show either to my few white hairs or to the fact that I have a number of books listed after my name in *Who's Who*. In my thoughts I am inclined still to assume myself a contemporary of these youngsters, and when one of them addresses me as "sir" it is like an unintentional slap in the face for my self-esteem. But what fetches me up most sharply against the fact that I have now entered on middle age (which not so long ago seemed to me, as it does to all the young, old age) is when I come out of my reveries and discover I have been remembering people I knew well but who are now dead and passed to history. I could even, I perceive (but I will not), make a book of reminiscences, fat with anecdotes and period photographs like those which used to be turned over to me, half a dozen at a time, by literary editors in the days when I tramped up and down Fleet Street, cadging for books to review.

Perhaps they are not so numerous, after all, the faces of the dead whom I remember in all the energy and purpose of life. Allenby, walking apparently unattended in the streets of Cairo, like a private English gentleman of the old school, with none of the cavalry thrust which earned him in the Army the nickname of "The Bull": and George Lloyd, who succeeded him as High Commissioner, by ancestry a Quaker but hardly to be seen unless surrounded with the pomps of power, sitting in a limousine, his face grayish with talcum powder, dark-browed, consciously stern, and looking, with his gray top hat and pearl-buttoned waistcoat and silk cravat, like a bookmaker who had had the good or bad fortune to be educated at Eton. "Lawrence of Arabia" I knew only as T. E. Shaw. He had a big head, a long, flat, impressive face, and controlled lips from which there emerged, delicately and incongruously, a tenuous, donnish, Oxford voice. He was thicker-necked and fuller-fleshed then than in his desert days, and when he got off his motorcycle after the long ride from Plymouth the wind had made his face and neck red, a strawberry color, not unlike the rash of measles. Gradually that would fade, and with it there would ebb out of his eyes the remote and dispassionate focusing due to driving at speed, his passion and pleasure, his means of deliverance from self-consciousness.

Hugh Walpole, who escaped from the inquisitions of self criticism by cultivating optimism and *bonhomie,* also appears most vividly in my memories with a flush on his face. He had a very clear and translucent complexion—the complexion of a baby, in color like the pink of some sea-shells but with no rigidity, no hardness of texture. The last time I saw him was one morning in the spring of 1941, not long before he died, the morning after a heavy Luftwaffe raid. We went through the London streets together in search of luncheon, past burned and blasted ruins, with the sunny air polluted by dust and soot, stepping over fire hoses and puddles of dirty water, untidy debris, and crackling heaps of broken glass. I was depressed, but presently I perceived that my companion's face had turned from pink to red, and this was due to excitement. Fire and explosions, at least in the aftermath, stimulated him. He was more natural that morning than I had ever known him, and I guessed that the destruction of war touched and titillated one of those obsessional neuroses he would sometimes talk about, though defensively, and which produced the grotesque characters and the sadistic or masochistic incidents in many of his novels. Hugh Walpole had little in common with T. E. Shaw, but they were both men in whose personalities there raged a secret civil war, and neither of them fully understood what the conflict was about.

In Alexander Woollcott there was a different sort of dissension. He turned his private life outward and kept it always on show, making a public character for himself so flamboyant and extensive that it was hard to imagine what he could be like apart from it. It might be that in his rare moments of solitude his sentimentality enveloped him like the enervating vapors of a Turkish bath; or the sardonic malice with which he offset this trait may have had all its own way; or quite likely he panicked before the onset of unaccustomed loneliness and ran to the telephone, the radio set, or the writing-desk as a refuge from the caprices of undirected private thought. I never really knew him, but I was interested in his writings, his broadcasts, the legends exported from New York, and the play, *The Man Who Came to Dinner,* in which (it was the openest of open secrets) he was pilloried as the egoistic hero and, characteristically, had seen to it that the pillory became something between a regal throne and a publicity platform. When on his last visit to London he invited me to a dinner-party at the Ivy Restaurant, with Thornton Wilder, John Dos Passos, Michael Redgrave (then wearing the bare neck and bell-bottomed trousers of an able seaman),

and Tom Harrisson, my curiosity was tickled. I find public characters appalling but fascinating, like prisoners who have built their
own jails on the model of a huge and ornate palace and are determined that everyone shall admire their voluntary penitentiaries.
Woollcott turned out to be a small man, much smaller than I had
expected, rotund, with a dark complexion and a squared, soft, rather
sagging face, constantly and variably animated. But not an unsym-
pathetic character. Far from it. The selfishness, the assertions of
opinion and desire, the overbearing despotisms of the legend, were
either absent or muted. He could switch on vivacity, and superlative endearments, which meant nothing; but these are commonplaces
among theater people on social occasions. Between voluble encounters with old friends, kissings and huggings and back-slappings,
he was an excellent host, attentive, ready to listen, even sensitive.
He went back to New York, was taken ill during a broadcast, and
died almost at once. Perhaps that night in the Ivy Restaurant in
London he knew, beneath the levels of consciousness, that death lay
not far off in the future, that the masquerade he had enjoyed so
much was nearing its end. Other people, I gather, have very different memories; but for me, who met him only a few times in a
few busy days, he lingers in memory as gentle, kind, and young
behind the walnut-brown, creased, mutable mask of his public face.

Two other writers, of a very different kind, I was privileged to
know much more intimately: Winifred Holtby and Stefan Zweig.
It seemed impossible that Winifred should die young; she had so
much vitality, so much to give to life and take from it. No portraits
convey what she looked like, tall and heroically built, a kind of
Viking with a sense of humor. She dressed badly, often choosing
purples and greens which screamed out against her gold hair and
her blue eyes, brilliant but never cold. Her face was big and long,
with boldly carved features; it could look ugly, almost crude, but
sometimes beautiful in an exalted fashion of which she seemed quite
unconscious. It was her generous and lively spirit which made her
beautiful, and it was impossible, knowing her, not to love her: to

do less would have been a mean failure, a degradation. Stefan Zweig shut himself out from the life of affairs in which Winifred adventured boldly and prodigally. He was not, by temperament, inclined to consider the present at all, only the past: in the past, by study and contemplation, the disorderliness of life could be tidied up and analyzed. He was a connoisseur of biography and psychology, and out of his exquisite discriminations he was able to find a creative faculty which consoled his natural melancholy. He was a spectator of life, an analyst and something of an erudite hero-worshiper of other men, dead and living: he needed distance in time to give him perspective, assurance, a steady vision. He was extraordinarily kind, and devoid of the brash exuberances of egoism.

A rather thickset man, Stefan Zweig had a face of some pallor imposed on a natural swarthiness, with a prominent nose and a full brown mustache; his sensitiveness showed in his mouth, full but delicately shaped, and in his lambent eyes, at once dark and luminous. Before he went to South America and committed suicide, in a student's despair at the horror of history reaching with barbarian force into the European civilization he loved, he took a house at Bath. It was a characteristic gesture: Bath was the nearest English approximation to Salzburg before Hitler grabbed at it. He loved both the Roman and the eighteenth-century classical architecture. But I remember him best in the small rooms of his flat in Hallam Street, behind Broadcasting House, rooms full of the modulated chiaroscuro of soft lighting and shadows, and decorated in browns and unemphatic greens and golds. These, too, were the colors he dressed in most often, and they were the colors in his meditative, benignant eyes, which would light up whenever he saw you, however inopportune the visit: the colors of a river pool, out of the main current, clear, pellucid, undisturbed. If Lady Macbeth should for her husband's convenience have died hereafter, Stefan Zweig ought for his own sake to have been born in an earlier age, before war acquired the intrusive adjective 'total,' before high explosive was invented, before the noises and alarums could be heard through the study door. His spirit grew no hard protective shell of its own; but it was a fine, sensitive and gentle spirit.

The other evening I had a strange experience: at times it had the overpowering quality of a dream. I went to see a performance of Shaw's *Saint Joan*. Although I have read the play several times, I had seen it only once, and then in an odd though interesting open-air version in the provinces, since the original production at the New Theater in the summer of 1924—the summer in which I was married—when Sybil Thorndike (not then Dame) played Saint Joan. Now I saw it again, after twenty-one years, with my wife and my fifteen-year-old daughter. And Saint Joan was played by Sybil Thorndike's daughter, Ann Casson, who in voice and bearing not only closely resembles her mother, but in a peasant gown, black prison garb, and shining armor, with gold hair dressed in what is called a page-boy's crop, and the bright ardor of her face, was so much like the Sybil Thorndike of 1924 that at times my wife and I clean forgot the years between. It was as if we were back in our honeymoon days, seated not in the front stalls but near the back of the pit, having waited for hours in the queue stretching round into the court off St Martin's Lane. To complete this tangle of past and present, two members of the original cast had returned: Eugene Leahy, all Irish conviction and intensity, as the Bishop of Beauvais, and Lewis Casson, the producer, but now playing the Earl of Warwick. And Sir Lewis is Sybil Thorndike's husband, and Ann Casson's father.

Now that I think of it a large number of the faces I remember most distinctly and persistently are faces seen on the stage and—not so many of them—on the cinema screen. For, with all respect to those who saw Irving and are unable to forget the pleasures of being hypnotized from behind the Lyceum footlights, I think the present era of British acting far superior to its immediate predecessors: indeed, I find it hard to believe that any other generation has known better acting, year in and year out, from so many brilliant, powerful and resourceful players. It is true that I never saw Irving, and so

PLATE XVIII: VENUS (Detail from "The Birth of Venus"),

by SANDRO BOTTICELLI

Uffizi Gallery, Florence

154

PLATE XIX: NEFERTITI, ARTIST UNKNOWN

Berlin Museum

155

cannot make the cardinal comparison; but then those who make it are pitting the present experience of their maturity against youthful memories sanctified by the passage of time and the ready laurel leaves of legend. And it is well to remember Ellen Terry, whom Bernard Shaw, enraptured but not light-headed with love, believed to have wasted herself playing second fiddle to Irving. There are few women I reverence more than Ellen Terry, so far as I know her through her autobiography, her letters, the reminiscences of others, the lovely soft-focus camera portraits of her youth with strength and tenderness and mischief blended in the unforgettable profile. But Ellen Terry as an actress—I have a gramophone record made by her, the "Quality of Mercy" speech from *The Merchant of Venice*. The voice is excellent, full, easy, flexible, and rich: but the phrasing, the emphases, the conveyance of meaning through intonation—oh dear, oh dear! I fear this sort of acting would seem tinsel and fustian today. About Irving I am prepared to believe everything his admirers credit him with, but, accepting his achievement at this valuation, I still see him as a one-man exhibition, a spellbinder, a purveyor of personality, an actor of genius—a genius he abused largely because he lived in an age of uncertain theatrical taste.

In my young days I saw Forbes-Robertson, Benson, Lewis Waller, H. B. Irving, Gertrude Elliott, Beerbohm Tree, Mrs Patrick Campbell, Fred Terry, and Martin-Harvey as Hamlet—and no other Hamlet has made such an impression on me. I possess, therefore, certain standards of comparison, and use them; for I have often been told I am an uncomfortable person to visit the theater with: I analyze and discriminate too much for other people's enjoyment. Yet, looking back on the last twenty years, I know I have seen on the London and provincial stage acting so accomplished that all my memories are pervaded with gratitude. There is too much to choose from: it is possible only to pick here and there, by favor. I saw Diana Wynyard, girlishly plump but already beautiful, already a mature actress, at the Liverpool Playhouse under William Armstrong's tutelage. She was serene of brow and eye in *The Cradle*

Song; and a few years later, in London, sophisticated, chromium-plated, poised, in *No Time for Comedy,* only to abnegate both loveliness and glitter and wit to the austere demands of a comparatively small part in *Watch on the Rhine.* Michael Redgrave, son of an actor and an actress, also started at Liverpool. In Turgenev's *A Month in the Country* he made himself a little foppish, devoted, languid, defeated by life, vulnerable to every emotionally charged atmosphere. In Patrick Hamilton's *The Duke in Darkness* he became nerve-tortured, pitiable, and in *Uncle Harry* acquired an Edwardian-period face, a genteel, small-town face, mild and pettifogging until vanity and secret scheming contorted it into dementia. Best of all, perhaps, I remember his extraordinary touching gaucherie as the Baron in *The Three Sisters,* and the ingenuous, and truthful, rendering of Arthur Kipps in a classic film made during the blitz months of 1940-41. The drawing by Mr Augustus John (Plate XVI, page 138) shows him as he is in private life. It is this face of professional potentiality which is his starting point when he goes into the theater. Makeup is little more than auxiliary: the metamorphoses, the intensities, the subtleties of expressiveness, the emotions precisely communicated, these are the products of a genius for the theater. He can discharge the full electric sensation of power upon the audience, and all his playing is subtle and finished. He is master of several kinds of comedy, and of the romantic, the poetic, and the tragic. His career is reaching to its summit, and I could not put any limit to the possibilities open to him.

Of Vivien Leigh all memories are exquisite: as Titania she glimmered through the Athenian woodlands, as if the horns of elfland had blown their filigree tunes visibly upon the air. There was an enchantment on her face, and in her face, and some of it lingered for the more sophisticated fantasies of *The Happy Hypocrite.* And in *The Doctor's Dilemma,* when she appeared in the superb crimson gown, the whole audience knew with what sort of visionary splendor, a painter's vision, Bernard Shaw had been in love. Vivien Leigh offers a challenge to any painter in the fine, clean, delicate delineations of her face and the contrasts of her dark hair, pale complexion, and eyes the color of a green sea in sunlight. The portrait by Dietz Edzard (of which the head only is reproduced in Plate XVII, page 139) is a study of a stage part. And in Korda's excellent film of *Lady Hamilton* how much more lovely, and more interesting, she was than all Romney's renderings of the original Emma. She played too, it will be remembered, Scarlett O'Hara in the prodigiously successful film of *Gone With the Wind,* and her beauty has become legendary. She has achieved a fame which for once can fairly be described as world-wide, and her very name is invested with an aureate glamour. It is all the more astounding, therefore, that she should have avoided both the blatant and the insidious temptations of the public life, the brassiness, the affectations, the insincerity and pettiness, the vanity, the self-absorption. Good manners must be natural to her, impregnable to every circumstance, and her charm is never reserved for celebrities only. Her head was not turned even by the triumph she earned as Sabina in Thornton Wilder's *The Skin of Our Teeth,* which in the spring and summer of 1945 burst like a fanfare of trumpets first on the great provincial cities and then on London. This is not only her latest stage rôle but so far the apotheosis of her career, a sustained feat of acting of infinite variety, witty and richly comic, authoritative, having dignity in spite of all indignities, satiric and poignant and boisterous by turns, something that will be treasured in memory for years to come and brought out whenever the conversation turns to the supremely great performances of players past and present.

Vivien Leigh's husband, Laurence Olivier, is an actor of exceptional dynamic force. What is most impressive about his playing is the sudden, dominating unleashings of power, in gesture, in voice, in the dark clouding of a dark face with the urgency of the will. He is genuinely an actor: he transforms himself, inside and out, with every part he has to play, but this virility of appearance and manner and speech is proper to the man. His Macbeth ranted too much, and in too dim a lighting, for my taste, but as both Romeo

157

and Mercutio he was poetry presented to the eye and the ear. His Richard III made drama out of melodrama. His Henry V was, without quibble, kingly; and he made the legendary Nelson into a human being, and moreover contrived to look, on the screen, the living image of the great admiral. Laurence Olivier has a face not plain, not ugly, but certainly not handsome in the old Matinee Idol style. The complexion is clear, fine-textured, brown, but there is no smooth beautification of the shape. The flesh clings lean and firm over the bones, and the bones emphasize, not unduly but unmistakably, the jut of brows and jaw. It is a face to build heroic conceptions upon.

He plays comedy too, with adroitness and polish. And there lies one of the prime characteristics of these contemporary stage faces I delight in: they change continually, they will not be allocated to one type, they do not bring to a new part in a new play all the habits and mannerisms of the last. They are truly actors and actresses, these people for seeing whom at the height of their powers posterity will envy us. There are so many of them, too—such richness. Ralph Richardson, Leon Quartermaine, Leslie Banks, John Gielgud (a scholarly player, with every tiniest movement weighed and timed, but by temperament, I think, better powered for the comedy of manners than for tragedy and romance), Robert Newton, Donald Wolfit (some of the Irving mesmerism there, not so lean of shank), Margaret Rawlings, Flora Robson, Angela Baddeley, Robert Donat —superb in *Heartbreak House,* with Edith Evans and Deborah Kerr—Charles Laughton (now lost to Hollywood), Cedric Hardwicke, Herbert Lomas (more Lincoln-like than Lincoln himself), Robert Morley, Wendy Hiller, James Mason, Roger Livesey, John Mills, Emlyn Williams, Beatrix Lehmann, Fay Compton, Sara Allgood—and as I must close this extempore list somewhere, let me close it magnificently with Irene Vanbrugh, Lilian Braithwaite, and Henry Ainley.

I could add dozens of other names. It is something—it is, in fact, a great deal—to have seen such players as these. It is to live, despite fascisms and slumps and wars, in a Golden Age. And now that I look back on what I have written here I see there is another reason why memories of the theater should occupy so large a part of my recollections. For of all human faces the stage-player's is, in one fundamental respect, the most intensively representative: it does to perfection, by art, craft, science and practice, what other faces contrive only imperfectly and between times—it expresses and communicates the further margins of meaning beyond what speech and action can convey. The player's face is a substantial part of his artistic fortune. It may be beautiful; it must be variable at control and precisely responsive to every modulation of thought, mood, and feeling. Unless required to body forth hypocrisy or reticence, it must contrive, without the contrivance showing, to impart the conviction of sincerity and spontaneity, though all has been rehearsed a hundred times over. It must transform itself first to a character other than the player's own, and then to all the miscellaneous but, in sum, coherent variations of experience which make up this assumption. It must seize, hold, sustain and satisfy the attention of hundreds of spectators, each with a pair of eyes turned attentively upon this one limelit face. It must furnish the adequate answers to a series of questions, telepathically emanated from the audience, each at its appropriate moment. The player's face is the human face specialized to its most subtle function: expressiveness. It is the visible index to a myriad characters, created by dramatists more lucidly, more simply, and yet more consistently and understandably, than any of the haphazard characters of real life. It is the magic mask which so many undramatic persons aspire to wear; the deliverance from the harsh strait-jacket of one ego; the power to be, not perhaps better than we are, but at least different, and different in more ways than one; the way of escape into the endless possibilities of all human nature.

CHAPTER EIGHT

THE GROTESQUE

In a sense the face is distorted whenever it passes from repose to the activities of eating, drinking, yawning, speaking, singing, laughter. But such mutations lie well within the compass of everyday experience, and make no undue impact on the attention. Only the extremes of intense emotion, the first access of anger, joy, fear, pain, astonishment and grief, express themselves in what can properly be called facial distortions. Between all these different emotions, as they show in the face, there is a disconcerting similarity. The mouth opens and expands or is violently twisted; the eyelids fall apart to reveal the white above and below the pupils, or are almost shut tight, enclosed in a sudden complication of wrinkles; the cheeks are violently creased; and the delineatory outline of the face alters its curves and proportions. The precise interpretation of intense emotion revealed in the face needs a context. Those who come casually and unprepared on a scene of personal drama in the streets are often puzzled to guess whether the strangers whose conduct attracts their attention are laughing or crying, sick and in pain, or merely enjoying themselves exuberantly.

On the stage, for fear the player's facial expressions be misinterpreted, the climaxes of tragedy have to be carefully prepared, not only by antecedent action and dialogue but by the deportment of other players which gives the lead to the audience's reaction. On the cinema screen, where every 'close-up' showing a face enormously enlarged is a hazardous promenade along a knife-edge precipice over the abyss of bathos, similar broad hints are dropped to the audience, and in addition a sympathetic mood is evoked by 'background' music. The pictorial and plastic arts are exposed even more nakedly to the dangers of misinterpretation, of arousing the opposite reaction to the one intended. This is because pictures and sculptures can show appearances only at one selected moment of time, and it is an essential characteristic of the emotional expressions of the face that they are not sustained for long: part of their vividness lies in their evanescence. With crucifixes and in sacred pictures the difficulty is to some extent modified by the surroundings in which they are viewed. They attain the requisite effect by being exhibited in churches or shrines: the appropriate environment is provided. Transported into art galleries and museums, sacred art may easily seem more ludicrous than moving. Spanish, early German and sometimes Flemish religious art, depicting the sufferings of Christ or of martyrs, is especially likely to arouse, in those who do not bring to it devout associations of a very ascetic, if not neurotic kind, inappropriate mental associations. There is a drawing in Berlin, by Matthias Grünewald, called *Lamenting Angel*. It shows a big, plump, babyish face bent so far back that it is almost horizontal, and the foreshortening, technically skillful, makes the writhing lines of the open mouth the focus of the picture—a central pit of darkness to which the vast receding chin leads upward like a hill-slope. It is, in effect, a grotesque study of a mouth emitting a howl, and despite the title and the intention of the artist, it strikes the eye as caricature. Similarly there is in the British Museum a drawing by Dürer of a *Head of Christ* which is evidently a study for a Crucifixion picture, for the head is crowned with thorns. Again the face is tilted back and slightly to one side. No doubt the drawing was made from a posed model, or even from a corpse. The vantage point is in front and from below the level of the chin, with the result that the gaping mouth, with tongue protruding, is shaped in a distended double cupid's bow, and the nose is all nostril vents. It is almost impossible to avoid the impression of a circus clown in an act of sacrilegious parody. And a very unpleasant impression it is.

Wounds may distort the face with scars and burns, with alterations of shape due to the removal of bones, muscles, and flesh tissues.

Here, fortunately, plastic surgery can do a great deal to remedy the injuries wrought by other branches of science. Diseases discolor the face, making it pallid or flushed, or, if the blood is infected, turning the complexion yellow or brown. All these have an indirect effect on the apparent structure of the face, by altering the interplay of light and shadow. Some maladies produce swellings, local or general; and wasting diseases make the flesh shrink inward against the bones. Elephantiasis, thickening and inflaming the skin, malforms the face most violently, and both hydrocephalus and giantism may enlarge and misshape the whole head. Compared with such pitiable misfortunes, the excrescences of goiter, wens, carbuncles, boils, and pimples seem tolerable. Drunkenness—alcoholic intoxication to the point of incapability—has been very rare in Great Britain for more than two decades now, but on occasions of festivity it is often possible for the observer who keeps his own mind and eyesight clear to note the effects of partial intoxication on other people's faces. Besides an enlarging of the pupils of the eyes, accompanied by the wider opening of the lids and the secretion of excess moisture from the tear-ducts along the lower lids, hard drinking produces a grayish pallor and sometimes facial sweat. The prominence of small purple veins on and around the nose does not usually occur until later—it arrives with a sick headache—but under the immediate stimulus the general aspect of the face may often be seen to change, most noticeably in a swelling of the mouth round the lips and of the cheeks under the eyes, while the nostrils distend: the face becomes at once coarser and less mutable in expression. No doubt one of the reasons why vocational drinkers insist on their companions keeping pace with them is that at the back of their clouded minds there jigs a suspicion—the conscience of the self-indulgent is always suspicious— of what the drunken and the semi-drunken look like to the sober.

These are natural distortions of the face, but man's imagination has never been bounded by the wide limits of nature. He cannot create out of the void, but he can analyze and reassemble what he knows into new and surprising combinations. This is the same faculty from which art proceeds, and art may be bold or imitative, revolutionary or traditional, governed by good taste or bad. So that faces, more or less recognizable as human, can be and are invented by the imagination and depicted by the hand. Sometimes they are bogey faces, designed to frighten those who made them, for there is pleasure as well as pain in being frightened. Primitive man enjoyed himself in this way, and at the same time placated his elementary religious sense. The early Greeks included in their mythology the Gorgons, the terrible or loud-roaring monstrous women of whom Medusa is the best known. The faces of the Gorgons were round— not for them the classic oval—and flat-nosed, and they had project- ing teeth, or tusks, and long tongues which they protruded spite- fully. Æschylus gives them only one eye and one tooth between the three of them. Instead of hair they had coiling serpents. Medusa alone of the Gorgons was mortal, and Perseus killed her by cutting off her head. This head of the slain Medusa had the power of turning anyone who looked on it into stone: it was either given to Minerva, who carried it on her shield, or buried by Perseus: there are alternative versions of most of the old legends. But representa- tions of Medusa's head were used on the walls of cities, and on the shields and breastplates of soldiers, to intimidate approaching ene- mies. Others, smaller, were worn as charms against the evil eye. A later legend, reacting against these crude conceptions, presented Medusa as no ordinary monster but a nice and personable girl, who made the mistake of choosing a temple dedicated to Minerva as the site for a love affair with Poseidon, the sea-god. As a punishment, Minerva changed Medusa's hair into snakes. This revised version was favored by later sculptors and metalworkers, to whom it gave the opportunity of portraying beautiful models with an unusual coiffure. Later still in the Ancient World, rationalization got a foot- hold in the old myth. Diodorus explains away the Gorgons as a Libyan tribe of warlike women, like the Amazons; Alexander of Myndus makes them wild animals (perhaps lions, with their manes looking like snakes), the sight of whom petrified men with fear;

and Pliny, allowing that they were women after all, attributes the snakes to the wild appearance of their long, unkempt hair. The most vividly up-to-date exegesis of the Gorgons is to be found, incidentally, in Robert Graves's novel, *The Golden Fleece*.

Mr Graves also gives us an excellent rationalization of those other classical monsters: the satyr, or goat-legged man; the harpy, or bird-woman; and the centaur, half horse, half man. If I understand his argument aright, the primitive Greeks among whom these myths were first evolved did not literally believe in the existence of such creatures. The monsters were pictographs, or pictures used symbolically, almost as signboards, and comparable to the heraldic badges of bears, buffalos, tigers and so on which often form divisional signs in the British Army. To the early Greeks such pictographs were the badges of clans or religious associations. Scholars suggest that the original centaurs were Thessalians who learned how to tame horses and ride them bareback: to neighboring tribes, as to the Indians of South America thousands of years later, horse and horse-man would appear as one creature, and doubtless the centaur clan, having discovered this horrifying effect, triumphantly exploited it in their communal badge. As time passed, this natural origin would be forgotten, and to the later Greeks and the Romans, informed only by vase-paintings and poetical descriptions, the centaurs became fabulous monsters, literally half man and half horse.

Both animals and human beings occasionally give birth to physiological monstrosities, although fortunately human monsters are very rarely born alive: the notable exceptions are giants, dwarfs, hermaphrodites and Siamese twins, who, we may hope, do not live too unhappy lives. But among these human freaks there are some whose malformations correspond closely to the monsters of ancient fables. The commingling of the human with an animal body is not known in nature, so that the conception of the satyr, the sphinx, and the harpy, so far as it was believed in, probably arose by an extension of the imagination from what was sometimes to be observed on farms and hunting-grounds. Cerberus, the hound of

Pluto, with its fifty or its three heads, was not difficult to imagine in a pastoral community where two-headed calves might be born to an apparently normal cow and so furnish a subject for local gossip for years to come. The hydra, another monster credited with up to a hundred heads, must have had a similar origin. But the hydra's capitalistic plenitude was unlimited, for when one head was cut off two others replaced it, unless the wound was cauterized by fire. This additional complication can be ascribed to the macabre fancy of a mind fed on observation of lizards and crabs which develop a new limb or tail to replace one lopped off.

The origin of the sirens is less anatomical. These nymphs of the sea (like the Lorelei of the Rhine) lured ships to destruction by means of their singing, and it is one of the oddest developments of language that their name should in modern times be used for a warning whistle to call workers to a factory, for a ship's signal (to landlubbers a 'foghorn'), and lately for the melancholy and exacerbating undulations of sound which announced the approach of hostile aircraft or self-propelled bombs. The early Greeks pictured the sirens as birds with women's heads or women with birds' feet; later they became simply beautiful young women, expert swimmers, with very long hair. They symbolized the treacherous nature of the sea. In view of the Greek inventiveness in other directions, it is strange that the sirens do not appear to have been invested with fish-tails, like mermaids, whose origin is Celtic and Teutonic, and who also symbolize the fatality of shipwreck. There is enough similarity at a distance—where they are usually seen—between walruses, seals, porpoises, and, still more, manatees and dugongs, and the fabulous mermaids to make their origin in human fancy understandable; and porpoises or dolphins at least were known to the Greeks. But even more striking is the fact that one of the standard types of monstrous human stillbirths has both legs joined in a single tapering limb, so that the lower half of the body looks like that of an heraldic dolphin. In all these inventions of myth and fable the human head is either retained on an inappropriate body or replaced by the head of a non-human creature. But there is one remarkable exception—the cyclops, deified giants, each of whom had only one eye, and that in the middle of the forehead. This monocular characteristic is explained as arising from the custom of a Sicilian tribe of fighting with a small shield or helmet over the face, in which was an aperture through which one eye only was visible. Here perhaps rationalization goes astray, for again there is a standard type of human stillbirth in which, at the root of the nose, just above the bridge, there is a kind of eye-socket, sometimes empty, sometimes containing a more or less normal eyeball. Cyclopean monsters also occur quite often among animals, and there can be little doubt that this Greek myth had its origins in first-hand natural observation.

Nature, it is evident, possesses sufficient power to affright human sensibility, although we have to remember that what is freakishly horrible to our eyes is so chiefly because it differs from what we expect. One eye, centrally placed, is not necessarily less beautiful than two; but instinct clings to the familiar, and it is only by a deliberate decision of the intellect—and the will—that we are able to discount our nervous recoil of horror. Our minds are still clamped within the eternal dilemma: each of us desires to be recognized as different from his fellows, but not too different, and different only in ways he approves of. And mingled with our horror at monstrosities there is always a furtive element of pleasure, which, if we confess to its existence at all, most of us are willing to concede is probably morbid and reprehensible. The pleasure may be due to finding an outlet for irreverence, a sop for the petty rebel in our nature, or it may be ascribed to the intensity of the shock to our nerves; all intense experience is a deliverance from tedium. Whatever the explanation, there is a secret fascination to be got out of human monstrosities, and this accounts for the success of freak shows in fairs and circuses, and photographs of 'war atrocities,' delectations for which some sections of the more educated classes have substituted displays of all-in wrestling and exhibitions of surrealist pictures and 'objects.' Cruelty enjoyed, passively or actively, by the vicarious use of the imagination operates in all these spectacles. They would lose their power if they were seen otherwise than against the background of normal experience. If we were all cyclops a two-eyed man would become a freak, and if the outward world resembled a surrealist picture the Royal Academy would be a society of revolutionaries. Indeed, Surrealism has already more or less lost its power to shock, and when it is tucked away into its place in the historical record its chief influence may be judged to lie in what so far has been its least noted characteristic: the faithful, pre-Raphaelitish representation of appearances.

Taking hints and stimulus from freaks of nature, the human mind can easily invent astounding monstrosities in its dreams, although, because of their hallucinatory and unstable nature, it is not often that these are satisfactorily recorded in pictorial art or in literature, where reason refuses to let go its last hold. German artists of the Middle Ages and later return again and again to the theme of the Dance of Death, with grisly detail; death seems to have a fascination for the German temperament, as blood for the Spanish. Demons, genii, and the witches, wizards and priests of black magic who profess to conjure them up, are depicted in the art of all places and periods, obviously to satisfy a popular demand. They are almost invariably ugly and horrific: they represent the evil which human nature feels within itself, and which it at once finds fascinating and seeks to repudiate. The persecution of old women alleged to be witches is probably a case of bad conscience coupled with the repulsion of the nerves confronted by extreme old age—not that all alleged witches were old. Yet there have been in Europe and white America cults of witchcraft, and some witches, accused of devoutly kissing the devil's posterior, have ingeniously defended themselves by saying that the devil's are no ordinary buttocks, but an additional and presumably worshipful face.

Gargoyles of carved stone or cast metal are commonly explained as representations of evil spirits being exorcised from consecrated buildings, although their primary function is to act as spouts for the ejection of superfluous rain water. On Greek temples gargoyles were often carved into the shape of lions, and the Romans used terra-cotta casts depicting various animals. The more familiar demoniac monsters still to be seen on many cathedrals are medieval, and probably to be classified with that license of ribaldry which made the devil a figure of fun in many morality plays, encouraged subordinate craftsmen to carve grotesque and satirical heads (some of which may be caricatured portraits of local worthies) on choir-stalls and pew-backs, and even allowed monkish scribes to make droll pictures in the margins of illuminated manuscripts. The Middle Ages, just as certainly as the Renaissance, had its own cult of beauty, and with the cult went its obverse, a rebellious delight in the ugly and the horrific. The painted wooden figureheads which sailing ships carried in the eighteenth and well into the nineteenth century may be viewed as in part a continuation of several traditions, reaching back to the wooden beaks of ships in the classical and Viking periods and also transporting to the sea the separate medieval conceptions of the grotesque carved figure and the colored statue modeled on some attractive young woman but representing the Virgin or a saint to be reverenced. The figureheads of ships, usually larger than life-size, were crudely shaped and crudely painted, and though they were admired, and even cherished, few can be reckoned beautiful. It is said that one figurehead—probably a religious figure, for it came from the prow of a galleon in the Spanish Armada—was washed into a cave on the west coast of Ireland, and within living memory caused scandal among the parish clergy because it became a focus for local superstitions.

Soon after the invention of printing came the etching, the copper or steel engraving, and the woodcut, a much cheaper process which could be used to illustrate comparatively inexpensive books. It was the woodcut, we may assume, even more than the engraving, which made the grotesque fancies of Bosch, Pieter Breughel, Cranach, and Dürer widely known. By the eighteenth century copper engravings had become popular and cheap, and there were print-shops which sold them plain for sixpence each, a shilling if colored by hand. Many of these prints were 'after' pictures in oils, mostly landscapes and portraits, and quite serious if not sentimental in intention. But others were originals and professedly comic and topical; they depicted an amusing situation in everyday life, a pictorial anecdote; or else they portrayed with grotesque distortions some well-known person in public life. The first kind foreshadowed the comic journals which are with us today, from *Punch* to the *New Yorker,* as well as, in cruder form, the serial story 'comic strip.' The second kind of prints was a development of the Italian Renaissance *caricatura,* practiced by Leonardo and Carracci, and later popularized by cheap reproduction and almost exclusively applied to members of the governing classes as they came into the news for one reason or another. A third kind of comic print developed its greatest popularity a little later, although its origin can be traced to woodcuts of the time of the Thirty Years War. This was the political cartoon, which also has since passed from the loose print to the line-block illustration in modern newspapers. The political cartoon often included portrait caricatures of home and foreign statesmen, but also allegorical and symbolic figures like John Bull, Britannia, and, later, Uncle Sam. It was a composition, not a single or group portrait, and it did not so much tell a story as picture a fable.

The British caricaturists of the eighteenth century drew nearly always for the print-shop market. The most successful were Rowlandson and Gillray, neither of them men of refined sensibility—with Rowlandson, to judge from his work, a good deal the coarser. It is possible to conclude from such evidence, and from the contemporary popularity of Smollett's novels, that under its paint and powder eighteenth-century England was pretty brutalized and insensitive. The blubbered, pock-marked, and pimpled faces which Rowlandson delights in are revolting to look at, and it is hard to believe that they were ever regarded as amusing. One has to remember that the British monarchy and the Court in the greater part of the eighteenth century were German, and German-speaking.

Moreover, the intermingling of 'Anglo-Saxon' blood with Irish, Welsh, and Scottish, which had occurred on a minor scale since Tudor times and earlier, had yet to gather impetus when the population at the end of the century began to desert the countryside for the expanding towns. The Industrial Revolution is lamented for many sound reasons, but I have never seen justice done to it for this unintended effect: the new urban populations intermarried, mixing many diverse racial elements, and so the modern English people, almost every one of whom has Celtic blood, while they retain the obstinacy and the gift for political commonsense of their 'Anglo-Saxon' predecessors, are less insular, more imaginative, more sensitive. The mental climate of the twentieth century in Britain is worlds removed from that of Hanoverian England, of which a good deal of the literature, the politics, the social customs—and the popular prints —can hardly be understood unless they are seen as typically Teutonic in their grossness and their grotesquerie.

Caricature nowadays usually dispenses with color and chiaroscuro: its technique is black and white, either in fine line or in washes, where the 'black' may be varied by gray tints applied, in the press reproductions, mechanically. But there has been little alteration in the pictorial devices used for representing human beings with sufficient distortion to make the comic intention clear but not to destroy the likeness. Sometimes the head is enlarged so that it overwhelms the body; sometimes the whole face is thinned (Gillray's method) or fattened (Rowlandson's). More often one feature is selected for enlargement or some other form of undue emphasis. The eighteenth-century device of distorting the face with an angry or agitated expression is not very much in favor nowadays. Symbolic figures, lions, eagles, bears, and stalwart young women in never-never costumes, half classical robes and half armor, are still intermingled with portrait figures in modern dress. Especially in time of war, national and racial characteristics are simplified and exaggerated to form easily identified types, which symbolize, favorably or unfavorably, allies and enemies. The nineteenth-century

Frenchman with gesturing hands, waxed imperial and mustaches, and a shiny silk hat with a tapering crown is rarely seen, but in the European press the English are still often caricatured as men in thick tweeds with a pipe clenched between protruding teeth, as very lanky soldiers in kilts, and as gaunt middle-aged spinsters with heavy boots and a disapproving expression. Paunchy John Bull in breeches, tail-coat, and high boots still represents Britain, and tall, slim, goateed Uncle Sam the United States, although not only the costumes are long out of date but the average Englishman, even before the war, was considerably thinner in face and figure than the average American.

In general, the caricaturist depicts the face by simplification and selection, and from first-hand observation or photographs he evolves a calligraphic formula which he uses over and over again. Repetition produces familiarity, which does not necessarily breed contempt. Caricature—in contemporary Britain, at least—has become kindly, and its indignation is more likely to be directed against abstracts and principles than against individual persons. The caricaturist's formula for public faces soon becomes as well known as the popular tunes of the moment, and people suddenly confronted for the first time with a well-known politician enjoy the diverse pleasures of identifying him by his likeness to newspaper photographs and to newspaper cartoons. The caricature is essentially different from the straight portrait only when it exaggerates its distortions, for none but the most academic and unimaginative portrait painters seek to obtain an exact physical likeness. Whether or not Hogarth was a caricaturist is a subject for argument: Fielding, his contemporary, thought not. But in many of the paintings of Breughel, Brouwer, El Greco, Hogarth, Goya, and Lautrec the elements of distortion and fantastication from which caricature grows can all be traced, while at the other extreme Tiepolo, best known now for his sketches, Daumier, the maker of newspaper cartoons, and Steinlen, the maker of posters, all figure as considerable artists.

It can be argued that all comedy arises from unexpected proportions and juxtapositions. The man in the audience, the reader or the observer, is jolted out of his customary view of things, and startled into laughter. This theory hardly accounts for the fact that many jests owe their success to the fact that they are seen approaching, and theater, music-hall, and even cinema audiences, so far from holding it against a comedian that his routine of merry making is familiar, value his 'business' the more the oftener they have followed it before. But perhaps this has rather to do with social festivity and good humor than with true comedy. The surprise is properly effective only once: repetition makes it familiar, and that arouses pleasant memories and the affections from which friendship is constructed. We laugh because we remember we have been amused in this way before, and we applaud out of sentiment and communal excitement. If the surprise theory of comedy holds good, then farce and burlesque are the theatrical techniques which most closely resemble pictorial caricature. There must be in what goes on on the stage a minimum resemblance to normal human behavior. So long as that remote point of reference is maintained, the more extravagant the comedian's antics the better. And as farce is, in situation and dialogue, highly artificial, the more seriously the players comport themselves, the more amusing they are likely to be—just as, in the standard situation of the comic draftsman, the old gentleman who slips up on a banana skin must be inherently dignified: if he is shown enjoying the joke against himself the onlookers are robbed of half their fun. Similarly, pictorial distortions of the face, whether they are intended to amuse or to horrify, depend for their effect on the observer's having, as a point of reference, a clear conception in his mind of the common standard—what scientists call the norm—of the human face. Consider the drawing of a *Grotesque Head* (Plate XXI, page 203) by Mervyn Peake, whose fantastic and original imagination marks out for this branch of his work a high place in the tradition of Goya and Daumier. Here is a face which does not so much appall as sadden us. It has an air of unviolent idiocy. Its laughter is out of the compass of ordinary amusement. And yet it is only just beyond the limits, and there is enough in this face to remind us of the norm that has been lost, the cheerful, oafish heartiness of a hard-working yokel.

Ghosts and other apparitions, discarnate monsters, depart from the norm in several ways. They are dead, yet they have the mobility of living beings. They may even speak, but in voices notably different from those we hear in everyday intercourse. And though visible, they are not tangible. They have form, they may have color, but they proceed through substantial obstacles like walls and doors, and the investigating hand which endeavors to clutch them closes on nothingness. These are the traditional attributes of phantoms. In addition they often affright us by their faces, which may be pallid masks of death, or skulls, or flesh with a phosphorescent glow. The representation of spirits is almost impossible for sculpture: the solidity of the material forbids. Nor has painting been very success-ful with these subjects. Dürer, Goya, and Fuseli (called by Blake "both Turk and Jew" although he was a stolid Swiss), when they seek to be ghostly, are more impressive in drawings and etchings than in oils. Blake, on the whole, remains the most vivid and con-vincing artist of the supernatural, and this despite the fact that he does not wrap up his spirits in clouds of shadow, or even suggest that their forms are transparent: he straps them with muscles in the classical manner of Michelangelo. The convincing quality of Blake's colored drawings is probably due to the fact that he believed himself to be copying visions manifested to him by a special dis-pensation. When his brother died Blake saw the departing soul rise through the ceiling, "clapping its hands for joy." Walking along the Strand one day, his companion asked to whom he had just taken off his hat, and Blake replied negligently, "Oh, that was the Apostle Paul!" And when he was dying he sang happily, one of his friends reports, of "the things he saw in heaven."

Coleridge, another visionary, but more dependent on dreams, im-parted his conception of the supernatural rather by means of the sound and rhythm of words than through specific imagery. We know little of what Kubla Khan looked like beyond

> His flashing eyes, his floating hair.

And the phantasmic woman on the ghost ship in *The Ancient Mariner*—

> Her lips were red, her looks were free,
> Her locks were yellow as gold:
> Her skin was as white as leprosy,
> The Nightmare Life-in-Death was she,
> Who thicks man's blood with cold——

is little more than a vivification of the conventional moralist's conventional warning to young men. Her place is in the long queue with the Strange Woman of the Old Testament, the Scarlet Woman of the Book of Revelation, Faustus's Helen of Troy, and all the feminine vessels of sin who are so much more alluring in print than in real life.

Shakespeare, who could always bring his feet down to earth when he wished, whether or not he believed in ghosts, was able to make them credible on the stage. In *Hamlet* the ghost speaks: he is not merely an apparition, but a character who actively influences the plot, and attention is drawn to the pallor of his face and his "sable silvered" beard. In *Macbeth* the apparitions are multiplied, yet none of them speaks except under the magic conjurations of the weird sisters. For the most part they are figments of Macbeth's disordered mind, and Macbeth is obsessed by faces. Stage by stage he builds up the details of his vision of the murdered Banquo, reporting its ghostly appearance to his guests who cannot see what he sees: its "gory locks," its silence, its communications by nods, its general aspect which "might appall the devil," its glaring but lifeless eyes. At the end, when Fate gathers vengefully around him, and he feels that there is no deliverance, Macbeth's obsession, fed upon murders and apparitions, grows more powerful. He rounds on the servant who comes to bring him ill news with one con-

temptuous and hysterical reference after another to his fear-stricken
face:

MACBETH. The devil damn thee black, thou cream-faced loon!
            Where got'st thou that goose-look?
SERVANT. There is ten thousand——
MACBETH.   Geese, villain?
SERVANT.   Soldiers, sir.
MACBETH. Go, prick thy face, and over-red thy fear,
            Thou lily-livered boy. What soldiers, patch?
            Death of thy soul! those linen cheeks of thine
            Are counsellors to fear. What soldiers, whey-face?
SERVANT. The English force, so please you.
MACBETH. Take thy face hence.

A little later he is killed by Macduff, and the play, a tragedy
written in the crimson of bloodshed and the pallor of fear, ends
with Macbeth's severed head brought on to the stage, red with blood
and white in death, its eloquent tongue silenced, its greed satiated,
and as little speculation in its eyes as in those of the vision of
Banquo which once affrighted it.

Ghosts are monsters, their faces necessarily blank or distorted.
They are evoked out of the fear of death, both the act of severance
from the body and the unknown that lies beyond the dying moment. The faces of ghosts are corpse-faces on which the awed and
sickened imagination has played. They are the obverse of the fanciful revolt against normality which produces caricature. Sometimes
an additional twist is given to the monstrosity by endowing it with
the substance and faculties of living humanity. The cinema, which
can play endless illusionist tricks with the three dimensions and
depends for much of its success on the human face, has been quick
to seize the opportunities offered by the imaginative conception of
monsters. It has dramatized the neurotic mind in *The Cabinet of
Doctor Caligari,* in *The Golem* and *Dr Mabuse,* in *The Student
of Prague, Warning Shadows,* and *M;* it has used spirits for charm
and comedy in *The Ghost Goes West,* and, after the stage play,

Blithe Spirit; and more realistically, though not more satisfactorily, it has exploited the idea of the human or pseudo-human monster in *Frankenstein, Dr Jekyll and Mr Hyde, The Invisible Man,* and *King Kong.*

Nevertheless, most people lack the visionary's ability of compelling the senses to perceive what exists only in the mind, and when phantasms and monstrosities are projected, however skillfully, into the material world they lose some of their power. The private vision of horror can best be communicated to others through words, injected by symbols which need to be reinterpreted in the receptive mind. No one has done this more effectively than James Joyce (who at the other end of his imaginative tether is as earth-bound as Shakespeare) in the 'Nighttown' phantasmagoria in *Ulysses.* This unacted and perhaps unactable drama begins and ends with a realistic encounter, in a disreputable Dublin slum, between the young Stephen Dædalus (or Joyce) and the middle-aged Leopold Bloom, a newspaper-canvasser of Hungarian-Jewish descent. The middle, and much the longer, part of the action, however, is occupied by a compost of decaying memories, fears, desires, shames, and glorifications, all hallucinatory, all taking place in Bloom's mind. Not only people but personified and voluble objects appear to him in this superbly variable and horrific waking nightmare, and among them is the corpse of Stephen's mother: "emaciated . . . in leper gray with a wealth of faded orange-blossoms and a torn bridal veil, her face worn and noseless, green with grave mould." Joyce was as obsessed with death and guilt as with sex and the excretory organs of the body.

But the most terrible aspect of this protracted scene is not the apparitions which rise and gibber in Bloom's mind (at times seemingly identified with Stephen's), but the fact that over and over again, as his neuroses are laid bare, Bloom changes not merely his appearance but sometimes his identity. He reverts to his adolescent self in a "Youth's smart blue Oxford suit with white vest-slips, narrow-shouldered, in brown Alpine hat, wearing gent's sterling silver waterbury keyless watch and double curb Albert with seal attached." Then, older but still young, he is a "squire of dames, in dinner jacket with watered silk facings, blue masonic badge in his buttonhole, black bow and mother-of-pearl studs, a prismatic champagne glass tilted in his hand." At other times he wears a purple Napoleon hat; an oatmeal sports suit; a red fez, a lascar's vest and trousers (here he has "tiny mole's eyes"); workmen's corduroy overalls with an apache cap; the crimson velvet robe of a Lord Mayor elect; the seamless garment of a martyr; the caubeen hat of the Irish emigrant of drawing-room ballads; Svengali's fur overcoat (here he has an "eagle glance"); a 'juvenile' suit striped black and gray, with a red school cap; and the plum plush breeches and powdered wig of a footman. He is put in the pillory, with ass's ears clapped on his head, like Bottom; when a harlot calls him a baby he appears at once "in baby linen and pelisse, big-headed, with a caul of dark hair," with big eyes and a moist tongue lolling out; and when he speaks he lisps infantile babble. And at one point Bloom changes his sex and is transformed into "a charming soubrette," but with "large male hands and nose" and a "leering mouth": compared with these giddy transformations the hobgoblin, "hydrocephalic, prognathic with receding forehead and Ally Sloper nose" is sane, traditional, innocuous. One function is common to the caricature, the monster and the apparition, and all forms of the grotesque: they reconcile us to the normal human face despite its countless limitations and deficiencies.

CHAPTER NINE

MASKS AND TRANSFORMATIONS

IT IS possible to use one's reading to provide furniture for the mind or ready cash for the exchanges of social conversation, and there are people who can make lengthy quotations impromptu from their favorite authors. This social accomplishment is not, to my mind—but then I lack it myself—so rewarding as the ability to take endless mental stimulus from what has been memorably but succinctly expressed, to "ponder these things in the heart." Passages from books which, unaided by conscious effort, linger in the memory afford their own satisfaction; if, moreover, they have the appropriate quality they also leave stings and seedlings in the mind. Hardly a week goes by, for example, but I find myself recalling and studying something from the Bible, from Shakespeare or Donne or Keats, from Dostoievski or Tolstoi, from Shaw or Joyce or Blake. These seem to be the authors on whom I draw for sustenance and stimulus most often, and I dare say it is not a very far-flung or fashionable list: no Baudelaire or Rimbaud or Kirkegaard, no Pascal, no Kafka. If I have made a confession no doubt some will hold it against me and mark me off as heading for the limbo of old-fogeyism, and I shall not be saved by remembering at this last moment to include Yeats and Proust.

Of all this familiar reading Blake occupies the smallest bulk, and it is very rarely that I do more than skip through the prophetic books: to me Blake means the lyrics and the epigrams. For years I have puzzled over one short lyric, not a very good one, which Blake included in a letter dated August 16, 1803. It refers to certain quarrels with his friends, and begins:

> Oh, why was I born with a different face?
> Why was I not born like the rest of my race?

The use of the word 'different' here is odd. It is employed by Blake as an absolute adjective of description, needing no preposition and noun to complete the sense, and in this function it seems to belong to contemporary American slang, not to the time in which Blake lived or the Elizabethan period from which he drew most of his poetic vocabulary. Even if the solecism is accepted as just another of Blake's premature modernities, the awkward couplet sticks in the mind: it expresses so directly one of the recurring dissatisfactions of human nature, and the vain desire (which is at the back of a good deal of 'exhibitionist' behavior) to escape from an established personality into another. Because the face identifies the individual, this dissatisfaction and wish for change often takes the form of adopting an artificial false face with which to go out into the world. The disguises of detectives and criminals fascinate children, and among their favorite toys are sure to be papier-mâché or cardboard masks. There is also a long tradition of fables about great princes, from Haroun el Raschid onward, who, weary of the pomp and publicity of their status, go out among the common sort, unrecognized because they conceal or disguise their faces. The encounter between Shakespeare's Henry V and the private soldiers on the eve of Agincourt depends for its irony and bite on the fact that the king is not recognized. Disguises and mistaken identities are scattered all through Shakespeare, from Viola wooing Olivia by faint-hearted proxy to Romeo wandering masked among the Capulets in order to fall in love with Juliet. Half the charm of amateur theatricals (for the players) lies in the excitement of escape from everyday identity; and when the classical gods metamorphosed themselves into mortal shepherds and bulls and swans we may be sure that those who invented the legends were letting off the leash their own desires for protean changes of appearance. To acquire another face is to become another person, to be born again, without the birth-pangs and the helplessness of infancy. It cannot be done in nature, but any illusion of achieving it is everywhere attractive. A prospect of novel adventure is opened up, whether the face is transformed, concealed, or half concealed.

The history of the face-veil (except in one Arab tribe, the Tuareg, worn exclusively by women) is a fine study in the adaptation of motives. The veil was at first merely the upper part of a loose mantle covering the whole body; then it became a separate garment draping the head and shoulders; finally two garments, head-veil and a face-veil. All three variations are still in use in Moslem countries. The original purpose of the veil was simply exclusive: it marked a woman as the property of one man, her father or her husband. It prevented other men from seeing her face. It was a portable and personal harem, for Moslems, whose religion by no means prohibits sensuality, are severely logical in concentrating the sense of feminine modesty in the face. Moslem veils are worn only outdoors, and discarded inside the harem quarters. In Egypt peasant women, who use the folds of their long black cotton robes to provide an improvised veil, if they are caught off their guard by the approach of a man will pull the robe up over their heads, leaving the lower part of their bodies bare. The original Moslem veil, or burka, covering the face below the eyes downward, was black and opaque; the veil of thin, semi-transparent white muslin possibly came from Turkey, and for long has been popular with well-to-do women. A variation is the Turkish yashmak, which is head-veil and face-veil in one. In sunlight the white veil reveals quite clearly the shape and color of the cheeks, nose, mouth, and chin. It makes no more than a polite pretense of concealment, and is an ideal instrument for coquetry, for it lends an air of mystery to the face just sufficient to invite inquisitive and philandering glances. In Turkey the veil has gone. In the cities of Egypt, Palestine, Syria, and India it has been abandoned by many women. Thus the white semi-transparent veil can now be seen as an intermediary stage on the way to emancipation from the harem, the West making its influence felt at last on the Orient. Yet it was doubtless extraneous Oriental associations which brought the veil, along with Christianity, to the dissolving and reforming Roman Empire. In the Dark Ages women often went veiled outdoors and within the churches, although the emphasis was placed on concealing the hair rather than the face. From the veil, the wimple and the high, stiff linen headdress developed. Compulsory asceticism was quickly turned to decorative effect.

The Renaissance encouraged women, or at least ladies of birth and position, to glory in their hair and to expose their faces, but a little later a charming and even more coquettish substitute had been found, in the eye-mask, which is not strictly a mask at all. Made from a narrow strip of velvet or silk, with holes cut where it fits over the eyes, and fastened behind the head with tapes or bands, the eye-mask remains indissolubly associated with Venetian carnivals of the seventeenth and eighteenth centuries. It was worn by both men and women; and by night at least, on the piazzas and canals and in crowded ballrooms lit by candles, it provided, if not a disguise (a domino or loose-fitting robe was usually worn as well, to baffle identification), an enchanting sense of anonymity. Made of white or black cloth, it left a great part of the face exposed, so that both lady and gallant could be sure they were not wasting the philandering hours upon someone old or ill-favored, but it covered enough to mystify and to make the final removal of the mask, in the privacy of a gondola cabin or some secret apartment, an adventure almost as intimate as what the discreetly scandalous chroniclers of the period call "the granting of the last favors."

It is said by some that eye-masks first came into use in Renaissance Italy, rather deeper in shape than afterwards, as shields to safeguard the delicate complexions of ladies against the blaze of the sun, and they were used for this purpose, in the carriage or the garden, by young ladies throughout the eighteenth century and well into Victorian times. Whether or not its original purpose was to protect the complexion, the eye-mask attained its highest popularity in Venice and elsewhere as a device for promoting flirtation and intrigue. It goes with moonlight, with the laughing encounter and the well-planned rendezvous, with the shadowed walls, the arched bridges, the fluttering flags and romantic cloaked figures of the little exquisitely sketchy capriccios of Guardi and Tiepolo. It survives in the language in the more eloquent name for a masked ball—masquerade. It was used to more utilitarian purpose also, by highwaymen and footpads who did not wish to be put too often to the inconvenience of killing those they robbed lest they should afterwards provide the magistrates with a description by which the criminals might be caught. In this function the eye-mask lasted right into the middle of the nineteenth century, for, with the dark (or shuttered) lantern and the jemmy, it was part of the professional equipment of Charles Peace and other burglars, whose sordid habits have since been made picturesque by the passage of time and the growth of legend. The masks worn by the public executioners, who regarded themselves as master craftsmen and to a certain extent made their office hereditary, were rather larger, covering most of the face. Only on special occasions was the identity of the executioner a secret: to this day no one knows who beheaded Charles I.

The 'Man in the Iron Mask,' about whose identity so many novelists and critics have speculated, in all probability wore no more substantial disguise than an eye-mask of black velvet. The device was not uncommon in seventeenth-century France, when it was thought expedient to conceal the identity of a prisoner and yet allow him to take exercise occasionally in places where he might be seen by the general public. Often the prisoner himself did not wish to be recognized, and wore the mask voluntarily; otherwise he could always be intimidated into wearing it by threats of torture and execution. The man in the mask of legendary iron was a prisoner in the Bastille from September 18, 1698 (he was brought there from an island fortress near Cannes), until November 19, 1703, when he died. He was buried next day, and the entry in the parish register gives his name as Marchioly, and his age as about forty-five. There can be little doubt that he was a political prisoner, confined by the direct order of Louis XIV, and various guesses at his identity were made while he was still alive and for long afterwards. He was said by the Princess Palatinate to be an English nobleman who had conspired against William III. Voltaire suggested he was an illegitimate brother of Louis XIV, born to Anne of Austria and Mazarin, and put away as a possible rival for the throne of France. By 1790 he had become a legitimate brother, and a twin, of Louis XIV, and eleven years later it was alleged that while in prison he had a son born to him, who grew up to settle in Corsica, took the name of de Buona Parte, and became the ancestor of Napoleon. He was even identified with the rebel Duke of Monmouth (who was beheaded in 1685, thirteen years before the masked prisoner arrived in the Bastille) and with Molière. Later theories make him out to be either a Count Mattioli, an Italian who doublecrossed the French King over the sale of a fortress, Eustache Daugier, who may or may not have been a valet, or James de la Cloche, one of those select natural sons whom Charles II in his merry monarchical moods chose to acknowledge, but without overmuch publicity. Who he was will probably never be certainly known: his misfortune and his mask are his only genuine claims to a place in history, and if he did not die to make a Roman holiday his story has since contributed to the livelihood of several novelists.

The full face-veil was probably always used by women when traveling in summer along dusty highways before asphalt and the municipal water-sprinkling wagon came into general use, and in the days of the early open motorcar women attired themselves for the journey—speed limit twenty miles an hour—not only in long dustcoats down to the ankles but by draping over the whole head, including a wide-brimmed and high-crowned hat, yards and yards of fine-meshed motor-veiling. Before then, however, the veil had come into fashion purely as a decoration. It was a veil with a difference, woven of fine silk or cotton, but usually fairly wide in mesh, for except on widow's weeds and heavy veils used by women keeping assignations (the four-wheeler cab driving discreetly to the door of the little house in the side street) its true purpose was not to conceal but to set off the face: just as a pumpkin may look more attractive netted in a string bag than exposed for sale on the bare boards of a shop counter.

The late-Victorian and the Edwardian lady often went out in daylight wearing a veil on which she had expended not only much money but a good deal of time and forethought in the choice. The veil was square or oblong. It fitted over the brim of the hat and was pulled tight in front of the face, the tip of the nose and sometimes the lips just touching the mesh, to fasten under the chin. It might be of any one of numerous colors: black (and not at all funereal), red, green, blue, brown, rarely yellow, and not often white. It might have designs woven through the mesh, like lacework, or it might be ornamented with opaque dots, of the same or a different color; sometimes these dots were made of glistening metallic threads like gold or silver or blue sequins. The effect was comparable to that of the Venetian eye-mask: something was withheld from view, and an air of mystery imparted. A handsome face behind a veil became majestic; a beautiful face was invested with an additional piquancy; and a pretty one seemed beautiful. In restaurants and teashops the veil would be unfastened and lifted up to fold on the hatbrim so that the teacup, the bread and butter, and the chocolate éclairs could reach the mouth; and this utilitarian rite also could be made into an act of indulgent intimacy, like the removal of the eye-mask at a gallant's persistent demand. In the last ten years or so the veil has returned to fashion, in a modified form: at first it was worn to hang loose but straight from the hatbrim, either just to cover the eyes or to touch the nose, but is now more often fastened tight under the chin. The charm of the old style made something of a 'sensation' on the London stage in 1942, when Vivien Leigh was playing Mrs. Dubedat in an Edwardian-dressed production of *The Doctor's Dilemma,* and in the first act came on wearing, over a tilted rose-adorned hat, a full veil of open black mesh which roused sighs of nostalgic memory from all the old gentlemen in the audience.

The mask proper, which fits close over the whole face or even over the whole head, and provides either a duplicate or an alternative for the real face, has a very long history. Possibly its origin is the death-mask, a mold taken by pressing clay or wet plaster or a metallic foil over the face of the recently dead. In the ancient world death-masks were either preserved as molded or used to make portrait-busts, and so had their place in the early development of art and in that aspect of primitive religion which cultivated ancestor-worship. Life-masks were also made, by similar methods (the subject closing his eyes and vents being left for breathing), from very early times. But the mask which is designed to be worn as a kind of alternative face belongs to drama and to the rituals of magic and war. It played an important part in primitive cultures in many parts of the world, including Negro Africa, 'Red Indian' America, India, China, Japan, Ancient Egypt, and Maori New Zealand. Probably the mask began as a kind of helmet made from drying an animal's head and stretching it on a wooden frame, and from this developed helmet-masks of stone, pottery, metal, carved wood, painted with conventional devices. Such masks were worn in ritual dances, for propitiating gods and demons, in wardances preparatory to battle, and in battle itself to terrify the enemy. They were also often exhibited as objects of worship.

The actors' masks worn in Greece and later in Rome were hollow helmets, considerably larger than the natural human head. They may be regarded as foreshadowing the cinematic device of the closeup, for their purpose was to make the various characters, drawn from familiar myths or legends, immediately recognizable even to the back rows of the audience in the large openair amphitheaters. These dramatic masks were fitted with metal mouthpieces intended to make the actors' voices carry farther, so that to some extent they were also prototypes of the microphone and amplifier. Because the theater mask could portray only one facial expression, the technique of acting was confined to speech, to movement about the stage, and to gestures, and in the Roman theater there was at last a revolt against this limitation. The players began to dispense with masks, but they returned to favor, either because the public disapproved of the break with tradition or else because, as some say, the great actor Roscius insisted on masks, he himself being disfigured by a squint.

Greek and Roman dramatic masks were conceived in three types: tragic, comic, and satiric, of which the last was the most grotesque. Conventionalized, tragic and comic masks often are incorporated in the decorations of theaters today. In the Italian Commedia dell' Arte, which flourished from Renaissance times to the eighteenth century and was improvised, with a good deal of miming, from outlined stories or scenarios, the male players wore masks, but these were, however crudely, designed to characterize much more fully than the classical masks the parts undertaken by the actors. Harlequin wore not only a patchwork costume but a black mask, and was perhaps originally a Negro. Pantaloon, neatly described by Shakespeare as "lean and slipper'd . . . with spectacles on nose . . . and his big manly voice turning toward childish treble," wore a brown mask with a big nose, spectacles, mustaches, and a long, thin white beard. The Doctor, an absurd cuckold, had a mask which covered only his forehead and his nose, but his cheeks were painted a bright red. On the mask of Pulcinello, the ancestor of Punch, the most prominent feature was a big, thin, hook nose, colored red, and it was only towards the close of the seventeenth century that he was made a hunchback and given cocks' feathers to wear in his hat. The Commedia dell'Arte introduced women characters, inamoratas, soubrettes, duennas, matrons, played by women, perhaps the first actresses of the European stage; but they did not wear masks.

Thereafter the mask disappears from the drama and, except for the eye-mask worn by robbers, and at masked balls, and masks and false noses worn facetiously at carnivals or parties, it disappears also from everyday life. But the fascination of the artificial face, the alternative to the solitary choice offered by nature, remains. Theatrical makeup, the use of cosmetics, shaving, the trimming of beards and mustaches to different shapes, affectations of facial expression, are all attempts to create a false face not so easily detectable as a mask. The face being, by common consent, the most accessible index to the mind, we all feel that if it can be altered a new and improved personality will be acquired. This somewhat pathetic human yearning forms the basis for two fantastic stories, each in its way a modern myth, which retain their grip on the imagination. It is worth noting that both were written in the *fin-de-siècle,* or decadent, period, when the literary imagination was obsessed, however artificially, by the problem of the fascination of sin and the dual nature of man. In *The Picture of Dorian Gray* Oscar Wilde told the story of a man magically exempted from the natural law by which debauchery in due time reveals its effects in the face. His portrait ages and grows wicked; he himself remains young and apparently innocent. Despite the tinsel style in which it is written, *Dorian Gray* is a moral tale, and follows an ancient tradition in bringing the sinful man in the end to calamity and retribution: the characters of the painted face and the face of flesh and blood are violently reversed. In *The Happy Hypocrite,* Sir Max Beerbohm's Regency fantasy, a nice variation of this theme is achieved: the wicked man, being granted a false face of innocence, falls sincerely and happily in love and learns the charm of unsophistication: a different face produces a different nature.

When we strive to understand those who lived in ages remote from us we come up against the same problem in a different aspect. Carlyle said that when he undertook any biographical study he set out first to obtain a contemporary picture of the man whose life he intended to write: the portrait told him more than stacks of historical documents. This method of interpretation, even of living faces, invites endless potentialities of error, as will be discussed later on. But Carlyle was a highly subjective historian, not likely to be bothered if he read into the past what was in fact never there. Different people will 'read' the same face in very different ways, and portraits of historical personages may be technically incompetent, or, consciously or unconsciously, flattering. Nor are they always adequately authenticated. Among the many portraits of Queen Elizabeth, for example, some, it is fairly certain, were never painted from the life, and others are quite likely not contemporary at all. And of the residue, in sum total they tell us little about the great Queen except that she was thin, regal, and red-haired, and wore elaborately ornamented gowns and rich jewelry. We cannot be sure whether she always retained the natural redness of her hair or whether it was dyed in her later years; nor do we know if the pink in her cheeks, as depicted in any particular portrait, was her own or came out of a pot. Without the testimony of gossips, the royal portraits would be extremely dumb and recalcitrant witnesses to the character of the Queen.

Shakespeare is another example of inadequate portraiture. The only picture of him which can with any degree of reliability be regarded as authentic is the engraving by Martin Droeshout which forms the frontispiece to the First Folio edition of the plays, issued in 1623, seven years after his death. The memorial bust in the church at Stratford-on-Avon is obviously posthumous, though the face may have been modeled from a death-mask or from the First Folio engraving eked out by the criticisms and suggestions of local inhabitants. Neither portrait has much merit as a work of art, though both have been excessively depreciated by enthusiasts looking, in vain, for a face resplendent with the grace and genius of the world's foremost poet. Engraving and bust clearly represent the same man, the only notable difference being that in the bust he is a little balder, his mustache is fuller and curls upward at the ends, and besides the tuft of hair under the lower lip he has a short chin-beard. The face of Shakespeare thus immortalized is long and smooth, with a high, domelike forehead, narrow, arching eyebrows, heavily lidded eyes, a fairly large but not ill-shaped nose, a wide mouth whose shape may be interpreted as either sensual or good-humored, and a rounded chin. The delineatory outline of the whole face describes an elongated oval, varied only by the indentations beside the eyes. Sufficient physical comeliness is represented to give substance to Aubrey's rather post-dated assertion that Shakespeare was "a handsome, well-shaped man," but of wit, imagination, creative power, fancy, passion, intellect, there is little or no evidence in either engraving or bust. Shakespeare, on this basis, must have been pudding-faced and dull-eyed. And so—for we must face facts—he may have been, at any rate towards the end of his life: a man of ponderous moods. Some outraged students, faced with the Droeshout engraving, have argued that it is either not a genuine portrait of Shakespeare or else that Shakespeare was not the author of the works ascribed to him. But there is no need to rush to such extreme conclusions.

It is worthwhile taking into account Ben Jonson, Shakespeare's devoted friend "this side idolatry." Writers, unless they happened also to be aristocrats or men of affairs, were not held to be of much account in the England of the sixteenth and seventeenth centuries. They did not make fortunes or cut a figure in society. They were not sought out as subjects for portraits. For the matter of that, English art was in low water, and such good painters as there were in London came from abroad. There are no portraits at all of Marlowe, of Webster, of Dekker, of Beaumont and Fletcher. We know as little, or less, of their private lives as we do of Shakespeare's. And the anonymous portrait, painted on a small panel, of Ben Jonson himself, which is now in the National Portrait Gallery, reveals little more of the sitter's character than Martin Droeshout's engraving. Skilled artists depicted notabilities—and Shakespeare, to his contemporaries, however popular his plays and however he might pride himself on obtaining a grant of arms, was neither statesman, courtier, soldier, nor even an alderman of the City of London. If his portrait was painted while he lived, most likely the job was done by some inferior workman or an amateur. Perhaps Martin Droeshout, himself a clumsy engraver, worked from such a portrait, or from a death-mask—or merely from descriptions and rough sketches furnished by men who had known Shakespeare and remembered him seven years after his death. One thing is certain: Ben Jonson had no high opinion of the likeness in the First Folio. He says as much, in a roundabout, formal way, in the verses printed over his initials opposite the engraving:

> This Figure, that thou here seest put,
>   It was for gentle Shakespeare cut:
> Wherein the Graver had a strife
>   With Nature, to out-doo the life:
> O, could he but have drawne his wit
>   As well in brasse, as he hath hit
> His face; the Print would then surpasse
>   All that was ever writ in brasse.
> But, since he cannot, Reader, looke
>   Not on his Picture, but his Booke.

In interpreting this we have to remember that Ben Jonson may very well not have been familiar with good pictures or a sound judge of what pictures he knew. It seems that he considered the Droeshout engraving solely for its faithfulness as a portrait of Will Shakespeare, and what he is telling us, surely, is that it gives the physical facts but not the vitality, the spirit or the character of the man. To know Shakespeare as he was, you must read what he wrote. That advice still holds good.

Portraiture is comparatively a modern art, little older than the novel. It has indeed much in common with the novel, for the novel is not just a story which happens to be told in prose and at some length, but a story which illuminates character and personality. In the classical world and the Eastern civilizations which preceded it, in the Dark Ages and the Medieval period, the mind was simpler, less introspective, and more taken for granted than it has ever been since. It was an instrument used for specific purposes in the business of living, but not itself examined with any close or sustained interest. The apparent exceptions to this generalization are Greek philosophy and religious mysticism, but in both these activities the mind was employed, subtly and skillfully, to an end. The beginnings of that comprehensive and highly intricate science which is applied by everyone every day—psychology—can be traced in Greek and Latin texts, but they are no more than beginnings. This is not to say that human nature was radically different then from what it is now: it was merely unselfconscious. The distinction can be clearly marked by comparing the great narrative literature of the different periods. In Homer, Sophocles, Vergil, Rabelais, Dante, Malory, Boccaccio, the interest—apart from verbal beauty—lies in the story, and the story is made up of what people do and say. Their emotions and their motives, so far as they are explained at all, are simple, direct, unambiguous. Character is sketched in outline, and the reader of today is continually tempted to read more into the people in the story than the author put in. That is one reason why the literature of the ancient world appears to us myth-like in its essential nature: the stories belong to the common stock, and every age feels free to elaborate and reinterpret them in its own way.

It would need a considerable work of scholarship to track down exactly when the change in emphasis began, when writers and their public shifted the interest from action (which may include speech) to the secret workings of the mind. But for convenience we shall not go far wrong if we regard Chaucer as the first of the moderns, and the Wife of Bath as a character study—the revelations being made in the first person—such as later became a mainstay of fiction. It is Shakespeare, however, who is, if not the father, at least the uncle—the benevolent uncle leaving behind him rich legacies—of the modern novel. The range of his explorative voyage into a new world of the mind—a new world infinitely more important than that discovered by Columbus or whoever it was reached America first—can be appreciated by reading some of the originals from which Shakespeare worked. He used Plutarch, in North's translation, when he was writing *Julius Cæsar, Antony and Cleopatra* and even *A Midsummer Night's Dream*. He used Holinshed's *Chronicles* for *Richard II, Henry IV,* and other historical plays, and Boccaccio for *Cymbeline* and *All's Well That Ends Well*. Now, it is not sufficient to say that Shakespeare was a mighty genius who transformed his borrowings out of all recognition. The point is that he retold old stories in an utterly new way. He peopled them with characters which so vividly disclose their inward nature that they are better known to us than most of the people we see and talk to every day. And that was something that had never happened in the world before. Humanity began to discover itself, and it is from Shakespeare, the poetic dramatist, rather than from any prose or verse story-teller that the modern novel, whose outstanding characteristic is the analysis of hidden motive, the novel of Dostoievski and Proust and Joyce, originates. Possibly, too, the modern biography (which, as Mr Peter Quennell has pointed out, begins with Boswell, a good Shakespearean) derives from the same slowly operating stimulus.

The portrait, created like all pictorial art within the dimensions of space and compelled to leave time out of count, cannot compete with the novel in range and complexity. Its function is limited to the depiction of human appearance at one chosen moment, but within these confinements it is able to make a very powerful impact on the imagination. It can achieve psychological analysis and synthesis. And, in fact, the portrait which reveals character and temperament preceded, in time, both Shakespeare and Chaucer. Less than a century after Boccaccio worked out in his *Decameron* tale after tale all dependent on plot, with one hero or heroine hardly to be distinguished from another, painters in Florence and other Italian cities were recording the faces of their contemporaries with such a subtle appreciation of the interplay between spirit and flesh that, looking at the pictures now, even in small reproductions, we feel we know the long-since dead men and women almost as intimately and fully as we know Falstaff, Hamlet, and Viola. The only trouble with Renaissance portraiture is that it was almost exclusively devoted to people of position, important where they lived and when they lived, but not always identical with the people of the period we should like to know about. And when a religious picture, or a composition on a mythical or legendary subject, incorporates portraits which interest us, all too often the identity of the models, still more their personal history, must remain unknown. It is only from the eighteenth century onward that we have any reliable store of portraits of all the great personalities: and even so the members of Parliament, the inheritors of peerages, the stockbrokers and company promoters, with their women and children—worthy folk, perhaps, but unexciting—far outnumber the gay, the powerful, the eccentric spirits who have other claims to immortality beyond the ability to pay a portrait painter's fee.

Earlier than the Renaissance all is oblivion and dubiety. What pass for the portrait busts of Plato, Socrates, Sophocles and Euripides, Julius Cæsar and Virgil are doubtfully contemporary and doubtfully identified as portraits of those great men. There is nothing to show what face Homer had, or even, to leap far forward in time, Rabelais or Villon, St Augustine or Abélard; and we have not one contemporary portrait of any person in the Biblical narratives, from the patriarchs to St Paul. The old world survives in monuments, traditions, and later copies of early texts. But it is a world filled with false faces or missing faces. Just where character and temperament should be most visible there is always a blank space. But human nature is not made to be content with such voids in knowledge, and what the record has omitted each of us fills in by the exercise of the imagination. We people the headless myths with portraits of our own devising. When the physical sight is baffled there is an inward eye which conjures up its own visions, perhaps more satisfactory than the images of actuality would have been. Most remarkable of all this belated portraiture, as will be shown in the next chapter, are the varied efforts of different ages to create and stabilize the facial appearance of Jesus Christ, of whom we have not only no contemporary portrait but not even, in all the four gospels, the briefest incidental description.

CHAPTER TEN

GOOD AND EVIL

DISTINCTIONS between good and evil may be broad and self-evident, or fine, elusive, perceptible only after the scrupulous weighings and balancings of casuistry. And whether good and evil are absolute or relative values, whether evil exists except as a negation and defiance of established good, whether good can be known as good without the contrast of evil, these are questions for theologians and philosophers to argue. For the present purpose—which is to consider the manifestations of these opposed qualities in the human face—it can be assumed that a distinctive conception of good and evil, clear enough for empirical use, exists in every adult mind. If more precise definitions and discriminations are needed they will be attempted as the argument proceeds. Few will deny that human faces communicate to those who look at them intimations of good and evil. One face, both in repose and in mutability, may convey a comprehensive impression of goodness; another, an impression of active or passive evil. More often, the same face will express at the same time both good and evil, or it may vary with mood and occasion, one quality alternatively prevailing over the other. Moods transform faces, and an evil that normally is latent, scarcely discernible, in certain circumstances will take possession of the face and make it, in a style and on a scale either petty or grand, an unintended exhibition of vice. On the other hand, there are faces which reveal no remarkable qualities at all, faces blanked out to a commonplace incommunicative average, until some crisis of personal life wakens them into a manifestation of unsuspected virtues. Good and evil in the face are, with most people, associated with another contrast of quality, between beauty and ugliness; but this is stretching words to cover widely different meanings, for the 'beauty' of goodness is not identical with physical beauty, and the 'ugliness' of evil is not necessarily repugnant to the senses, and, given dynamic intensity, may be invested with a kind of unmaterial beauty, that of power or diabolism.

These overlappings of our mental conceptions, good and beauty, evil and ugliness, may best be understood as so many aspects of that quest for ultimate truth (a principle, not a collection of facts) which is the most fundamental and persistent purpose in human history; and Keats may not after all have been clanging the empty vase of a platitude when he proclaimed that "Beauty is truth, truth beauty." The unending quest is twofold in its nature, and with the discovery of ultimate truth mankind undoubtedly seeks for itself spiritual and physical perfection: that is to say, the consummation of the qualities we call goodness and beauty. For it should be noted that, however resolutely and lucidly we distinguish in our minds between physical and spiritual beauty, in practice, and especially in the unconscious assumptions by which most of our behavior is directed, again and again we unite the two into one.

This integrating tendency can clearly be seen in the almost universal assumption that certain configurations of the face, certain shapings and proportions of the features, symbolize definite traits of character. For example, large, well-shaped eyes, set well apart, are taken to indicate sincerity, candor, honesty. A wide mouth, with lips neither thick nor thin, to most people means a generous nature; and a prominent chin, particularly if it be slightly squared, stands for determination. Conversely, small eyes, set close to the nose, are regarded as a sign of cunning and treachery; eyes over which the upper lids droop, half concealing them, betoken suspicion; and for eyes which avoid the direct glance of other eyes, moving their focus to some other object, we have an adjective, 'shifty,' which implies an adverse moral judgment. In this rough-and-ready system of interpreting motives and characteristics from the physical appearance of the face (it is in use every day almost everywhere) a long nose with a thin, pointed end is infallibly the sign of undue curiosity, the mark of the Paul Pry clan; thick lips mean sensuality; thin ones meanness or envy; and a narrow mouth indicates self-righteousness. And notoriously a small or receding chin stands for a weak will, a habit of indecision.

Such judgments are unfair. The shape and configuration of the face are physical accidents, the products of heredity, influenced to a minor extent by health and environment, but hardly at all by character. If by taking thought it is impossible to add a cubit to one's stature, it is equally impossible to enlarge the eyes or the mouth, to alter the shape of the nose or to transform a 'weak' chin into a 'strong' one. The physical appearance is inherited; the heir may be grateful (he has no right to be proud) or indignant, but it is manifestly unjust to blame him for what he did not make and cannot alter. Predictions and condemnations of this kind belong to the same order of irrationality as those racial and social prejudices which condemn people for being born to Jewish or Negro parents, or even for being natives of certain parts of the world. This method of interpreting the physical form of the face as an indication of character is not only unjust; it is fallacious. One does not have to live long in the world, provided one keeps the mind alert, to discover that people with small, close-set eyes may be devoid of cunning, that a hero may have a 'weak' chin and a poltroon a 'strong' one, that "a man may smile and smile, and be a villain." Life is not so simple as many proverbs and rule-of-thumb philosophies would have us believe.

But if experience gives the lie to this method of relating the physical accidents of appearance to personal character, how has the system come into use, and why, in defiance of justice and observation, does it persist in all of us, whether or not we make efforts to discount it? There are, I suggest, three answers to this question, each complementary to the others. For one thing, humanity, intent upon its age-old quest for ultimate perfection, feels in the depths of its instincts that beauty ought to be identical with goodness, and therefore that people whose faces are physically attractive should possess comparable attributes of the spirit, while those who are known to be wicked should be visibly ugly. For another thing, human nature is only spasmodically and incompletely rational. Quite properly, in my opinion, most people feel that reason is a key which cannot turn all the locks guarding the mysteries of life; but from this assumption we all, at one time or another, proceed to another not so proper: we conclude that we are being rational whenever we make any use at all of our reasoning powers. So long as the machine works, it does not matter much what raw material we feed into it, and we are quite satisfied with the manufactured product. We possess the reasoning machine; we work it; therefore we are rational beings. Yet very often we reason not to attain a conclusion hitherto unknown to us, but to achieve a confirmation, apparently justified by logic, of conclusions we already hold, conclusions which are in fact prejudices. Having observed someone's face and having decided that it is the face of a voluptuary or a liar or a sadist, we then observe his behavior, as often as not at second hand, picking up gossip and rumor. We use our reason to sort out and interpret the evidence thus obtained, and find little difficulty in ignoring what does not fit in with our preconception and magnifying and distorting anything that suits our unconscious purpose. And so we decide that our instincts were right, or our first impression was a true one, and no one must dare to call our judgment a prejudice because we have been at some pains in order to reason our way to it.

The fallacy of seeing character in the physical appearance of the face, however, is not utterly baseless. It arises, by confusion and over-simplification, from a real and intimate relationship between the flesh and the spirit, which is set up whenever the face loses the passive aspect of repose and, with or without any transient mobility of its parts, becomes expressive: when it is, so to say, played upon from within by emotions. Imagine a face—a man's, a woman's, a child's, it does not matter which—of average comeliness, the features pleasingly shaped and proportionate: a face not noticeably beautiful or ugly in its physical attributes. There is no need to characterize it further: it will do that for itself as it registers and reveals the moods, the reactions, the desires which enter and dominate its owner's mind. All these effects will be observed by other people, but they will not be observed with scientific detachment and precision. Just as a good artist painting a portrait does not set himself to copy in slavish imitation the evidence of his eyesight, so any human being watching the play of expression on another's face distorts and exaggerates in his mind what his eyes actually record. Let us suppose that the owner of the face is in a mood of indecision. The muscles controlling his lower jaw will probably relax and the chin will, either in fact or by illusion, slide down and back. If he changes his mood, and turns obstinate, the chin will come forward and up. The actual physical adjustment may be infinitesimal, or on this occasion there may be no movement of the chin at all; but the eye of the observer, prompted by expectation, by a changing tone of voice, by an alteration in bodily demeanor, will either note the movement of the chin and mentally enlarge it, or imagine it if it was not to be seen at all. For people very often do express decision and indecision by such flexings and slackenings of the jaw muscles; and, as every reader of Chesterton's Father Brown stories knows, what the eye is accustomed to see it tends to see whenever an appropriate context of circumstance is provided.

Similarly, when the owner of this imaginary face is being sincere and speaking from his heart, without pretense or reservation, his eyes will either be enlarged by an additional opening of the lids or, by illusion and association, will appear larger. But if he be feigning an emotion his eyes may very well be partly closed, to conceal his thoughts, and to the observer they may actually seem smaller and closer together—the shifty, pig's eyes of popular judgment. If he is inquisitive, the head will be slightly protruded at the neck, and the eyes will stare sharply, both actions contributing to the illusion of an elongated nose. In smiles and laughter the mouth will broaden, thus creating the conception of the wide mouth as a symbol of generosity and good nature. Petulance often rolls the underlip outward, thickening it, and so any thick underlip may be read as indicating a pampered disposition. In a voluptuous mood the whole mouth may swell and relax, both lower and upper lips exposing their damp surfaces: and so a thick-lipped, wet mouth becomes the mark of a sensualist. Similarly with the thin, sucked-in mouth which accompanies cautious thought and dubiety, and is thus associated with miserliness, and the pursed, narrowed mouth, which becomes emblematic of envy. Whether jealousy can in fact transmute the color of blue or gray or brown eyes to green is more than I know, but jealousy is a sickness of the mind, and as such it may lend sudden pallor to the complexion of the face, and this, in combination with new lusters in the eyes due to the intensity of the jealous emotion, possibly induces an illusion of green coloration.

Not all faces are noticeably modified by the emotions, although almost all will exhibit these changes of appearance if the emotion is aroused so suddenly as to penetrate the guards of custom and watchfulness. As pleasing and displeasing expressions appear in this imaginary face of average comeliness, it will be distorted in its general effect, now more beautiful, now uglier. And so far as real faces in their physical constitution approximate to these variations, so they will, unjustly and irrationally, be interpreted, not by the emotions they express but by their permanent and largely inherited characteristics, which will be deemed signs of good or bad character. This arbitrary judgment is long-established in the human mind. It is the basis of traditional stage makeup, established long before Robertson and Ibsen brought realism into the theater. It is the foundation of the popular demand that the heroes and heroines of romances should be beautiful, and the villains ill-favored. It even appears in the formal procedure of law courts which insists that the accused should be on view throughout his trial, so that judge and jury may form an opinion of his demeanor—that is to say, to a considerable extent, an opinion of his face as an instrument revealing character.

Charles Le Brun, a formal and pompous painter, but a talented draftsman, who was ennobled by Louis XIV, among many other activities produced a number of drawings of heads, almost abstract heads, designed to illustrate the principal emotional expressions. Le Brun's fame, eclipsed now, lasted a long time. When Napoleon was exiled to St Helena, after Waterloo, the victorious Allies not unnaturally set about getting back some of the 'treasures of art' which, along with bullion and furniture and plate and what not, Napoleon had plundered from other countries. Connoisseurs were sent to France to track down the loot, but they did not find it all, and when they did they did not always succeed in recovering it. Veronese's great picture, *The Marriage Feast at Cana,* for example, as Professor Bodkin tells us in *Dismembered Masterpieces,* was alleged to be too large to be transported across the Alps easily and cheaply, and the Austrian diplomats took, as fair exchange, a picture by Le Brun. Today it seems absurd that a Le Brun should be considered comparable with any Veronese, much less the *Marriage Feast,* but it has to be remembered that in 1815, although he had died in 1690, Le Brun's reputation was still high. I have, for example, on my shelves a book of engravings by Le Brun, published in London in 1813 at the then high price of fifteen shillings. These are the engravings which illustrate the expressions of the face. They are magniloquently described on the title-page as "Heads representing the various Passions of the Soul as they are Expressed in the Human Countenance: Drawn by that Great Master Monsr. Le Brun and finely engraved on Twenty Folio Copper Plates nearly the Size of Life." Obviously Le Brun's work retained its popularity, even outside France, a century and a quarter after his death, and people were prepared to see in the physical variations of the face reliable indications of what goes on in the mind.

It would seem, however, either that Le Brun's observation was inexact, or his deductions unjustified, or else that people in seventeenth-century France had minds which affected their flesh more violently than ours do. Concerning Desire, the text under the engraving says: "This Passion brings the Eye brows close together and forwards towards the Eyes, which are more open than ordinary: the Eye ball is enflam'd" (presumably this means the pupil or iris is enlarged) "and places itself in the middle of the Eye, the Nostrils rise up, and are contracted towards the Eyes." Sadness "makes the Eye brows rise towards the middle of the forehead more than towards the Cheeks . . . ye white of the Eye is Yellow . . . all about the Eyes is livid . . . the head carelessly leaning on One of the Shoulders; ye face is of a lead color, the lips pale." With Horror, "the Eye ball placed at the bottom of the Eye is half covered by the lower Eye lid: the Mouth is half open, but closer in ye middle than ye sides." With Fright the eyebrow muscles are "mark'd, swell'd, pressed one against the other, and sunk towards the Nose, which draws up as well as the Nostrils . . . the end of the Nose is pale:" and (this is not apparent in the illustration) "the hair stands on end." Anger has "a cruel and disdainful Grin." With Hatred or Jealousy, the nostrils are "drawn backward so as to make wrinkles in the Cheeks," and "the mouth is so shut as to show the teeth are closed." While under the influence of Despair (in this engraving the hair really does stand on end) "the forehead wrinkles from the top to the bottom . . . ye end of ye Nose sinks down, ye muscles tendons and veins are swell'd and stretch'd."

Extravagantly phrased as these descriptions are, they correspond to what is depicted in the engravings, and though our later taste will tend to moderate the distortions a little, it nevertheless remains true that a face which expresses intense emotion becomes, however momentarily, a distorted face: and, except for grief and fear, the greatest distortion is caused by emotions commonly regarded as reprehensible. This should make it easier to understand how physical malformations and disproportions in the face come to be associated, unreasonably and unfairly, with bad character. One final example is the traditional diabolic or Mephistophelian face, of which the outstanding characteristics are eyebrows rising diagonally outward from the bridge of the nose, large, flashing eyes (due to an excessive exposure of the whites), hollowed and creased cheeks, and a wide mouth turned down at the outer corners, as we say, sardonically. If we consult Le Brun we find once again that the physical appearance which symbolizes a permanent character is a stilling and conventionalizing of transient distortions produced in the face by a mood. The devil, it should be remembered, is conceived as an angel fallen from grace, and his besetting sin is pride. This is the same passion which Le Brun illustrates as Scorn, and the text beneath the engraving particularizes its attributes in words which apply just as well to the diabolic face which any competent makeup man can produce for the footlights or the cinema camera. "The Eye brow is knit, the side of it next the Nose sinks down, and the other side rises very much: the Eye is very open, and the Eye ball is in the middle; the Nostrils rise and draw towards the Eyes and make wrinkles in the Cheeks; the Mouth shuts, its sides sinking down, and the underlip is pushed out beyond the upper one."

Good and evil, within the limits of normal human experience—that is to say, where there is no remarkable deviation towards either extreme—reveal themselves in the face, in youth, as moods or evanescent emotions. With maturity, the recurrence of these moods leaves a record in the face, producing characteristic expressions, and in time may actually modify the physical appearance. The child's character, at least so far as it is visible in the face, is unformed, all possibilities and alternatives; the young man's or young woman's is merely hinted; by middle age the mold is set; and in old age it either hardens or relaxes. But the disentanglement, among the mutabilities of any face, of mood from trait, of character from temperament, and both from heredity, is a much more difficult and subtle task than is commonly realized, and as it involves many other factors besides good and evil it must be deferred for discussion in the next, and last, chapter. Goodness may be manifested in many ways, all within the compass of normal human nature, neither saintly nor wicked. It shows itself in unmalicious laughter, in modesty and admiration, in compassion, in sensitive awareness of other people's feelings, in courtesy, in courage, in trustfulness, in

PLATE XX: HEAD OF AN OLD MAN, *by* G. B. TIEPOLO

Formerly in Wendland Collection

PLATE XXI: GROTESQUE HEAD, *by* MERVIN PEAKE

comradeship, even in serious thought, in all spontaneous affection, in loyalty, and in the taking up of responsibilities. Evil passions, which time and habit can confirm as vices, show themselves in the faces of human beings not to be accounted predominantly wicked. Such evil passions are for the most part failures to achieve the normal good. Often their pettiness makes them ludicrous, as in conceit, which is a shadow of arrogance and springs from a combined lack of modesty and humor, in surliness, suspicion, envy, jealousy, and those sensual indulgences, half-hearted and furtive, which are due to lack of purpose or of the ability to resist environment. Anger, indignation, scorn, ambition are not necessarily evil: they must be judged by what arouses them and the actions they stimulate. And there is a wide tract of the emotions which cannot safely be generalized, for morality does not go, throughout its course, by common consent: what is priggishness to one will seem virtue to another, and qualities which repel in one small society may be welcomed and esteemed only a few miles away.

Of all forms of evil, cruelty seems to me the ugliest, and I imagine that most civilized people will agree with me in this. Cruelty takes up into itself most of the major sins: it is arrogant, it is irresponsible, it is sensual, it denies pity and comradeship and affection. It is active, and therefore a major sin, but by some acrobatics of the imagination it is passive also; the sadist intuitively knows and rejoices in his victim's sufferings. Cruelty does not consist merely in the infliction of pain: the doctor, the schoolmaster, the parent, the soldier, have on occasion to cause pain to others, and they are not necessarily made cruel by their occupations. Nor is cruelty the same as brutality, for it is sensitive and self-conscious: else it would be robbed of its keenest pleasures. Better to call the fox-hunter a brute —that is to say, in this respect, an animal without the human faculty of imagining himself the prey instead of the hunter—than a sadist; for it is his imagination which fails him when he has none of the kindness he lavishes on horse and hound to spare for the fox. Brutality, cultivated and sustained, will coarsen the face, even making the features swell and lose shape. But cruelty may refine it, may hollow the cheeks, sharpen the line of the nose, impart new curves to the lips and new lusters to the eyes. Cruelty, in fact, can produce some similitude to the diabolic face which, once its confidence is threatened, is apt to become a maniac face.

There are many theories which seek to establish and account for criminal types, predisposed by mental defects and faults to transgress the laws of society. Perhaps the best known is still that of Cesare Lombroso, the nineteenth-century psychiatrist, who investigated and classified the physical attributes of thousands of convicted criminals, not by any means all Italian. Lombroso paid particular attention to the face, and among the facial characteristics of the born criminal he included sharp, prominent incisor teeth, like those of rodents; the absence or scarcity of beard growth in males; premature wrinkling; chins either small and receding or large and flat; and bushy eyebrows meeting across the nose or rising upward, in the diabolic style, at the outer ends. Criminal types, he maintained, rarely go bald or even gray, and among murderers dark hair is more common than blond, while swindlers run to curly hair. Lombroso's theory might be summarized as a contention, backed by considerable evidence, that habitual criminals are more subject to diseases of mind, body, and nerves than are law-abiding citizens, and that most of them can be considered degenerates, akin in certain respects to savages and lunatics. Among criminals also there flourish some odd superstitions, perhaps handed down by word of mouth for many centuries. One of the most horrible is a belief that the pupils of the eyes of a murdered man retain after death the image of the face of the murderer. It is surmised that it was to destroy this mythical evidence against himself that Frederick Guy Browne, in 1927, bent over the corpse of the policeman he had killed on an Essex roadside and fired his revolver into each of the dead man's eyes.

Lombroso also developed theories about genius, which he tended to think of as a disease, often associated with epilepsy and not very different from insanity. His observations offered an adequate explanation for the behavior of some criminals and some men of genius. Certain diseases undoubtedly act like a stimulant on the mind, perhaps not improving the quality but increasing the rate of production, and to epilepsy might be added tuberculosis, whose feverish effects can be traced in the work of Keats, D. H. Lawrence, Katherine Mansfield, and many others. But not all consumptives and epileptics are creative or in any other way eminent, and many men of genius have been quite free from disease; while, as a further anomaly, the emotional intensity, the sharpening of the senses, the almost stereoscopic vision of life which characterizes the work of many writers afflicted by tuberculosis, is hardly to be found in the gently reflective last essays and letters of Robert Louis Stevenson, who died of the disease.

It will perhaps be wiser to doubt if any artistic talent is created as a by-product of a physical malady, although if it already exists it may be modified and intensified. Much more probably some forms of criminality are symptoms of inherited or acquired diseases, just as they can be fostered by environment. But not all. The normal man possesses, within roughly definable limits, free will, and it does him less than justice to deny that when he chooses to commit crime he cannot help himself. And as the consideration moves from one abnormality to another, it is not surprising that a relationship between them should become apparent. Lunacy, genius, mysticism, violent crime, and the extreme vices all have this in common: they set up an intense, and usually a secret, conflict in the mind. It is not necessary to conclude that a man who commits murder must be insane, but I find it hard to believe that if he goes on committing murders—or any other kind of cruelty—he will not become a madman, whether his madness is recognized or not. From the stresses caused by evildoing both the genius and the mystic are emancipated: they do not live always upon the dizzy peaks of private experience, and many of them, between bouts of enlightenment, will be found to be thoroughly sane, commonplace, and even earthy in behavior.

All intense emotional experiences transfigure the face, not merely with the muscular contortions depicted and analyzed by Le Brun, but with more subtle variations of color and often by an emanation of some unphysical but perceptible force perhaps analogous to diffused light, for its effect is not unlike that of a glow of heat. Fear often drains blood from the face, producing a pallor tinged with yellows, blues, and greens; and, often renewed, fear upsets the metabolism of the whole body, and this in turn shows in the complexion. Both anger and shame suffuse the blood vessels beneath the skin of the face, turning it red, but whereas anger makes the eyes more brilliant, shame may cloud them and disorder their focus. Love unsatisfied is notoriously a kind of sickness, and in the face it may produce an actual or illusory thinning, with shadows in the cheeks and round the eyes, comparable to the effects of physical privation and nervous strain. By contrast, those who know they are loved confront the world with glowing faces, and seem to smile even when their expression is serious. And the plainest woman when she is tending her baby is invested with a spiritual beauty which seems to have a physical luminosity.

All these are normal characteristics, which any and every face may reveal from time to time. There are others, however, to be met with only rarely, in the faces of men and women so dedicated to goodness that, whether or not they are with due rituals and investigations canonized after death, we speak or think of them as saints. Joan of Arc is perhaps not typical: her austerities were those of a soldier rather than a religious, and the voices which counseled her gave suspiciously practical advice on military and political problems. Admirable as Joan's character was, one may surmise that she was elevated in theological status after her execution rather as a martyr and patriot, a leader in a nationalist war, than as a devout woman. But one characteristic she certainly shared with many other saints. It will be remembered that in the epilogue to Mr Shaw's play Joan, returned to earth as a phantom in the Dauphin's dream, asks her former friends, enemies, and acquaintances, who have just recited a litany of praise at her feet, whether they would welcome her return in the flesh. And one by one they excuse themselves. Doubtless the fault is in them, but the point not to be evaded is that saints are more comfortable to read about, to see on the stage or in pictures, than to live with. Like genius, saintliness consists not in the attainment of an even standard of faultless achievement (many saints, St Augustine notorious among them, have been great sinners) but in super-normal devotion to one purpose—in this case, a religious purpose. The saint, if only intermittently, puts all his eggs in one basket. He ignores and withers away nine hundred and ninety-nine potentialities of experience in order to concentrate the energy they would consume on the outstanding thousandth part. While others can get along very well appreciating what we may call the particles of God's nature as they are to be met with in everyday life, the saint searches along a narrow inward path for the quintessential abstract of divinity. In this sense he is to be classified with all specialists who leave themselves no private lives and no casual interests. And ordinary humanity, while it admires and may be grateful for the product of this intensity, shrinks from spending overmuch time in the company of the devotee. The saint, in fact, taken day in and day out, may be a bore or a positive nuisance, and his self-dedication not easily distinguishable from selfishness. He is trying to live intimately in his thoughts with God, and the human society of which he is a member, preoccupied with affairs much nearer at hand, is apt to regard him as an obstacle on the highway, to be avoided respectfully but with determination.

Most pictures which portray saints are made either out of the artist's imagination or from models of more or less unsaintly character. Unless the painter has in himself something of the saint's asceticism and mystic rapture, as Greco had, what he paints is not very convincing testimony to the qualities of the saintly face. Tiepolo, in his drawing of the *Head of an Old Man* (Plate XX, page 202), intent only on draftsmanship and simple composition, comes nearer to communicating holiness and devotion than in most of his elaborate and highly decorative paintings. The saintly face may be physically beautiful or ugly or nondescript: it will not be truly saintly unless the forms and colors are subordinated to a transcendent spiritual quality. Similarly, the saintly face may be young or old, simple and innocent of temptations or ravaged by conflicts and passions, but the flesh must, to a far greater degree than in the normal human face, symbolize and give expression to the aspirations and extra-sensuous perceptions of the soul. It need not be a wise face—saints are often confused with sages—nor need it bear marks of suffering: a person may become a martyr by chance, and for a diversity of causes. But necessarily the saintly face will, by common standards, be austere. It will be intense, also, for the Kingdom of Heaven is taken by storm, and also it lies within us, so that the saintly face will be contemplative, if not downright introspective. The tensions, however, will not be unresolved, and we may look for serenity also. Saints renounce a great deal that others value, but they receive ample compensation. And finally the saintly face is a face illuminated from within, a face of benediction, for despite all its tautened abstraction, its private vision of a superhuman goodness is emanated to human society.

The saint is one who sees God with the clarity and immediacy of optical vision, and the face of God, as Christians conceive it, is the human face transfigured yet further than in the faces of saints. The savage worships tribal gods, not easily distinguishable from demons, and invests them with few notable attributes of goodness and little likeness to humanity. The pagan conceives a community of gods and goddesses who are physically idealizations of human beings, endowed with magic powers, and capriciously intervening in human affairs, but subject to human passions and foibles. Phœbus discovers Aphrodite's amour with Mars, and betrays them both to Vulcan; Juno, Minerva, and Aphrodite submit their beauty in competition to the judgment of the mortal Paris; and the lordly Zeus is heartily philoprogenitive in his love affairs, siring not only Venus but the Graces, the Fates, the Seasons and the Nine Muses, as well as Helen of Troy and innumerable semi-divinities. As the Greek and Roman civilizations became philosophical, they also became more rational, and for the literate part of the population the old story-laden conceptions were mentally set apart from serious thought on the nature and destiny of human existence. The gods and goddesses were organized into a conservative institution, useful to the State, and they retained an anomalous grip on parts of otherwise emancipated minds. But the primal simplicity of belief had been lost long before the Christian bishoprics were established.

Religions which are devoted to a single God not only align themselves better with the trend of philosophical thought but introduce a new and revolutionary element into man's idea of himself in relation to the universe. The single God possesses not only enormous power (it is not always omnipotence), both creative and administrative, but goodness also. He has still to be propitiated, with sacrifices and laudatory rites, but his favors are no longer capricious. He enjoins his laws on human beings in a code of conduct not in every detail explicit or free from anomalies, but coherent and precise, and those who obey the code are rewarded not merely with material profits but with spiritual grace. In the Jehovah of the Old Testament goodness takes the form of righteousness, and the divine favor is extended only to the chosen people. The Allah of the Moslem world is a kinsman, or descendant, not too closely related, of this Jehovah. But in the New Testament doctrines the whole world, every human being, is seen as a vast family, the children of God the Father; and through the intercession of God the Son and the operation of God the Holy Ghost, inexorable righteousness is transformed into mercy. Here is a new ideal of behavior, a conception of loving-kindness between one man and another as something good and desirable in itself, and moreover in harmony with the purposeful development of the universe. Because this ideal has been realized only rarely and briefly and locally, because those who profess it so often fail in its practice, because wars and contentions still flourish nearly two thousand years after its inception, many have despaired of the practicability of the ideal, and many have questioned its validity. But the truth is that the world has not been, and could not be, the same after Christ. Evil is clearly separated from good in the minds of everyone influenced, however remotely, by the Christian way of life. In brief, it is still possible to commit sin, but hardly to be unaware that what is committed is sin. The conflict is no longer a chaos. The forces of good have a permanent rallying-point, a standard in more senses than one. Human aspiration may falter and lose ground, but it is no longer in doubt of its objective.

Because the ancient Jews made neither pictures nor statues, the only visual conception we have of the One God, either as Jehovah or as God the Father, comes from the Christian Church. And it does not come very early in Church history—later, in fact, than the first surviving portraits of Christ. The depiction of God has been attempted comparatively rarely, and always within a convention determined by theological doctrines. God is conceived as a man because in Genesis he is said to have made man after his own image, and also, perhaps, because human imagination is balked if it strives to create except from the evidence of the senses. If God is not conceived as a sublimation of man it is hard to see how he could be represented to the eyes, except as a machine or an abstract pattern, both devoid of the essentially godlike principle of vitality. As God is the father of all, not merely of children and young men and women, he is depicted as a very old man, though necessarily vigorous. His face is wise, serene, benevolent, majestic, and as little of it as possible is revealed: the hair is long, and the beard, beginning high on the cheeks, covers the greater part of the face. The beard, plainly, serves to enhance majesty and mystery, and also, with its soft, intricate lines, to soften the awfulness of the general conception.

In depicting Christ artists were confronted with a very different problem. The Son of God is specifically human, fully invested with the flesh and the nature of man, from infancy to maturity, and subjected to violent death. Many reasons have been adduced for the absence of any authentic contemporary portraits; it is probably sufficient explanation to recall that none of the apostles and disciples (themselves unportrayed and undescribed) thought it necessary to mention even in passing the appearance of Christ. The new religion was one of austerity and humility, holding the physical life as of little value and likely at any moment to be gladly exchanged for a resurrection life of perfection. All portraits of Christ, therefore, are imaginary portraits, and date from long after his death. In the *Confessions* St Augustine says, "His true likeness is unknown to us." Responsible Catholic commentators do not claim any authenticity for the various veronicas—cloths treasured as relics—on which Christ is said to have wiped his face, miraculously leaving a portrait impress, or shrouds alleged to have been wrapped round his head after the crucifixion, with a similar after-effect. The word 'veronica' is by some derived from the Latin *vera,* true, and the Greek *icon,* image, but the name seems to be a variation of 'Berenice.' The relics are to be regarded as a testimony to faith rather than fact. Moreover, the face of Christ which they depict is invariably bearded, more or less conforming to the conventional Christ face established in religious art some centuries after the founding of the Church: whereas the earliest imaginary portraits of Christ that we have, painted on sacred vessels and the walls of Roman catacombs in the fourth century, show him as beardless, young, and of some physical beauty.

Earlier written references by the Fathers of the early Church, however, had described Christ's appearance as plain and unremarkable, and it is assumed that at first it was, consciously or unconsciously, considered politic to contrast the God of the new religion with the strapping and handsome deities of pagan Greece and Rome. The contrast emphasized that Christianity was designed for the salvation of the soul rather than of the body, and that within the Church not only the poor and the enslaved, but the crippled, the diseased, the deformed, the weak and the insignificant were equal with patricians and gladiators. A further assumption is made that, as Christianity later extended its missions through the Roman Empire, artists inheriting the pagan tradition tended to depict the new God in a convention such as their predecessors had used for Apollo and other handsome, young and heroic deities; and so the earliest portraits of Christ have something in common with a pre-Christian and non-Jewish tradition.

From the fourth century the head of Christ is often enveloped in a nimbus or halo, later to be used as a symbol for all kinds of sanctity; the halo had previously been reserved for depictions of Roman emperors. Later still the Christ face is given a beard, and some have seen in this an approximation to the idealization of the Greek philosopher, the halo (with sometimes a throne) and the beard together symbolizing Christ as ruler and teacher. This, however, is surmise. Similarly there is surely little reason to see in the portraits of the early Christian era—some showing Christ bearded, some depicting a clean-shaven face—a rivalry between two conceptions, each striving for supremacy as convention and tradition. It is more probable that the two different kinds of portrait conformed to local prejudice and were perhaps taken as representing Christ at different stages of human development, as youth and as man. In the eastern, Byzantine Empire the convention hardened quicker and lasted longer, and here the portrait was less representational: the artist depicted not so much a human being as an abstract and austere, even grim, design of shapes and colors made out of down-flowing hair, beard and mustaches, with heavily marked features, sometimes not easily recognizable as a portrait at all. And when Christianity spread to Northern Europe other artistic traditions came into play. In the eighth and ninth centuries Irish monks were incorporating into the illuminations of manuscripts portraits of a bearded Christ in which the face is subordinated to an intricate pattern of spirals and other geometric figures; while in the Teutonic Empire of Charlemagne the imaginary portrait was clean-shaven and youthful, but not classic. By the eleventh century this had evolved into a Gothic convention, in which natural shapes and proportions were deliberately distorted, and realistic representation was ignored as deliberately as in the Irish convention.

With the late Middle Ages and the Renaissance naturalism came into favor (it is only in comparatively modern times that artists have attempted to depict Christ except as a recognizable human being) and by that time the convention of the short-bearded, sad face of the mature Christ was established. Leonardo in the *Last Supper,* Michelangelo in the Sistine Chapel frescoes, and a few others reverted to the shaven or the youthful Christ face, but in the minds of the devout the question was probably settled when in 1492 the Pope received from the Sultan an emerald on which was carved a portrait of Christ said to be contemporary. Medals were struck representing this portrait, and imitations of them circulated far and wide. The emerald has disappeared, and it is not certain that the Pope ever received such a gift from Turkey. But the conventional Christ face as we know it had come to stay.

From the Middle Ages onward painters, sculptors, woodcarvers, and metalworkers made not only portraits of Christ for churches and shrines, but pictorial narratives of events in the gospel biography. Everyone is familiar with pictures in which Christ is shown as a baby in arms; as a small child at his mother's knee, often with his contemporary St John; as a boy in the Temple and in Joseph's house; as the man with a mission preaching and performing miracles; at the Last Supper; on trial before Pilate; undergoing all the ordained ritual of a Roman crucifixion; dead; transfigured; and in the miraculous state of resurrection. In the Middle Ages the Church was almost the only patron of art, and the subjects of nearly all pictures were religious. The intimate connection between the Church and art persisted, though no longer as a monopoly, through-out the Renaissance, the deist and rationalist eighteenth century, and the industrialization of the last century. Today, however, few artists attempt religious subjects, and probably this is due to the fact that Christian doctrine and practice have lost their hold on the communal and individual mind. But when powerful artists do produce work of a religious nature large numbers of people who might be expected to applaud proclaim instead their indignation. Rightly or wrongly, artists feel that the conventions founded in the late Middle Ages and the Renaissance are exhausted. Those who experiment with new conventions, like Roualt, are likely to find their work appreciated solely for its æsthetic achievement by a comparatively small public not deeply interested in religion.

The face of Christ, then, as it is conceived by most people, is an imaginary portrait created by common consent five hundred years or more ago: the face of a young man, highly sensitive and sympathetic, with long hair and only partly concealed by a beard which is both short and, on the cheeks and the chin, thin enough to let the form of the face show through. Unfortunately this representation reaches many people in a diluted and falsified version, through the sentimental, effeminate variations, popular in the eighteenth and nineteenth centuries, of Guido Reni (who could draw well enough), Carlo Dolci, Pompeo Batoni, Peter Mignard, T. M. H. Hofman, Munkácsy, and Holman Hunt (whose *The Light of the World* was denounced by Carlyle as fit only for worldlings). In its purest and grandest form, the conventional Christ face is to be seen in the works of the great masters, when painting emerged from its primitive efforts (now so often overpraised) and before the religious impulse was subordinated to the decorative elaborations of baroque and rococo. There is Verrocchio's *Baptism*, Piero della Francesca's *Resurrection*, Raphael's and Leonardo's drawings of the head of Christ (both in Venice), Titian's *Entombment*, and Bellini's *Dead Christ*. Nevertheless, it has to be said that the face of the Jesus Christ of the Christian doctrine, God as well as man, remains unrealized. It lies beyond the horizons of pious imagination and artistic skill. What we are shown in even the greatest paintings is the face of an exceptionally good man. As a baby in Mary's arms, as a child playing with a bird or raising a curly head towards the light, as a man in non-period robes among other men similarly attired, as a figure on a cross or in a tomb, or even in the emancipation of life after death, the Christ of the medieval and Renaissance artists remains a man. Divinity shows in his face only at second hand, by reflection. He is saint and martyr, but hardly God.

It is likely that this is how Christ appeared to those who saw him in Galilee and Jerusalem, and more than likely that he had less physical beauty and more Hebraic characteristics than most painters have given him. But Christ cannot be seen in that way now, just as, in another department of our apprehension, after the plays and the music have passed into the common stock of experience, neither Shakespeare nor Beethoven could appear to us as they appeared to their contemporaries. What we look for in portraits of Christ is the revelation of a character transcending the human, and this neither paintings nor sculpture, nor the human minds which conceive them, can supply. Those who come nearest are the mystics, particularly Greco and Blake, both of whom used and transformed the facial convention established long before they set to work. But when these mystic pictures are examined it will be seen that the face plays only a subordinate part in the composition, and the transcendent effect is achieved chiefly by attitudes, colors, and the grouping, deliberately unrealistic, of various figures and objects in a not-easily penetrable symbolism. The face of Christ, so far as we know it, is a product of the human imagination, to which strict limits are set. It is a face which remains unknown and unknowable.

CHAPTER ELEVEN

READING THE FACE

Look at any man's face with interest and intensity, and in a few seconds you know a good deal about him. We all make summary judgments of this kind every day of our lives, and as we judge so we are judged by others. Usually the process is casual, unsystematic, and arbitrary. We decide on the evidence of his face that this man is likable or repulsive, or, perhaps, interesting to us, or not interesting at all. The more specific information given by the face we assimilate so rapidly and automatically that we are hardly aware of it, for the face tells us approximate age, race if not nationality, the state of bodily health and nerves, and the mood of the moment. It is mood to which we pay most attention, and if the person we are looking at is a stranger we are apt to identify the transient mood expressed in his face with a permanent character we imagine for him. To note the moods of a face is comparatively easy: even if it is almost blank of expression we can usually make a guess at whether this is due to introspection, fatigue, boredom, shyness, or a cautious fear of disclosing the thoughts. But to interpret a face fully, to discover the abiding nature of the person who carries that face about with him all his life—this is a much more difficult, intricate, and subtle task, and one full of potentialities of error.

It is first necessary to make a clear division in the mind between what is meant by character and by temperament. Etymological derivations are not always a reliable guide to the present meaning of words, but here they do serve to emphasize a fundamental distinction. 'Temperament' comes from the Latin, where it means 'combining in due proportion': while 'character' in the Greek means 'an engraved mark or imprint.' Applying these basic ideas to the abstract of any human being, the unmaterial part of an entity which is called a person, it should be clear that his temperament is, to a large extent at least, what he inherits as a new combination from both of his parents and from his racial and national origins; while his character is what is impressed on him by what he does and what is done to him. A baby will have, in an elementary form, temperament, a predisposition to a certain outlook and certain forms of behavior; but not until it grows up sufficiently to make decisions of its own, however trivial they seem, can it begin to form its own character. This important distinction is easier to draw in the mind, between two ideas or conceptions, than in practice, when action and speech, and the motives causing them, have to be accounted for. It may, for example, be only a matter of a few weeks, or even days, before the newborn baby begins to impose character upon inherited temperament. In every human activity both temperament and character, sometimes in conflict, sometimes indissolubly intermingled, come into play but unless their differing natures are realized there can be no hope of limiting the confusion. In any adult face, then, evidence of both temperament and character may be looked for, and it will be no simple process to tell t'other from which. Moreover, the mind, which sorts out, analyzes, and interprets what the eye sees, is not itself a scientific or infallible instrument. It contains and is influenced by instincts and prejudices which it does not always recognize for what they are, and of whose existence it is often ignorant even while it obeys their promptings and wheedlings. The mind's reasoning faculty is limited and faulty, and can be used for self-deception; and it dislikes and revolts from any suggestion that its conclusions may be erroneous. Where such an imperfect and variable instrument, never wholly under control, is employed there need be no surprise if human faces are misread, and if judgments about the person who lies, so to say, behind the face vary from time to time and from one observer to another.

Again, the task of interpreting the face, complex in itself, is not confined to separating evidence of temperament from evidence of character. The face presents a great deal of other data, which may or may not be relevant. There is physical beauty or its absence or its negation. Facial loveliness stimulates in the observer not only æsthetic appreciation but, between the sexes, desire—faculties which complicate if they do not confound the judgment. Love is blind not to what delights the senses, but to manifestations of character and temperament which, if noted and understood, might cool off desire: and the last thing desire can tolerate is the lowering of its temperature by common sense. Moreover, physical beauty is powerful even when, as between normal people of the same sex, it provokes no desire. There is first a mental link, arising from the aspiration to perfection and simplicity, between physical and spiritual beauty, and this predisposes us favorably towards those who are unusually lovely: we feel subconsciously that a beautifully formed and colored face ought to be accompanied by beautiful thoughts and feelings. Conflicting with this, if we are ourselves not beautiful—or if we are beautiful in the same or in a different way—may be jealousy and the urge to compete for attention. And again, unhappy experience of beautiful people who have proved disappointing on further acquaintance, or a habit of jealousy, may set up a further opposition to the natural tendency to see in a beautiful face an indication of a beautiful nature: we may have acquired a prejudice, such as that which makes many men assume that a handsome man is likely to be a cad, and this prejudice will automatically come into operation to influence our judgment of a stranger whose looks other people publicly admire. Plainness is a negative quality: it leaves judgment suspended. But ugliness produces the opposite disposition to that aroused by beauty. So far from the judgment being half won over at first glance, it immediately swings to adverse. And again many elements of physical ugliness, such as small eyes, a long nose, a thick underlip, are identified in our minds with momentary distortions of the normal face due to displeasing moods, and so are liable to be taken as evidence of a displeasing personality.

What we are trying to do when we seek to read a face is to disentangle the individual from the type: for, while each of us is a

PLATE XXII: PORTRAIT OF A MAN, SCHOOL OF RUBENS

Author's Collection

PLATE XXIII: SELF-PORTRAIT, *by* SAMUEL PALMER

Ashmolean Museum, Oxford

unique being, it is only in certain respects that we are different from other people—indeed, the common factors in the face, as in the blending of temperament and character which we may call personality, far outnumber those which are peculiar to any one person. Racial inheritance determines the predominant appearance of any face, and parental heredity, as well as environment, operate only within the limits set by race. The thickened lips, the round skull, the flattened nose, the curly hair, as well as the darkly pigmented skin of the Negro, are all determined long before his birth. To one or other of the great racial groups, whatever admixtures of ancient history produced them, we must each of us belong, and in this, as in so many other matters, we have no say. From the first moment of life the individual is given a uniform of flesh which he cannot refuse to wear. This uniform has three main varieties. Ethnographers classify the races of mankind in various ways, but the basic subdivision is into White, Black, and Yellow. The use of these color names may be misleading, for the Whites are subdivided into dark and fair Whites, and fair ones are to be found not only in Western and Northern Europe but in the Mediterranean borders of Africa and in India; while the dark Whites, whose complexion is usually brown, include not only those we think of as Latins but many people of Celtic origin. In addition, there are innumerable Whites in whose ancestry fair and dark are intermingled. To add to the confusion, the skin of the Blacks is, as often as not, brown, and many varieties of the Negro race are to be found in the Philippines, New Guinea, and Malaya, as well as in Africa and North America. The Yellow races include not only Chinese, Japanese, Burmese, Siamese, Tibetans, but Lapps, non-Swedish Finns, many Turks, Russian and Manchurian Mongols, North American Eskimos and Malays.

It is obvious that the color classification is primarily a mental convenience, and that the racial inheritance of any one person is to be identified rather by the formation of the head, and of some other parts of the body, than by complexion. Nevertheless, the three-race classification of mankind in broad terms holds good today. There has been much intermingling of blood in the past between the sub-divisions of each race, but comparatively little mixture of White, Black and Yellow with each other. Moreover, these broad racial divisions correspond closely with historical and geographical cultures. But the apparent simplicity is undermined by the occasional, and not very rare, appearance among peoples of the White race of individuals with noticeable characteristics belonging to one of the other races—that is to say, people of White parentage or ancestry who closely resemble (not necessarily in complexion) Negroes or Mongols. This phenomenon might be ascribed to a biological sport, due to some more or less remote intermingling of another race in the individual's ancestry. Frequently, such an explanation is justified. But not always. Often the White of Mongol appearance is diseased and of arrested development, even imbecile: and indeed the medical name for one type of imbecility, characterized by the Mongol eye, defective breathing due to the formation of the nose, an open mouth, prominent cheek bones, and a disposition to sit in the Buddha posture, is 'mongoloid.'

The problem of accounting for these White mongoloids has been thoroughly discussed by Dr F. G. Crookshank in *The Mongol in Our Midst* (revised edition, 1931). To simplify a long, detailed, and controversial argument: Dr Crookshank maintains that the Mongol-like appearance of certain White people, while it may be complicated by disease, is not pathological and not necessarily a sport or freak of biology. He traces a physical and mental similarity between the three main races of mankind, White, Black, and Yellow, and the three great apes, the chimpanzee, the gorilla, and the orang-outang. And he argues that while man is not to be regarded as evolving from the apes as we know them today, the White race had a common ancestor with the chimpanzee, the Black with the gorilla, and the Yellow with the orang-outang. At some specific but now utterly indefinable point in history three families of creatures destined to become prototypes of both man and ape underwent a similar schism. One branch of a certain generation went its own way and began the long process of evolving the White Man, while another started to breed what were to become chimpanzees. And so with the Black Man and the gorilla, the Yellow Man and the orang-outang.

For myself, I find several difficulties in accepting this hypothesis, to which, in general terms at least, many ethnologists subscribe. How was it possible for the first generation offspring of the common ancestor to be so separated, not in one family but in three, that there could be no subsequent interbreeding between their progeny? This version of the evolutionary process seems altogether too neat and tidy to square with my notions of even prototypal human behavior. And if we follow Dr Crookshank's argument farther we find that, while he pays many tributes to mongoloid Whites (among them he numbers Clemenceau and Lenin) for intelligence, charm, even originality, he accounts for mongoloid and (by implication at least) negroid imbeciles as beings whose development before and after birth has been arrested, so that they are, compared with normal Whites, infantile, stupid, incapable of adult responsibilities. They ought to have evolved, in the womb and through childhood, into the full stature of the White Man, whose distant cousin is the chimpanzee; instead, because of retarded development, they stay at the lower level of the Yellow or Black Man, and in physical appearance and in habits remind us of gorillas and orang-outangs.

If this theory means anything it means that the Black and Yellow races are inherently inferior to the White. Many people will automatically revolt from such a conclusion, as hostile to the liberal conception of human equality. We have heard too much of master races, and suffered too long and too bloodily from them, and there is an obvious danger that, once White believes itself to be by predestination superior to Black and Yellow, it will exploit, if not tyrannize over, its 'inferiors.' Thus history and ethics produce reactions in the mind which immediately erect obstacles against any theory of racial inequality.

If, however, we are to form a detached opinion we must lay aside our sophisticated egalitarian conceptions, as well as our more primitive instincts which may tell us to distrust and perhaps despise those of a race different from our own. In brief, we must start by recognizing the possibility that Dr Crookshank may be right when he suggests that the White Man is mentally superior to the Black and the Yellow. If we assume that modern civilization is an advance on its predecessors, then the proposition is proved: written language, literature, pictorial art which is representational and has perspective, harmonic music, characterized drama, the sciences from physics to psychology and powered machinery—practically all these achievements are the work of the White race. It is true that Chinese philosophy, ceramics, poetry, and paintings are, and rightly, highly respected in the Western world, and that many White people derive pleasure and profit from such characteristic Negro productions as tribal sculptures and weaving, the religious songs called spirituals, and the form of improvised music known as jazz; but these entries on the other side of the ledger are infinitesimal compared with the advances made by the Whites. Egalitarianism, the discomfort of feeling that someone else, for no fault of his own, is occupying a status lower than ours, prompts us to argue that while all the foregoing may be true, it is true only because we are judging Black and Yellow by standards set up by White. Tempting though the argument is, I fear it is also fallacious, for there does seem to be an absolute standard of values to which all men, whatever their racial color, and however unwillingly, subscribe. Brought into intimate and sustained contact with a White civilization, the Black or Yellow peoples sooner or later yield to its attractions. The overriding tendency is for all non-White races, and for White peoples still incompletely adapted to modernity, to 'Westernize' themselves: the phrase speaks for itself. The assimilation may, at first, take merely material forms: a desire to wear suits and shoes, collars and ties, a desire to possess railways, motorcars, cinemas, radio sets. And there is giving as well as taking: the West learns from the East; Europe and America are modified by Africa. But, by and large, what the

White man has created the Black and the Yellow seek a share in. In reaching this conclusion I confess that I have had to struggle with certain psychological censors in my own mind. I dislike writing or saying or thinking anything which in any way appears derogatory to the Negro and the Chinese, for although I have met few of them, those I have known I have liked very much. As for Mongols, personally unknown to me, I have an idea that one of the two varying types of woman I am predisposed to find attractive might very well, in Dr Crookshank's view, be described as mongoloid in face. And if I turn to the great apes, those far-off cousins, though I know them only in zoos, I find the gorilla immensely more attractive than the chimpanzee. Long hours I have spent in front of the big cages, watching the dark-haired creatures lazing or exercising, puzzling and pondering their big heads with the almost human faces in which it is not difficult to trace, as if in a slow-motion cinema film, the aching, painful, obstinate processes of elementary cogitation. But when I take a rapid conspectus of history it does seem to me not unlikely (though how I cannot guess) that mankind is to be classified by its faces into White, Yellow, and Black, that each has its tenuous kinship with the great apes, chimpanzee, gorilla, and orang-outang, and that of the three the White race is, by proved achievement, clearly superior.

But either reason or instinct nags at me not to leave the problem there. The logical conclusion is accompanied by a sensation of profound uneasiness. I do not wish to feel—nor do I in fact feel—that I, as an individual, am superior to a Negro or a Chinese. How, then, can the reasonable hieratic judgment be squared with the egalitarian instinct? In this way, I think. The Western civilization in which I live, and in which most of those who read this book will be living, with all its defects and its suicidal manias the finest that man anywhere or at any time has achieved (for it incorporates the best of the past), is not of our making. We inherited it from long generations of our forefathers. We are ourselves, to a large extent, the product of the past of this civilization. We think and feel and behave as we do because of the lives led by our forefathers. This is not a merit in us. It is our good fortune, and our responsibility. We cannot help being what we are, any more than the Nigerian can help being a Nigerian or a Solomon Islander a Solomon Islander. It is in this recognition that true equality is to be found. And when a member of another race, given the opportunity, is able to live among White people, to absorb White education, to use his intelligence and his imagination in the way we use ours, so far from resenting his achievement we should honor him for it, because in a few years he has achieved what it took our ancestors ages to reach. Moreover, along with his White education, he probably retains knowledge and wisdom of his own racial inheritance unknown to us; and although over the whole extent his inherited culture may be inferior to ours, in specific elements it may have the advantage. Again, whether in the remote past the Whites acquired their enterprising characteristics because they lived in temperate climates or whether they sought out such climates because they were enterprising is an insoluble problem, like the precedence of chicken and egg. And in any event, it is probably bad for anyone to feel superior to anyone else.

In general, we judge a face more confidently if it belongs to the same racial group as our own, for then we are more likely to have in common both symbols and what they symbolize. Nor does the unmitigated shock of first setting eyes on people with a different pigmentation and facial structure occur very often nowadays: we are prepared for the reality by innumerable pictures. It is still not so easy for us to discriminate the individual from the type among other races, but most of us have learned automatically to adapt our æsthetic standards. Features such as wide, flexible, out-turned lips or the mongolian eye (not necessarily set aslant in the face but marked by a horizontal, uncurved lower lid and a fold of skin at the inner corner) which in a White might be displeasing, harmonize perfectly with facial structures appropriate to other races. We can tell, an any rate to our own satisfaction, a good-looking Sudanese from an ugly one, a refined Chinese face from a coarse one.

When we observe faces strongly marked by the characteristics of one of the subdivisions of the White race our discriminations, and perhaps our prejudices, are more finely drawn. The clearest racial distinction is between the broad- or round-headed people and those with a comparatively long and narrow skull, the length being measured from forehead to the back of the head. The round heads are sometimes called a Mediterranean type, and the long heads Northern, but these ethnological divisions do not correspond to modern nationalities. The White peoples of today are all mongrel Whites, and probably all the better for the impure pedigree, although among them there do occur individuals whose faces closely resemble the perfect model of an ethnological racial type. There are, for example, to be found in Italy women with the classical oval face, so often depicted from the time of Praxiteles to that of Raphael; in Scandinavian countries there are tall men and women with the straight gold hair, the blue eyes, the fresh complexion of the German 'Aryan' ideal; and in Ireland hair so black that it has red and blue tints in it often goes with a thin-cheeked, long upper-lipped facial structure, and clear blue eyes fringed with such dark lashes that Victorians loved to describe them as "put in with a sooty finger." These perfect types are always a small minority among faces which possess only one or two, or none at all, of the elements of the ideal beauty.

Conqueror races living privileged lives among a subordinate population may in quite a few generations begin to approximate in appearance to the native stock, and not always by interbreeding. To take two great soldiers as examples, it has been claimed that neither Wellington nor Lawrence of Arabia can properly be regarded as an Irishman because, although their ancestors had lived in the country for long enough, they had never intermarried with Celtic Irish. In Lawrence the problem is complicated by the fact that his mother was Highland Scottish: but then it has to be remembered that Ireland was known as Scotland before the country called Caledonia took over the name; Highlanders are in fact Irish colonials. The fact remains that both Wellington and Lawrence had faces which in structure and coloration are of types recognizably Celtic Irish: and if the story of their non-Irish ancestry is true this may mean that in a comparatively short time faces begin to conform, by a kind of protective adaptation, to their environment. The origins of racial characteristics as they show in the faces of White peoples, all mongrels, are so intricate and complex that they cannot possibly be traced: even if we know from records who married whom centuries ago we can hardly guess what alien mixture was brought into the strain, to 'out' perhaps several generations later. It is otherwise with Black and Yellow races, where intermingling is simpler, where individuals are less clearly distinguished from types, and where national civilizations have not been brought to the same pitch of elaboration. All the White peoples have a habit of assimilating other White peoples, as settlers, as conquerors, as voluntary or involuntary immigrants. The Berbers of North Africa are Moslem and have many Arab customs, but racially they are not Arabs; the Prussians are largely Slav, and Prussian facial types are to be seen plentifully in Bavaria and the Rhineland; and the people of the United States are not blended of more racial elements than those of Great Britain, although the process has been crammed into a shorter time and consequently has set up greater political and social stresses. Consequently White faces differ among themselves in the utmost variety, and although this feature or that conformation of the flesh over the bones may be attributed to some aspect or other of the racial inheritance, to locate its distant origin is more often than not a wide and unfenced field for speculation.

Yet the racial elements in any face may arouse a strong and instinctive attraction or repulsion in the observer. It is not always a case of like responding to like, although in mating and setting up a family many people are so influenced by tastes, interests, and manners that the range of choice open to them is automatically limited. Nine times out of ten we can forecast the kind of man that a girl brought up in a country house, and accustomed since her childhood to shoot and follow hounds, will marry: his tastes will be the same as hers. Many professions and occupations influence habits and so produce modifications in the face—particularly modifications of expression—and this evolves an occupational type, which tends to marry a type it considers suited to its professional needs. The peacetime Army officer is likely to marry a woman who will breed stalwart sons and whose manners and ideas will not embarrass his superior officers on social occasions. The lawyer and the civil servant will seek for a face that promises discretion, and the intellectual for one which he imagines will never look bored under the impact of his analytic and allusive conversation. But these are the conformists. There are others more adventurous, and often they are drawn towards people very different from themselves. When tall marries short, blond brunette, long-head short-head, it is commonly believed that nature is using them to restore her averages. More than physical appearances are involved, however, and in the offspring of a 'mixed' marriage of this kind there will be not only a compromise, probably unequally balanced, between the inherited facial characteristics of the parents, but a new amalgam of temperament. The children of two parents not obviously destined to mate may very well find in themselves a perpetual stress of opposing instincts—and all the innovations, discoveries, experiments, and artistic creations which jolt progress spasmodically forward are probably born from such inward stresses. Those who do not conform in their mating to what might be expected of them, therefore, are just as likely to swing nature's balance to one extreme or another as to move it gently back to average.

In relationships other than marital—that is to say, in early love affairs, in liaisons, and in friendships—the same distinction between the conformist and the adventurer can be observed. Some people are uneasy except in the company of their own kind, where they can feel that what is passing in other people's minds is much the same as goes on in their own. If they have to live in a foreign country they will confine their social acquaintance to people of their own nationality, and further restrict their friendships to those they imagine behave, and look, like their national ideal. One sort of Englishman will have no use, in India, for natives of the country, or other foreign residents, or for English people who are not 'pukka sahibs.' And some Americans are even more insular: everything must be presented to them in the American idiom and the American accent, and what they see and hear abroad with their own senses is not recorded faithfully but with the distortions set up in their minds by sentimental or prejudiced legends. Conformity of this kind, in whatever nationality it is found, is restrictive and impoverishing. Those who are open-minded delight in the society of people different from themselves. They find them interesting because they are different, and from the impact of an unfamiliar temperament and experience they draw not only increased knowledge but mental stimulus. It is possible that the conservative inertia and self-sufficiency of the conformists (whom I assume to be in a majority everywhere) is necessary to maintain stability, tradition, national character; but without the enterprise and the sensitiveness to novelty of the more adventurous, international intercourse would become merely a traffic in goods, with ideas staying at home and decaying for lack of fertilization. Not only that, but within each nation society would harden into self-sufficient castes and classes; ideas would all be communal and everyone obliged to subscribe to them; and in every human face racial inheritance would be, not one pervasive element among several, but the despot determining every mood and every expression.

Divested of clothing and any distinguishing form of hairdressing, an English face may be taken for an American, a French or Flemish, a German or Austrian or Hungarian, even an Arab or Indian; for each of these nationalities there is an archetypal distinctive face. But as, racially, all White nationalities are more or less mongrels, in many of them there is a wide range of individuality. The averages may be separable, but the variations often overlap, so that one particular face might plausibly be attributed to any of several nations. This is not to say that nationality has no formative effect on the face: it is one of the most powerful aspects of environment and tradition, and as such it plays a considerable part in fostering and guiding the development of personality. Born and bred in Dakota, of Swedish parents, a child may retain all its life Scandinavian characteristics in its face, but these will be intermingled and to some extent overlaid, as it grows up, by other characteristics distinctly American, and the product of American institutions and customs. And so with every nationality. The native language probably modifies the structure not only of the inner and normally invisible parts of the mouth and the throat, but of the outer lips, the jaw, and the areas of the face adjacent to the lips. The Dakota-born child with the Swedish parents will have lips, tongue, palate, and vocal chords adapted by long generations of inheritance to the speaking of Swedish; if, however, it is taught from infancy to speak nothing but American English this constant exercise will almost certainly produce some modification of the speech organs, and so of the face, if not in the Dakota-born, then in his offspring. But the influence of nationality is not so discernible as that of racial inheritance; race is a matter of ages, not of generations.

Confronted with a portrait head, an immobile depiction of one stilled expression, we can perhaps, if we are told its nationality, discriminate certain appropriate elements in its appearance. But without extraneous knowledge we are forced to guess, and we may easily guess wrong. Similarly, if we see a child with both its parents we may be able—not always—to say which aspects of its appearance are derived through the father, and which through the mother. Yet from the child's face alone we should be hard put to it to reconstruct mental images of its parents. Again, occupation is known to modify the adult face, but if a series of photographs or paintings of various people, of the same nationality and sex and age, is put before us we cannot tell which is the physician and which the dock-laborer, which the violinist and which the professional footballer. Magazine editors often take advantage of this difficulty to entertain their readers with guessing games in which no one can feel confident that his solution is the right one. The effects produced by occupation are rarely obvious and cannot be so much as tentatively traced unless we can compare portraits before taking up the occupation with others made after it has been followed for a number of years.

To 'read' a face, to discern the nature of its possessor, is never easy and often impossible. The most apparently simple and candid face is full of enigmas, barriers to understanding, accidental associations and misleading signs. In my opinion, no one, judging solely from the visible evidence, can be sure of correctly reading any face seen for the first time. Experience of the world, of the effects of behavior on the face, and psychological alertness help a great deal, and shrewd guesses can be made: but even the shrewdest may be far from the mark, and those that are apposite will generally be found not to reveal anything very profound. On the one hand the face is a recording instrument of extreme sensitiveness, and anything which permanently affects character may be written there. On the other hand, the language it is written in is neither very legible nor free from ambiguity: and character is a concurrence of intellectual, volitional and emotional processes arising from active and passive personal experiences, an endless sequence of conscious and unconscious decisions, great or small, taken by the individual in the course of his daily life. Complex in its workings and deep-sunk in its motives, character is not a quality which has a separate existence. It is not abstract, and although it is made, it is made from materials not chosen by the individual. He has to create his own character out of the temperament, the disposition toward certain forms of behavior, which he inherits directly from his parentage and more remotely from his racial origins; moreover, his temperament is from his infancy modified by his fluctuating state of health, by his upbringing, by the traditions and customs of his social, local, and national circumstances, and by every aspect of environment. These influences act upon the temperament simultaneously with the will power, the thoughts and the feelings which eventually evolve his character. Not one of these forces is to be separated from the others except as we catalogue them with names and descriptions for the sake of clearer thinking. It is small wonder, then, that in observing a face of which we know nothing, except what our eyes tell us, we are baffled in our attempts to imagine the personality belonging to it, and that, if we are temerarious enough to offer an interpretation, our deductions often prove to be erroneous.

It will not surprise me if some who read what I have written refuse their assent to my conclusions, if they withdraw their minds and reiterate their belief that they, at any rate, are skillful in judging character from the face. And I will not deny that they may possess such a faculty. My point is that it is a limited and a tentative faculty. Turn to the illustrations in this book, examine the faces depicted, and try to construct a full and detailed account of the character of the owner of each face. The *Woman's Head,* by E. R. Hughes (Plate VI, page 42), offers a profile portrait of a young woman with regular and handsome features. The eyes look forward with every appearance of candor, the mouth is full and sensuous without indicating sensuality, the expression of the whole face is contemplative and gentle. But is it possible to say that the qualities thus hinted are permanent and not a momentary mood? Can we be sure that they are not, in one so young, the product of inherited temperament rather than of character? Suppose this young woman (I have no idea of her identity) were in fact to be habitually petulant, secretive, weak-willed, would these defects of character have had time to show themselves in, say, a thickening of the lower lip, a narrowing of the eyes, a slackening of the jaw muscles? Next for consideration I suggest Dürer's *Portrait of a Man* (Plate XII, page 106), equally handsome in a different way. Here the face is exceptionally broad, the flesh over and beside the upper part of the jaw heavily embossed, the nose well shaped but long and thin, and the chin juts forward and has a slight cleavage in its lower outline. The expression seems to be one of slight amusement, and if there is self-consciousness in it there is no lack of confidence. This face might be attributed to a soldier or a brigand, a successful merchant or politician, almost certainly to a man of active life and extrovert interests. Yet it cannot have been the character he made for himself which gave this unknown man his broad cheek lines and his 'strong chin,' and it is possible to interpret the shape of his nose as indicating either curiosity of an impertinent sort or a Renaissance alertness of mind. And for all we know he may have let the good qualities inherited from his ancestry run to seed, and his character, as he formed it, may have been vacillating and self-indulgent. On the other hand, for all we can tell, he may have been imaginative rather than a man of action, a faithful husband and a doting father instead of the dashing and irresponsible lover of many women which, conventionally, his type of good looks would indicate.

When the self-portrait by Samuel Palmer (Plate XXIII, page 219) is examined, it soon becomes evident that here is not only a drawing remarkable for its technical skill—it is, indeed, one of the finest portraits ever made—but a picture, however apparently simple in composition, invested with a great though unflamboyant tensity of emotion. And it is, remember, a self-portrait, drawn by a man who was staring into a mirror as he worked. He seems to have set himself to record intimately, faithfully, with, so far as is humanly possible, no bias and no sentimental imputations, the appearance of his own face at that most profound and mystical moment when the eyes peer into a mirrored image of the fleshly form out of which they are looking. This self-scrutiny, which is more often than not taken lightly, diverted into an æsthetic appreciation or made to serve the practical purposes of the toilet, can be an exercise in metaphysics which strains the whole basis of the relationship between the ego and the universe. It was by the contemplation of his own face, reflected in the still water of a fountain, that Narcissus was driven to suicide. To stare at the image of one's face, and realize the experience imaginatively, is to mix the objective with the subjective, to suspend consciousness like a tightrope between inward and outward reality, and to walk to and fro, precariously balanced, over an abyss. The physical and the psychical instruments of observation are turned simultaneously upon themselves. In practice, self-scrutiny cannot be kept up for long: the mind revolts against the strain, irrelevant thoughts enter, the eyes turn away or cease to see clearly the pictured face before them. The artist making a self-portrait, however, has a double guard against this evasion. He looks at his face in the mirror with a professionally objective glance, and he looks at it only intermittently, to take evidence and stimulus for what he is drawing or painting. Nevertheless, in the portrait of his own face Samuel Palmer has contrived to render more than composition and likeness. He has left a record of his personality, his character and temperament combined, a witness to the sort of man he was. Well, what sort? There is no concealment by beard or mustache, and no tricks to enhance physical attractiveness: this is the face of a young man pleasant enough to the eye but not remarkably beautiful in any way. The hair and the thick eyebrows are untidy; the eyes, well spaced, appear to observe rather than to reveal; the chin is narrow but firmly molded, and on either side of the full, unsmiling mouth the cheeks are a little asymmetrical, as if an aching tooth had produced a swelling. What can we discover, from the portrait alone, about Samuel Palmer except that at this moment he was young, highly serious, and perhaps determined? Should we know from this evidence that he was influenced all his life by his youthful acquaintance with William Blake, that he was passionate and romantic by nature, and that he saw and depicted in English landscape a mystical loveliness transcending and transforming the physical reality of woods and fields, hills and rivers? Once something is known of Palmer's life, it is easy enough to begin to read his character into his face; but before then, and despite the emotional impact of the portrait, almost every deduction must be tentative and dubious.

Turning to Robert Greenham's *Auburn Victorian* (Plate XV, page 123), we find a very different technique and a very different face. In the original painting the hair under the slanting hat is red-gold, the white patches in the background are identifiable as snowdrifts, and the tip of the nose is tinted with pink, as if by cold air. The face of this girl is all smooth forms, simplified to a charming structure of youth and comeliness, and her attitude, with her head aslant and her hands crossed under it, if a little affected, has the sort of affectation young people easily fall into. As with the E. R. Hughes portrait, the expression is meditative, but this face is at once less adult and less like what we call aristocratic. Yet dare we say that this girl of the nineteen-forties is worse equipped to cope with life than the young woman pictured perhaps half a century earlier? And should we have any right to be surprised if we were told that she is the daughter of a noble family, while the subject of the E. R. Hughes picture worked in a shop or a factory? Such defiances of expectation occur in everyone's experience. Mr Greenham tells me that his picture was not painted from a model. It is a composition invented and executed for its decorative value, and so far as it is a portrait it is an imaginary one. The girl never existed except in the artist's fancy. But would anyone dare to say so much without the artist's authority? The girl has a young face, in which character has hardly had time or opportunity to impress itself on inherited temperament; yet from the portrait the observer could easily imagine how—if she existed—she would speak and behave in certain circumstances. The point is that his imaginings might, for all he could tell, be far removed from the fact.

To take the argument a stage further, let me consider another face which need not be reproduced for reference because events have made it familiar to everyone who is living today: the face of Adolf Hitler. Opinions will differ, and posterity may disagree, but to us who live in these days it seems certain that Hitler perpetrated more evil than any other man in history. He caused the death of many millions, he corrupted the minds of his own people, he was responsible for innumerable and sickening tortures, he produced fear and destruction and misery wherever he was able to reach. Hitler died in his fifties: there was ample time for character to show in his face. Let us discount painted portraits, as designed to flatter, for tyrants may like representational but not realistic art. Let us think of the innumerable photographs: photographs of Hitler orating, in conference, rejoicing in victory, glooming in defeat, threatening, exhorting, smiling upon social occasions, communing with the mountains at Berchtesgaden, receiving bouquets from little girls in peasant frocks. Can we see in any or all of these pictures of his face the truth of his character—the pride of power, the sickening cruelty, the boundless ambition, the megalomania, the self-pity, the self-glorification? Is it a face recognizable at once as the source of the world's catastrophe? Is it Satanic? Has it beetling brows, furious eyes, a predatory nose, disdainful lips, an aggressive chin? All the world knows that none of these features were to be found in Hitler's face, that, for all it discloses, not a single episode of his abominable career could be guessed from his face. Here is the most evil character in history, and his face is nondescript, neither beautiful nor ugly nor impressive, a haphazard conglomeration of ill-shaped and commonplace features, the sort of face we might expect to find on an obscure government employee, a little unbalanced perhaps by his hobby of painting water-colors—which are not bad but not at all original or powerful as the silly fellow imagines them to be. Perhaps this obscure Hitler-who-might-have-been frightens people occasionally, when his conceit about his artistic ability is affronted: then his face becomes contorted with rage and his eyes enlarge and blank themselves into a sustained glare, but the local doctor shrugs his shoulders and says it is a mild form of intermittent hysteria, not likely to become dangerous. This is what is discernible in Hitler's face: inferiority and pettiness, the unfortunate temperament he inherited and failed to make the best of.

If we imagine Hitler born, the son of an ill-paid excise man, not in the doomed Austrian Empire but in England or America, it is not difficult to imagine a little further and see him following an obscure but harmless career in some small town; earning a living without undue physical exertion; attending the debates of the local political club, where his vehement but incoherent speeches are a favorite 'turn'; and once a year sending in his imitative water-colors to the Exhibition at the Town Hall, where he believes that no one is fit to appreciate his genius but nevertheless relishes every casual word of praise he can elicit from the visitors.

Germany is a country apart from the main development of European civilization, a country full of anomalies and barbaric survivals; but nothing about the Germans is so little understandable as that they chose to subject themselves, and to idolize, such a man and such a face. The only possible explanation is one which affords no answer to 'why' but takes us part of the way towards 'how.' It must be that the majority of Germans could not see Hitler as sane and civilized people do. They had a conception in their minds which overcast and falsified the witness of their eyes. This is not an exclusively German error, from which other nationalities are exempt: it is peculiar to Germany only in its extremity of falsification, in its power to debauch the moral sense by excusing every vileness for the sake of martial victory, achieved or prospective, and in its application to such an unheroic figure as Hitler.

The fact is that human beings, instead of reading a face dispassionately, are more likely to read into it, to credit it with qualities of character and disposition they have perceived or heard of or imagined from other sources. If Hitler was seen as the savior of his people, a prophet, a great statesman and general, then to those who accepted him in such a rôle he began to look like the German conception of the hero. Conversely, we all expect a criminal to show in his face the traits which prompted him to crime. The swindler's eyes—once he is known as a swindler—begin to look shifty and deceitful, although formerly they may have seemed honest enough, if we bothered to notice them at all. The murderer, once

caught and convicted, exhibits blood lust in his every expression—
or, if his face is not very expressive, he is said to show his callous
indifference: yet there must be, going about in the streets of every
city, quite a few people who have committed murder but have
never been suspected. The tendency is always to see in the face
confirmation of what we already believe about its owner. I have
before me as I write a newspaper report, from an intelligent and
trustworthy journalist, on a number of German prisoners—"members of the Nazi party who have been caught around here, and
German soldiers of the S.S. who, after having disposed of their uniforms, have been found behind the Allied lines." Visited in their
cells, these men are described as "hard-bitten" and "sullen bullies":
one has "a pasty face" and all are said to reveal a "horrible, stupid
intensity of stare." Before he visited them in their cells, the journalist knew that these prisoners were guilty of disgusting crimes. It
is perfectly possible that he has given a fair and objective description
of their appearance, but what interests me is the speculation whether,
had he been told before he saw them that they were victims of the
Nazis, would he have seen the same "sullen" and "horrible" qualities in their faces? Some evil men undoubtedly look evil: but not
all. It is natural, instinctive, to expect character to show in the face,
but life is rarely so simple as that, and the expectation, not being
consistently gratified, may lead to very false judgments. During the
Rundstedt advance into the Ardennes, at the end of 1944, a number
of American soldiers, captured and disarmed, were massacred by
machine-gun fire from German tanks circling round them. If the
Germans who did that could all be discovered and brought to trial,
the rest of the world would expect to find them ugly, low-browed,
narrow-eyed, scowling, with brutalized faces. But it is likely that
many would turn out to be fair-haired, blue-eyed, rather handsome,
apparently fitted to play the hero in a cinema romance. That will
be one of the stiffest problems the armies of occupation and the
civil administrators will have to tackle: to reconcile the apparently

human and even attractive faces of Germans in defeat who, in the years of their triumph, were guilty of behavior which humanity must repudiate or lose its human status.

What is most easily seen in the face is temperament, the disposition towards certain sorts of behavior. But this is only the inheritance of race and parentage, which the heir may either squander, neglect, or cultivate responsibly; the record of his stewardship is not readily to be discerned, and hardly at all at first acquaintance. It is as we learn to know someone intimately, as we learn to watch what he does and what he refrains from doing, the endless sequence of tiny decisions which, coral-like, builds up his character, and to compare this with the mutable revelations of his face, that we learn to sift the individual from the type, the man as he is from the potentialities that were open to him at his birth. The human face is not inscrutable: it is an open book, but one written in several languages and in fine script, the lines intertangling. Although some may be scholars, none of us is master of these languages. Individual character is the last inscription made in the face, and it needs time to become even faintly legible. Richard II, in Shakespeare's play, when he had been deposed by Bolingbroke, sent for a mirror—

> I'll read enough
> When I do see the very book indeed
> Where all my sins are writ, and that's myself.

But when he looks into the mirror he marvels that all his follies and misfortunes have made so little change in his appearance,

> Give me the glass, and therein will I read.
> No deeper wrinkles yet? Hath sorrow struck
> So many blows upon this face of mine,
> And made no deeper wounds?

There is the truth about character in the face. It shows, but slowly, inconsistently, faintly, and enigmatically. It is like the bare statistical score sheet of a cricket match, which tells who got the runs and the wickets and who held the catches: but to form a true judgment it is necessary to have inner knowledge, to know how variably the pitch played, what runs came from the edge of the bat, the rate of scoring, and the catches that were not held. The face is never to be read offhand, and to obtain any assurance of correct interpretation we need further information than the face itself reveals; what is more, we need to verify our extraneous information lest we read false meaning into what we see.

All the good and all the evil in the world are to be found in human faces, the Divine 'Yes' and the Satanic 'No,' as well as, more often, the gibbered yea-and-nay, or the timid evasion of any decisive answer to the implied questions asked whenever an individual life is launched into the world. When we look at any human face we deal with a mystery, and mystery (in the purer sense of the word which obtained before stories of criminals became a fashionable entertainment) is at the core of what we regard as sacred. The mystery of the human face is part of the mystery of existence. We do not know what we are, or why we are here, or whither we are tending. We achieve apprehensions, but no certainty. We have to make our personal, tentative answers or we are not fully alive; and if we say we do not care, we anticipate judgment upon ourselves. Nor dare we impose our answers upon others, for if their mysteries are not sacred, then our own are cast into doubt. We are given each a face by which we are known, as we are given a name we respond to. And we are surrounded by other faces, like ours yet not like. Some we respect, some we love, some we turn from, some we hate or despise. But if we attain a little wisdom we try not to make our anger and our contempt absolute; we found them upon a lamentation for the debasement of what might have been. For while all portraits of God are fictitious and unsatisfactory, offering us only a man when we look for the unlimited Godhead, it is equally true that in man, and in man's face, there is to be discerned a faint reflection and diluted essence of the nature of our God, who is, who must be, we being what we are, a human God. The very fact that Divinity is conceivable in terms of the human mind is an indication of the status open to man. If the Christian story and the Christian doctrine is submitted to the harshest appraisal, it follows that we, as human beings, as man, have invented all this out of our imagination. Myself, I believe in a soldier Godhead existing objectively behind all our cloudy perceptions, nor am I disposed to lay the blame for what is done evilly in the name of any God elsewhere than upon humanity. But, accepting the rationalist and agnostic arguments on their severest levels, they surely do not overthrow the potential status and the better achievements of man? Our imagination creates only by analysis and synthesis, by reassembling into new combinations the elements of our experience. If we have invented an imaginary God, then at least it is a noble conception, and made out of the stuff of our existence. Nor does it distort the fundamental character of the human face, which remains a mystery, the frontal aspect of the topmost part of the body, a utilitarian collection of sense organs, a complex machine designed for seeing, hearing, tasting, eating, drinking, and speaking, which has also become the apocalyptic chronicle of all that passes in the mind, the heart and the spirit.

INDEX

INDEX

INDEX